DEVELOPING AND IMPLEMENTING IDEA-IEPs

DEVELOPING AND IMPLEMENTING IDEA-IEPs

An Individualized Education Program (IEP) Handbook for
Meeting Individuals with Disabilities Education Act
(IDEA) Requirements

By

EDWARD BURNS

State University of New York at Binghamton

Charles C Thomas
PUBLISHER • LTD.
SPRINGFIELD • ILLINOIS • U.S.A.

Published and Distributed Throughout the World by

CHARLES C THOMAS • PUBLISHER, LTD.
2600 South First Street
Springfield, Illinois 62704

© 2001 by CHARLES C THOMAS • PUBLISHER, LTD.

ISBN 0-398-07122-5 (cloth)
ISBN 0-398-07123-3 (paper)

Library of Congress Catalog Card Number: 00-060772

Printed in the United States of America
MR-R-3

Library of Congress Cataloging-in-Publication Data

Burns, Edward, -
    Developing and implementing IDEA-IEPs : an individual education program
(IEP) handbook for meeting Individuals with Disabilities Education Act (IDEA)
requirements / by Edward Burns.
        p.cm.
    Includes bibliographical references (p.) and index.
    ISBN 0-398-07122-5 -- ISBN 0-398-07123-3 (pbk.)
    1. Individualized education programs--United States. 2. Handicapped children--
Education--United States. I. Title: Individualized education program (IEP) handbook
for meeting Individuals with Disabilities Education Act (IDEA) requirements.
II. Title.

LC4031 .B82 2000
371.9'0973--dc21   00-060772

For Edward W. Stevens, Jr. and Claudette C. Stevens
Good friends and good support are ever so important.

PREFACE

*D*eveloping *and Implementing IDEA-IEPs* is comprised of eight chapters relating to the development and implementation of effective IEPs. Chapters 1, 2, and 3 relate to the history and purpose of the IEP and the overall IEP process. Chapters 4 and 5 consider need and determining present levels of educational performance. Chapters 6, 7, and 8 focus on writing measurable annual goals and short-term objectives or benchmarks, providing services, and evaluating IEPs and the IEP process. The ultimate goal of this book is to elevate the IEP from a form to show compliance to a dynamic planning document that clearly shows how to develop a specially designed program for each child with a disability that can be reviewed and revised to promote regular curriculum participation. When first introduced in 1975, PL 94-142 was regarded as the cornerstone of special education and "the centerpiece of the statute's educational delivery system for disabled children." For the Individuals with Disabilities Act (IDEA) amendments of 1997 the status of the IEP in the special education process has been reasserted and strengthened to achieve the role envisioned by PL 94-142.

The regulations for IDEA-1997 describe the IEP as the statutory vehicle for ensuring a free appropriate public education to children with disabilities. For school personnel, teachers, and parents the IEP represents the framework for providing specially designed instruction to meet each child's individual needs. The purpose of this book is to consider issues relating to the development, implementation, revision, and evaluation of IEPs in the context of IDEA-1997, the regulations, relevant court cases and best practices that have been employed by states and school districts.

Developing and Implementing IDEA-IEPs is supported by the following website which provides access to book updates, information relating to the most current laws and regulations for IEPs, links to IEP forms and publications, IEP court cases, and other relevant information for writing, developing, and implementing IEPs. This website also provides an opportunity for reader input relating to *Developing and Implementing IDEA-IEPs*, suggestions or other information or techniques that will improve the IEP process.

http://www.idea-iep.com

The IEP is about change and individual need. To this end, input from teachers, parents, and other professionals is essential for the continued growth of the IEP as an effective and viable planning document.

CONTENTS

DEVELOPING AND
IMPLEMENTING IDEA-IEPs

Chapter 1

INDIVIDUALIZED PLANNING

EDUCATION FOR ALL CHILDREN

PUBLIC LAW 94-142 (OR PL 94-142), the Education of All Handicapped Children Act (EAHCA), was signed into law in 1975 and provided the foundation for a systematic planning process to meet the unique needs of children with disabilities. This law, the culmination of legislation,[1] court cases,[2] and educational attempts to meet the needs of students with disabilities, mandated a *free appropriate public education* for every child with a disability.[3] The concept of a free appropriate public education (FAPE) provides the rationale for individualized planning, is the basis for much of the litigation concerning individualized planning for children with disabilities, and includes procedural safeguards to ensure that schools provide an appropriate education for every child with a disability. As discussed in *PARC v. Pennsylvania*,[4] *appropriate* refers to "training appropriate to the child's capacity" and "within the context of a presumption that "a least restrictive placement is preferable to a more restrictive placement" (p. 1260) (e.g., a regular classroom placement is preferable to a special classroom).

Prior to PL 94-142 children were receiving special education services, but the services were not necessarily designed to meet individual needs, were not always the result of a well-defined planning process,

and were often not appropriate. The essence of a law for the "education of all handicapped children" is not merely to provide special education but rather to provide a plan, centered about specific goals, for specially designed instruction to meet a child's unique needs.

Public Law 94-142 greatly expanded the services for children with disabilities by requiring that all children with disabilities are located and evaluated, and that each child is provided with an appropriate education. For PL 94-142, the key to determining the appropriate placement was individualization rather than programmatic concern. A self-contained special education class might be appropriate for one child but highly inappropriate for another. The least restrictive environment mandate requires that an appropriate education is determined by needed services and not the location of services. For example, a child should not be placed entirely in a self-contained classroom when some degree of regular classroom participation is possible.

Public Law 94-142 was an attempt to develop a comprehensive plan that would assist in meeting the needs of children by defining terms, requiring individualized educational programming, outlining services, developing centers and programs, training personnel, authorizing research projects, meeting technological needs, and providing services for infants and toddlers age 0 to 2, and children with disabilities. The underlying purpose of PL 94-142 was not simply to establish rules and procedures to demonstrate eligibility for Federal assistance, but to meet the unique learning needs of each child with a disability.

Curriculum Considerations

Before PL 94-142 the concept of curriculum for students with disabilities often meant a different curriculum, but not necessarily an appropriate curriculum. Special education was often viewed as a placement option that occurred apart from the regular education curriculum rather than a process to provide children with "an appropriate preschool, elementary, or secondary school education."[5]

For nondisabled students the curriculum is a plan of study for learning and achieving educational goals. For children with disabilities, the general curriculum is the same curriculum as for nondisabled children.[6,7] Wiles and Bondi (1998) stated that "through analysis, design, implementation, and evaluation, curriculum developers set goals, plan experiences, select content, and assess outcomes and school programs" (p. 11). The importance of the school curriculum for children with disabilities is underscored by the requirement that measurable annual goals must relate to needs that result from a child's disability that will "enable the child to be involved in and progress in the general curriculum."[8]

For children who are not disabled the task is to determine and develop a school curriculum; for children who are disabled the appropriate curriculum might be the school curriculum, a modified school curriculum, or a curriculum that is highly individualized and substantively different than the school curriculum. Because of highly individualized curriculum needs, a general curriculum for all children with disabilities is not possible. A visually impaired student might have above average verbal skills; a child who is deaf or hard of hearing might have unique communication needs; and one child with a specific learning disability might have a communication disorder, another a reading deficit, and a third a disorder in mathematics. The only solution to meet these varied needs is to develop a highly individualized plan for each child with a disability to ensure that needs are identified, goals set, and services provided. This is accomplished by providing every child with a disability an Individualized Education Program, or IEP, that addresses needs that result from the disability. The basic IEP goal of addressing needs resulting from a disability is achieved within a context of the least restrictive environment so that the child is educated with nondisabled children, and is involved in and progresses in the general curriculum, to the maximum extent appropriate.

Choate et al. (1995) stated that "the IEP is, by definition, the nucleus of curriculum development in special education" (p. 29). These authors reasoned that special education teachers often ignore the regular classroom curriculum and "the content of the special education curricula is often fragmented, limited to low-level basic skills and low-level texts" (p. 32). As can be seen by the renewed emphasis on participation in the regular education curriculum, the Individuals with Disabilities Education Act amendments of 1997 (IDEA-1997) authorized by PL 105-17 attempts to rectify this situation. Rather than treating the IEP as the special education curriculum, or as a license to remove a child from the regular education curriculum, the IEP should be conceptualized as a plan to maximize the extent that children with disabilities are educated with children who are not disabled. The goal of special education is not *special education* but the maximization of regular curriculum participation. The primary task of the IEP team is to design a plan to best achieve this goal.

The Cornerstone

In 1977 Hewett described the IEP as "the cornerstone" of PL 94-142 by requiring "a written, individualized education program for each child" (p. 568). Smith (1990) referred to the IEP as "the sine qua non of Public Law 94-142" (p. 6). McLaughlin and Warren (1995) stated that "few would dispute that the Individualized Education Program (IEP) is one of the hallmarks of the Individuals with Disabilities Education Act" (p. 1). The law and the regulations provide an array of requirements, services, and procedural safeguards, but the IEP represents the statutory vehicle for the implementation of the Act.

Public Law 94-142 defined the IEP as "a written statement for each handicapped child developed in any meeting by a representative of the local educational agency . . . qualified to provide specially designed instruction . . . the teacher, the parents or guardian of such child, and, whenever appropriate, such child."[9] This definition was redefined in IDEA-1997 to mean "a written statement for each child with a disability that is developed, reviewed, and revised in accordance with" specific content requirements detailed in the law.[10] Beginning with PL 94-142, and continued by IDEA-1997, the IEP signifies a written statement that is the result of a meeting in which "an annual description of services planned for students with disabilities" (Smith et al., 1995, p. 52) are developed. Using special education to develop individualized programs for children who are not disabled but who need additional attention (e.g., because of limited English proficiency or lack of instruction) abrogates the responsibility of the local educational agency to provide an appropriate education. Special education and related services under IDEA-1997, and therefore the need for an IEP, is not intended for children who do not have disabilities, and not for children with disabilities who do not need specially designed instruction.

Public Law 94-142 gave special education a purpose and a focus. The purpose was to provide a meaningful plan for meeting each child's unique educational needs; the focus concerned the development of an appropriate and individualized plan. The vehicle to provide an appropriate plan for services, and a method for accountability, was the IEP. The IEP was a comprehensive statement of the educational needs of a child with a disability and the specially designed instruction and related services required to meet these needs. The local educational agency was responsible for the development and implementation of the IEP to "establish or revise, whichever is appropriate, an individualized education program for each handicapped child at the beginning of each school year and will then review and, if appropriate revise its provisions periodically, but not less than annually."[11]

The purpose of PL 94-142 was not to make the IEP a bureaucratic requirement or ineffectual paper plan to give the appearance of an appropriate education; the IEP was intended to provide a viable education plan that would result in appropriate services. Unfortunately, PL 94-142 was not entirely clear as to how to best develop, review, and revise the IEP. Often the only IEP requirement that was met when the law was first implemented was a written document, but one in which needs were ill defined, goals vague, and services disconnected from both needs and goals. When an IEP is developed in this unplanned and amorphous fashion, a meaningful review and revision of the IEP to better meet individual needs is virtually impossible. Of course, when an IEP is written with no real planning or calculated educational intent, the primary purpose is generally to suggest compliance so that there is no real plan or services to review.

The Multipurpose IEP

The IEP document requirement is that the IEP is written, is developed by a team, contains the appropriate content, is in effect at the beginning of the year, and is reviewed and revised as necessary. In addition to specific regulatory requirements, the IEP is a multipurpose document that serves a variety of planning, communication, and collaboration functions.[12] As described in the IDEA-1990 regulations the IEP has six primary functions:

1. *Communication.* The IEP meeting serves as a communication vehicle between parents and school personnel, and enables parents, as equal participants, to jointly decide what the child's needs are, what services will be provided to meet those needs, and what the anticipated outcomes may be.
2. *Resolution.* The IEP process provides an opportunity for resolving any differences between the parents and the school concerning a child's special education needs; first, through the IEP meeting, and second, if necessary, through the procedural protections that are available to parents.
3. *Commitment.* The IEP sets forth in writing a commitment of resources necessary to enable a child to receive needed special education and related services.
4. *Management.* The IEP is a management tool that is used to ensure that each child is provided a free and appropriate education.
5. *Compliance.* The IEP is a compliance/monitoring document which may be used by authorized monitoring personnel to determine whether a child is actually receiving the free appropriate public education agreed to by the parents and the school.
6. *Evaluation.* The IEP serves as an evaluation device for use in determining the extent of the child's progress toward meeting the projected outcomes.

Compliance, as discussed above, is an important and necessary function of the IEP. However, a distinction must be made between compliance to develop a meaningful educational plan and compliance to complete a document that might be anything but meaningful, educational, or appropriate. One of the major criticisms of the IEP process is the emphasis on compliance rather than a concerted effort to provide appropriate educational programs. There is no doubt that many children with disabilities receive appropriate specially designed instruction, but often in spite of rather than as a result of the IEP.

Finally, the IEP attempts to focus on the need to achieve a thoughtfully planned set of goals. A teacher and school is obligated to make a good faith effort to help a child achieve the measurable annual goals and objectives or benchmarks. However, the IEP is not a contract in the sense that a teacher or public agency is responsible for a child's ability to achieve the goals and objectives or learning rate. Nonetheless, if goals and objectives or benchmarks are not achieved, procedural safeguards exist to correct the problem, and the IEP team is required to revise the goals as necessary.

PLANNING FOR NEEDS

The development of an IEP is preceded by an individual evaluation of the child's disability and educational needs. After a child has been referred for special education, a plan is developed by an evaluation team to "assess specific areas of educational need."[13] If repetitious data are collected and does not address areas of need, the determination of educational needs and levels of performance will be misunderstood and misdirected. Merely collecting test scores is not planning, and this lack of planning becomes most evident in the determination of measurable annual goals. If specific behaviors or skills that a child needs to participate in the school curriculum prior to the IEP meeting have not been assessed, these needs will probably not be addressed when the IEP is developed. The requirement that the individual evaluation is conducted by a group of qualified professionals and the parents[14] reflects the need to discuss, select and develop, if necessary, evaluations and assessments that explicate a child's unique needs. This is in contrast to a mechanistic evaluation plan that entails an unvarying protocol of tests in which specific instructional needs and levels of performance are not identified.

The individual evaluation should begin with a review of the referral, determining what existing data should be considered, and what additional assessments and evaluations are needed. McLoughlin and Lewis (1994, p. 33) discussed an Individualized Assessment Plan (IAP) that "describes steps and procedures in the assessment" and "must reflect the reason for referral and must yield systematically organized data." Wyoming requires a multidisciplinary evaluation plan[15] that "requires a description of evaluation procedures to determine eligibility and present levels of performance, hearing or vision evaluations if so indicated (e.g., by screening), and the names of those responsible for conducting the evaluation."

Strategic Planning

A successful IEP requires strategic planning. This means that programs and services are selected and coordinated to best achieve desired measurable annual goals. A child might need specially designed instruction relating to basic reading skills, but not instruction involving science or social studies; or strategic planning might result in specific test accommodations made so that the child can demonstrate content area proficiency, but the actual content is provided by the regular classroom teacher.

Strategic planning is characterized by appropriate and specific goals. One deficiency of many IEPs is the inclusion of excessively vague goals and questionable accommodations. Goals are listed for a child "to improve reading," "to develop writing skills," or "to improve classroom behavior," but these goals provide neither direction nor a meaningful and measurable end result. If a child is receiving special education, there should be a clear purpose for providing services, and this purpose is defined by explicit goals which bridge the gap between present and desired levels of performance. For this reason a statement of annual goals required by PL 94-142 has been redefined in IDEA-1997 to encompass measurable annual goals that "are instrumental to the strategic planning process used to develop and implement the IEP for each child with a disability."[16]

A well-planned IEP is characterized by appropriate and well-planned goals. However, planning appropriate goals can only be achieved by carefully considering the interrelationship among all IEP components (e.g., levels of performance, goals, services). For an IEP to be effective all elements must be thoroughly integrated. This means that levels of performance provide the beginning benchmark for goals, services are provided to achieve goals, and goals are reviewed and revised annually.

Measurable annual goals and short-term objectives or benchmarks represent the plan for specially designed instruction. Goals are designed to address a child's disability and/or educational needs. For a child with a specific learning disability, the primary goal is to remediate a specific area of performance (e.g., listening comprehension, basic reading skill, or written expression) rather than to focus on a possible underlying neurological or physiological cause. For other disabilities, both disability and educational need must be considered. For a child who is deaf or hard of hearing, maximizing the child's residual hearing via amplification might be just as important as providing appropriate instructional interventions.

After need has been established and goals defined, services are planned so that the goals can be achieved. Special education and related services are a logical extension of a child's unique needs and the goals developed to meet these needs, and services that do not address needs and corresponding goals are inappropriate. Also, services cannot be based on a child's disability (e.g., special education is synonymous with a self-contained classroom) but must be based on the child's individual needs that result from or are impacted by the disability.

In order for an educational plan to be viable, a provision must be made for evaluation and revision. After a period of time, certain needs might have been eliminated because of the effectiveness of services, because certain goals and services are ineffective, or new needs and services are identified. After developing an initial program, the child's progress might reveal more serious underlying needs. The written expression goals for a child might not have been successful because of an underlying reading disorder; or a child's reading might be secondary to receptive language needs. Only if goals and services are periodically evaluated can a program be adjusted to meet a child's unique needs.

Educational Planning

The House of Representatives report[17] for PL 94-142 defined the purpose of an individualized education program as an educational plan to help a child achieve his or her potential, to allow all principals an opportunity for input in the development of an individualized program of instruction, and that individualization means specifics and timetables. The Senate version[18] placed emphasis on the actual planning rather than the documented plan or IEP. The Senate envisioned an individualized planning conference that was defined "as a meeting or meetings to be held at least three times a year for the purpose of developing, reviewing, and when appropriate and with the agreement of the parents or guardian, revising a written statement of appropriate educational services to be provided for each handicapped child."[19] The Senate regarded the individualized planning conference as a way to ensure parent involvement and to provide appropriate services. The term *individualized instructional planning* advocated by the Senate was replaced by *individualized educational program* PL 94-142,[20] but *planning* was and is the essence of a successful plan or IEP. The goal is not to generate an IEP document, but rather to engage in meaningful planning with the parents and to develop a document that reflects this planning.

The need for parent participation has been re-emphasized in IDEA-1997, and strengthened by procedural safeguards to ensure, as much as possible, parent participation.

In the final draft of PL 94-142, the Senate interpretation of planning as "a meeting or meetings for the purpose of developing a written statement . . . with the joint participation of parents" (p. 1484) prevailed over the role of parents suggested by the House. The House version originally used the term *consultation*, while the Senate version elevated the role of parents to active participants in the planning process. Planning is essential for developing appropriate and effective IEPs, and parent input and participation is essential for planning.

Partnership

Parents are not merely consultants but equal partners with school personnel in making IEP decisions. Because planning requires the participation of school personnel, the parents, and when appropriate the child, an IEP is not a task unilaterally undertaken by the school district, and then presented to the parents as a fait accompli. The guidelines concerning parent participation state that an agency can come to an IEP meeting with recommendations

> but the agency must make it clear to the parents at the outset of the meeting that the services proposed by the agency are only recommendations for review and discussion with the parents. Parents have the right to bring questions, concerns, and recommendations to an IEP meeting as part of a full discussion, of the child's needs and the services to be provided to meet those needs before the IEP is finalized.[21]

Pre-prepared IEPs developed without parent input are inappropriate and contravene parent input and planning participation. Without parent input all IEPs are drafts, including computer-developed IEPs that often suggest document completeness, but for the addition of the parent's signature. If a school district does bring an IEP draft to an IEP meeting there must be "a full discussion with the child's parents, before the child's IEP is finalized, regarding drafted content and the child's needs and the services to be provided to meet those needs."[22]

An IEP completed before parents have an opportunity to provide input does not represent meaningful planning. The IEP meeting is intended to serve "as a communication vehicle between parents and school personnel," and parents should be treated as equal participants in making joint and informed decisions regarding needs, involvement in the general curriculum, and the achievement of agreedupon goals.[23]

The role of parents in the development of the IEP is not intended to be a gratuitous requirement, but rather the *sine qua non* of the planning process. Parents are now an integral part of the evaluation process, the determination of a disability, and the IEP team. Parents' "concerns, and information that they provide regarding their children, must be considered in developing and reviewing their children's IEPs."[24] The 1997 reauthorization of IDEA not only re-established the role of parents in planning but provides unequivocal mandates that will increase parent participation. Although IDEA outlines a variety of procedural safeguards to ensure participation, an appropriate education for children with disabilities is achieved by "encouraging parents and

educators to work out their differences by using nonadversarial means."[25]

By reasserting the role of the parents in planning, the unique needs of children can best be met by encouraging parents to "provide critical information about their child's abilities, interests, performance, and history," to participate in discussions about the needed services, and as part of the IEP team in "deciding how the child will be involved and progress in the general curriculum and participate in state and districtwide assessments, and what services the agency will provide to the child and in what setting."[26]

School districts are required to ensure the participation of parents in development of the IEP[27] by finding mutually agreeable and convenient meeting times, keeping records of attempts to ensure parent participation, and helping parents understand IEP proceedings (e.g., using an interpreter). The prior written notice that details the rights of parents and parental consent is intended to include parents in the planning and to provide parents with recourse if they believe they have been excluded from this process. The importance of planning with parents, rather than fostering a contentious and litigious relationship between parents and school personnel, is one of the primary reasons for adding a mediation process to the list of procedural safeguards[28] so that parents and schools are able to resolve disputes "amicably, making decisions with the child's best interests in mind" (p. 26).

COMPLIANCE AND PLANNING

The PL 94-142 IEP requirement provided a method for ensuring compliance so that an appropriate educational plan could be developed as a result of the collaboration between the school, the parents, and the

child when appropriate. If a child did not have an IEP, if the IEP was incomplete, or other IEP provisions were not met, the local educational agency was not in compliance with PL 94-142. Unfortunately, many schools did not focus on the type of compliance intended by PL 94-142 and what the Supreme Court[29] referred to as a "reasonably calculated" IEP; that is, an IEP designed to provide some benefit to a child and not merely to list a series of vague and disconnected statements. Compliance should result in "full participation of concerned parties throughout the development of the IEP," and not completing what was referred to in *Doe v. Defendant I*[30] as a "laundry list of items" (p. 1191).

The emphasis on documentary compliance is most obvious when educational performance is poorly defined and the goals for special education services are unclear or even nonexistent. Compliance has come to mean a mechanistic and shallow approach to planning, but the real purpose of compliance is to encourage planning and parent participation. This is the reasoning in *Hudson v. Rowley* when the Supreme Court clarified the meaning of compliance by stating that "Congress placed every bit as much emphasis upon compliance with procedures giving parents and guardians a large measure of participation at every stage of the administrative process . . . as it did upon the measurement of the resulting IEP against a substantive standard."[31]

There is no absolute guide for determining what constitutes an effective IEP, but compliance with the procedures results, "in most cases," with an appropriate IEP if parents are active participants. A school district might view compliance as only a prerequisite for funding but *Hudson* interpreted compliance as a means for achieving parent participation, planning, and the "substantive content" of an IEP. The court reasoned "that the congressional emphasis upon full participation of concerned parties throughout the development of the IEP . . . demonstrates the legislative conviction that adequate compliance with the procedures prescribed would in most cases assure much if not all of what Congress wished in the way of substantive content in an IEP."

Compliance is essential for achieving an appropriate education for children with disabilities. However, compliance is not a goal but rather the first step in the development of meaningful, viable, and effective IEPs. As discussed throughout this book, the purpose of developing an IEP is not simply to generate a document, but to memorialize the essential elements of the "planning conference" and to develop an effective educational plan.[32]

The House of Representatives report for PL 94-142 noted "the movement toward the individualization of instruction, involving the child, the parent and other educational professionals" to construct an individual education program or prescription based on the following fundamental tenets:

1. Each child requires an educational plan that is tailored to achieve his or her maximum potential;
2. All principals in the child's educational environment, including the child, should have the opportunity for input;
3. Individualization means specifics and timetables . . . and the need for periodic review of these specifics.[33]

Multifaceted Planning

Collaborative planning. Planning an IEP must be collaborative and must involve all members of the IEP team. A successfully planned IEP requires active participation from the regular classroom teacher, a special education teacher, the parents, the child when appropriate, and other qualified personnel. The "agency must make it clear to the parents at the outset of the meeting that proposed services are only recommendations for review and discussion and the team must engage in "a full discussion" of the child's needs before the IEP is finalized."[34] Until there has been consideration by the entire IEP team, which most importantly includes the parents, all matters brought before the IEP team are in the form of recommendations.

The role of the regular classroom teacher is especially noteworthy in IDEA-1997. The goal of achieving greater regular curriculum participation cannot be achieved without the participation of the regular classroom teacher. The change in IDEA-1990 from "the child's teacher" to "at least one regular education teacher of the child" for IDEA-1997 is significant.[35] The purpose of regular classroom teacher involvement is to have a teacher who does, or most likely will, implement a portion of the IEP rather than to have a single classroom teacher serve on the IEP team to represent all classroom teachers.

The composition of the IEP team also includes persons "knowledgeable about the general curriculum," "the availability of resources," and "individuals who have knowledge or special expertise regarding the child."[36] Collaboration is not restricted to specific team members, but entails cooperation among all interested parties to meet a child's needs. The IEP team is not defined by a static and unchanging membership that is bureaucratically advantageous for scheduling but represents a collaborative effort among all interested parties, qualified personnel and the parents to address the child's disability and needs. If necessary, other qualified personnel might be invited to an IEP meeting because of their special expertise. For example, a social worker,

occupational therapist, or guidance counselor might attend an IEP meeting in order to provide expertise relating to specific goals, services, or accommodations.

A further attempt to encourage planning between parents and school personnel is the limitation on attorney's fees in relation to the development of an IEP unless the meeting is the result of a mediation or judicial action.[37] The IEP meeting is intended to allow school personnel and the parents an opportunity to plan and "the bill specifically excludes the payment of attorneys' fees for attorney participation in IEP meetings, unless such meetings are convened as a result of an administrative proceeding or judicial action.[38]

The need to collaborate is not confined to school personnel and parents. By age sixteen an IEP must include a statement of interagency responsibilities and needed linkages.[39] This requires representation at IEP meetings from participating agencies, and a need to plan and coordinate services in order to promote an effective school-to-work transition plan. If employment is a necessary transition service, the school might need to collaborate with local employers to develop necessary employment skills, or to modify the student's curriculum in order to prepare the student for the transition from school to work.

An IEP can be integrated with other types of individualized service plans under another Federal program if the plan contains all of the information required in an IEP, and all of the necessary parties participate in its development. Examples of service plans that could be consolidated with an IEP include Individualized Program Plans (Title XX of the Social Security Act–Social Services), Individualized Service Plans (Title XVI of the Social Security Act–Supplemental Security Income), and Individualized Written Rehabilitation Plans

(Rehabilitation Act of 1973).[40]

Comprehensive planning. Planning an IEP must be comprehensive. The IEP team must consider each component of the IEP. Team members must determine whether all of the child's needs have been considered, what measurable annual goals will meet these needs, and what objectives or benchmarks will allow for a fair assessment of progress. The need for thoughtful and comprehensive planning is never more evident than in the development of a statement of transition services that "promotes movement from school to post-school activities."[41] In order to achieve this goal, an effective statement of transition services must plan for the identification and coordination of vocational activities, adult employment, independent living, postsecondary, independent living, and related services.

Focused planning. Every child will have a variety of educational needs, but not all these needs require specifically designed instruction. One of the major drawbacks of self-contained classrooms is limiting children who can benefit from the regular classroom curriculum. If a child is achieving satisfactorily in science or social studies, these areas should not be part of the IEP; if a child does not have a behavior problem, there is no need for goals to address behavior; if a child has a disability in speech and language, but is able to achieve in reading, the IEP should focus on speech and language and not reading. The focus of special education is specially designed instruction, related services, and support for areas of need resulting from the child's disability.

Logical planning. Each element of the IEP has a logical and meaningful purpose in the overall plan. The regulatory guidance concerning the relationship between IEP components is "a direct relationship between the present levels of educational performance and the other components of the IEP."[42] A good indication of a logical and integrated IEP is a clear relationship between the individual evaluation, the statement of present levels of performance, goals, and services. A reading of one IEP component should logically relate to preceding and succeeding components. If there is a question as to why a goal is included when there is no corroborating evaluation data, or why a service is included when there is no corresponding goal, the underlying logic of the IEP is suspect.

The basic logic of an IEP is represented, to some extent, by the statutory listing of IEP content; that is, present levels of educational performance provide the basis for measurable annual goals, measurable annual goals are used to designate services, and progress is evaluated and reported to parents. An IEP document is not required to follow this order, and the IEP team is not required "to include information under one component of a child's IEP that is already contained in another component."[43]

INDIVIDUALIZED PLANNING FORMAT

There are a variety of individualized plans and planning approaches that have been designed to meet the unique needs of children and adults. These include Behavioral Intervention Plans,[44] Consumer Service Plans, High School Plans, Individual Literacy Plans, Individualized Education Plans, Individualized Family Service Plans, Individualized Program Plans, Individualized Rehabilitation Employment Plans, Individualized Service Plans, Individualized Transition Plans, Individualized Written

Rehabilitation Plans, Plan for Achieving Self Support (PASS), Rehabilitation Plans, School Transition Plans, Section 504 Plans, and Service Plans for private school children[45] and among others.

In Virginia a Consumer Service Plan is defined as a "document addressing the needs of the recipient of mental retardation case management services, in all life areas" and an Individual Service Plan (ISP) is defined as a "comprehensive and regularly updated statement specific to the individual being treated containing, but not necessarily limited to, his treatment or training needs, his goals and measurable objectives to meet the identified needs, services to be provided with the recommended frequency to accomplish the measurable goals and objectives, and estimated timetable for achieving the goals and objectives."[46] In British Columbia a distinction is made between an Individual Education Plan for students with disabilities, and a Student Learning Plan (SLP) that is required for every student starting in ninth grade, including students with disabilities.[47] In Colorado a specific literacy plan is required for children below specified levels established by the state and that this "literacy plan may be incorporated into the individual education plan . . . ".[48]

The various plans that have been devised to provide services are often quite similar in format to the IEP. An overview of these planning formats reveals a focus on individual planning, identifying important needs, developing goals, providing services, establishing timelines, and evaluating progress. The following describes several planning documents that are particularly pertinent to the development of IEPs.

Individualized Family Service Plan (IFSP). Part H (or subchapter VIII–Infants and Toddlers with Disabilities) of PL 94-142 was devoted to infants and toddlers age 0 to 2. This contained a requirement for written documentation that paralleled the IEP in many respects. The Individualized Family Service Plan required a statement of present levels of performance, a statement of outcomes, services, and dates. For IDEA-1997, Part H was renamed Part C and the IFSP was expanded to include "a statement of the natural environments in which early intervention services shall appropriately be provided, including a justification of the extent, if any, to which the services will not be provided in a natural environment."[49] An IFSP also requires a statement of family resources, family concerns, and the identification of a service coordinator. The identification of a service coordinator is certainly an idea that would facilitate the development and implementation of many IEPs. The following is a list of the eight elements required in an IFSP for IDEA-1997:

1. Present levels of performance in relating to physical, cognitive, communication, social and adaptive development
2. Statement of family resources, priorities and concerns
3. Outcomes, criteria, and timelines
4. Specific services
5. Natural environment statement of inclusion or exclusion
6. Initiation and duration of services
7. Identification of a service coordinator
8. Transition to preschool steps[50]

There is a period of overlap between an IFSP and an IEP. For children three through five (or for a two-year-old who will be three during the school year), an IFSP can be used in place of an IEP if agreed upon by the agency and parents.[51] In doing so, the parents must be told the differences between an IEP and IFSP "because of the importance of the IEP as the statutory vehicle for ensuring FAPE to a child with a disability."[52] If an IFSP is selected, written informed consent must be obtained from the parents.

Transition plans. Transition planning for students fourteen and older is an essential element of IDEA-1997, but transition planning is also required for early intervention programs for infants and toddlers to preschool programs under IDEA. While the emphasis in school-to-work transition planning requires long-range planning, the transition from preschool involves the early intervention lead agency, the school district, and the parents and begins between three and six months before IDEA eligibility.[53]

Service plans. All children with disabilities must be identified, located, and evaluated, including private school children.[54] For each child with a disability in a private school who receives special education and related services a service plan is required.[55] The service plan, however, can result in partial services, a specific related service, all services, or a combination of special education and related services being provided on-site at the private school setting or at a public school location.[56] Because a school district *may* provide on-site services, but is *not obligated* to do so, a service plan might be substantially different than a regular IEP in terms of goals, where services are provided to achieve goals, and participation in the regular private school curriculum.

Individualized Written Rehabilitation Plan (IWRP). Participation of the individual with a disability in the planning process is especially important in rehabilitation planning. As a result of the Rehabilitation Act of 1973 (PL 93-112, discussed below) guidelines were developed to sufficiently include clients "in tailoring the rehabilitation program" to meet the clients individual needs.[57] As was the case when the IEP concept was first formulated, a major purpose of requiring an individualized written rehabilitation program is (1) involving the client in decision making, (2) documenting objectives and services, (3) evaluating objectives, and (4) revising the objectives if they are not being achieved.[58]

There is an obvious overlap between the "client-centered" approach that characterize rehabilitation plans, and the transition service IEP requirement. An IEP requires a statement of transition services that focuses on school-related programs by age fourteen, and a statement of actual transition services and interagency linkages by age sixteen. Although IDEA-1997 allows a child with a disability[59] to be a part of the IEP team if appropriate, a child is required to be invited to the IEP meeting if transition services are being considered. If the student does not attend the IEP meeting, the school district must consider the student's preferences and interests.[60]

The Rehabilitation Act amendments of 1998 expands the concept of an IWRP and includes criteria for an Individualized Rehabilitation Employment Plan (IREP)[61] that must include specific services, outcomes, conditions, timelines, and criteria and results in employment in an integrated setting to the maximum extent appropriate. An IREP must include the following:

1. specific employment outcomes chosen by the eligible individual;
2. vocational rehabilitation services needed to achieve the outcomes;
3. timelines for the achievement and for the initiation of the services;
4. who will provide the vocational rehabilitation services;
5. criteria to evaluate progress toward achievement of the employment outcome;
6. the terms and conditions of the IREP;
7. the extended services needed by the eligible individual; and
8. a statement of projected need for post-employment services.

The criteria for an IREP are similar to those of an IEP in many respects and have great import for developing effective transition services for students with disabilities. Both planning documents emphasize unique individual needs, specific outcomes (goals) and services to achieve the outcomes, and timelines and "criteria to evaluate progress toward achievement of the employment outcome" (IREP) and "progress toward the annual goals" (IEP). Both documents require a date when services are initiated and a timeline for achieving services (IREP) and annual goals (IEP).

As is the case with IEPs,[62] the purpose of an IREP is not "to burden the counselors and rehabilitation coordinators with unnecessary and cumbersome paperwork" but "to improve communication between the handicapped individuals to be served and the rehabilitation counselors who sincerely wish to see them served."

Section 504 plans. Section 504 refers to Title V or the Rights and Advocacy section of the Rehabilitation Act of 1973 (see PL 93-112, discussed below). Section 504 does not describe a plan, program, or specific accommodations, but prohibits discrimination because of an individual's disability.

A child can receive services under IDEA or Section 504, but Section 504 does not require a plan for specially designed instruction. A child might need an interpreter, help with an assistive technology device, or a specific test accommodation (e.g., large print), but not need special instruction. If the child does not need special education, the child is not eligible for services under IDEA, but the child could be eligible for all necessary services under Section 504 if the child 1) has a physical or mental impairment which substantially limits one or more of such person's major life activities, 2) has a record of such an impairment, or 3) is regarded as having such an impairment.[63]

If appropriate, an IEP can be used to meet a child's Section 504 needs. In 1992 the Council for Administrators of Special Education (CASE) developed a Student Accommodation Plan relating to Section 504 that includes a description of (1) the nature of the concern, (2) the basis for the determination of the disability (if any), (3) how the disability affects a major life activity, and (4) the reasonable accommodations that are necessary. The CASE plan emphasizes the need to address how the disability impacts a "major life activity." This is in contrast to IDEA which requires that the disability adversely affects educational performance. Unlike IDEA which requires that a child receive specially designed instruction, Section 504 can provide either instruction or specific accommodations that will allow the child to participate in and benefit from programs or activities.[64]

Behavioral Intervention Plans (BIP). An IEP team is required to oversee the development of a Behavioral Intervention Plan following a disciplinary action; that is, the IEP team is required to conduct a functional behavioral assessment and implement a BIP for the child's behavior that resulted in the suspension. Not later than ten days after taking a disciplinary action, the school district must "conduct a functional behavioral assessment and implement a behavioral intervention plan . . . that resulted in the suspension." The IEP team is responsible for developing, reviewing, and modifying the plan to address the behavior.[65] If the child already has a Behavioral Intervention Plan, the IEP team must review and modify the plan as necessary by considering "strategies, including positive behavior interventions strategies and supports."[66]

Individualized transition plans (ITP). An IEP must include a statement of transition services by age fourteen "that focuses on the child's courses of study (such as participation in advanced-placement courses or a vocational education program)" or by age sixteen to coordinate interagency responsibilities. A school district can meet this requirement by developing a separate ITP that includes a statement of vocational needs; the vocational strengths, needs, and interests of the student; measurable annual goals and short-term objectives; and services in a variety of areas (e.g., vocational counseling, or job coach).

IEP LAWS, CODES AND REGULATIONS

Federal legislation provides the basic guidelines for IEP development and implementation. The laws, codes, and regulations described below overview the chronology and historical development of the IEP. The basic five IEP elements were first outlined in PL 94-142 under Section 602(a)(19) and then codified in the United States Code as 20 USC 1401(a)(19). The 600 numbering used in the text of the PL 105-17 refers to title VI that was added to the Elementary and Secondary Education Act (PL 89-750) in 1966 (which also created the Bureau of Education for the Handicapped). This act was subsequently replaced by the Education of the Handicapped Act or PL 91-230 in 1970.

In 1990 the Education of All Handicapped Children Act (PL 94-142) was changed to the Individuals with Disabilities Education Act (IDEA) by PL 101-476. The most recent amendments to IDEA were made in 1997 by PL 105-17. These three laws, PL 94-142, PL 101-476, and PL 105-17 detail the increasing role of the IEP as the foundation for providing children with disabilities an appropriate public education. Table I provides a brief summary of the major statutory amendments in relation to IEPs.

Table I. IDEA Laws and Regulations Summary

The IEP in Public Law

Law	Name	Popular Title	USC	Public Law
PL 94-142	Education of All Handicapped Children Act of 1975	PL 94-142, EAHCA	20 USC 1401(a)(19)(A)-(E)	602(a)(19)(A)-(E)
PL 101-476	Individuals with Disabilities Education Act	IDEA, PL 101-476 (also IDEA-1990)	20 USC 1401(a)(20)(A)-(F)	602(a)(20)(A)-(F)
PL 105-17	Individuals with Disabilities Education Act of 1997	IDEA, IDEA-1997, PL 105-17	20 USC 1414(d)	614(d)

Code of Federal Regulations

The Individuals with Disabilities Education Act amendments is accompanied by a series of regulations that interpret the law and which are published in the Code of Federal Regulations (CFR, C.F.R., or simply the Code). The final regulations to PL 105-17 were published March 12, 1999 and appear in the Code as Title 34, Part 300, Sections 1 to 756 (or 34 CFR 300.1-300.756). These regulations also include Appendix A (Notice of Interpretation), which provide guidelines for interpreting IEPs. Although the regulations were not published until 1999, the regulations will be referred to in this book as the 1997 regulations or IDEA-1997 regulations in reference to PL 105-17 (IDEA-1997) which was passed into law in June of 1997.

The regulations are intended to implement changes made to IDEA amendments of 1997 related to areas such as eligibility, evaluation and IEPs; make other changes based on relevant, long-standing policy guidance (e.g., extended school year services, the determination of ADD as Other Health Impaired); and revise the requirements on state complaint procedures under both the Part B and Part C programs.[67]

Although much of the information heretofore contained in the Code of Federal Regulations are now incorporated in PL 105-17, the regulations provide an invaluable source for interpreting IDEA-1997. The primary regulations for IEPs concerning definitions, IEP meetings, team membership, and IEP content is contained in sections 300.340 to 300.350. Other important sections of the regulations in relation to IEPs include procedures for evaluation and determination of eligibility in sections 300.530–543, the evaluation of specific learning disabilities in sections 300.540–543, and least restrictive environment guidelines in sections 300.550-556. Appendix C of the 1990 regulations, which was devoted entirely to questions regarding the development and implementation of IEPs, has been substantially modified and renamed Appendix A for IDEA-1997. The regulations for IEP content and development, for the most part, are an exact copy of the statutory guidelines in 20 USC 1414(d). Table II shows the relation between PL 105-17 and regulations for areas that are especially relevant to IEP content and development:In addition to the federal

Table II. PL 105-17 and CFR Correspondence

IEP Statutory and Regulatory References

Area	CFR	USC	PL 105-17
Definitions	300.3-30	1401(1)-(30)	602(1)-(30)
Eligibility	300.110-156	1412-1413	612-613
FAPE	300.300-313	1412(a)(1)	612(a)(1)
Evaluation	300.320-321, 300.530-543	1414(a), (b), (c)	614(a), (b), (c)
IEP	300.340-350	1414(d)	614(d)
Private Schools	300.487	1412(a)(10)	612(a)(10)
Procedural Safeguards	300.500-529	1415	615

regulations, every state has laws and codes for developing and implementing IEPs. Prior to PL 91-230, federal support was mostly advisory[68] and state laws and regulations for providing services for children with disabilities were sporadic at best. With the emergence of federal requirements for developing IEPs, the regulations of states generally parallel federal laws and regulations concerning IEPs (especially with respect to basic IEP content). Because IDEA-1997 offers extensive guidelines for how the IEP should be developed, and what should be included in an IEP, state laws and regulations for IEP development may not comply with the most recent amendments. Nonetheless, to be in compliance with Federal laws and regulations as of July 1, 1998, all new IEPs must conform with IDEA-1997 IEP requirements.

Public Laws

PL 89-750. The Elementary and Secondary Education Act (ESEA) amendments of 1966 amended the ESEA of 1965 (PL 89-10) by providing state grant programs for handicapped children under a Title VI–Education of Handicapped Children.[69] Prior to PL 89-750, financial assistance was available primarily to meet "the special educational needs of educationally deprived children."[70] In order to receive a grant a under PL 89-750 a state educational agency was required to submit a state plan that specified certain assurances, and the special educational needs of children with disabilities was first addressed as a matter of law so that "effective procedures, including provision for appropriate objective measurements of educational achievement, will be adopted for evaluating at least annually the effectiveness of programs in meeting the special educational needs of, and providing related services for, handicapped children."[71] This very general requirement for a state plan created a need to develop an effective procedure for evaluating educational performance at least annually.

PL 91-230. PL 91-230 further amended the ESEA of 1965 in 1970 by repealing the existing Title VI and creating a new Title VI, the Education of the Handicapped Act (EHA). This act was composed of two parts:

Part A (General Provisions) and Part B (Assistance to States for the Education of Handicapped Children). An important change in EHA entailed assisting states in the development of programs designed to meet special educational needs.[72]

PL 93-380. The Education Amendments of 1974 (PL 93-380) to the ESEA of 1965 further amended EHA (PL 91-230) by adding two important sections that provided the basis for what would become PL 94-142. Section 613(a))12) is the foundation for a free appropriate public education and established "a goal of providing full educational opportunities to all handicapped children."[73] Section 613(a)(13) dramatically enhanced the role of parents to cope with inappropriate educational programs by requiring prior notice and due process procedures in order to voice complaints. Most importantly, PL 93-380 established the philosophical basis for special education by mandating "effective procedures . . . in decisions regarding identification, evaluation and educational placement,"[74] and requiring that "to the maximum extent appropriate, handicapped children . . . are educated with children who are not handicapped."[75] Section 613(a)(13)(B) has been referred to by the courts as "IDEA's mainstreaming provision,"[76] "a preference for mainstreaming,"[77] and mainstreaming directive,[78] but would later become the least restrictive environment provision of IDEA-1997 or 20 USC 1412(a)(5). The text for 613(a)(13)(B) originally directed

> procedures to insure that, to the maximum extent appropriate, handicapped children, including children in public or private institutions or other care facilities, are educated with children who are not handicapped, and special classes, separate schooling, or other removal of handicapped children from the regular educational environment occurs only when the nature or severity of the handicapped is such that education in regular classes with the use of supplementary aids and services cannot be achieved satisfactorily.

Public Law 93-380 did not require an IEP but did create a need for comprehensive planning and documentation in order to provide a range of procedural safeguards and to memorialize the process involving evaluation, placement, and services.[79] By requiring procedural safeguards relating to identification, evaluation and services, mandating a least restrictive environment, and requiring that these programs be evaluated "at least annually," PL 93-380 provided the basis for the procedural safeguards and due process rights detailed in IDEA-1997.

Public Law 93-380 also added Section 513,[80] the Family Educational Rights and Privacy Act (FERPA), to ensure confidentiality and the right of parents to review education records and to challenge misleading or inappropriate data.[81] Although the IEP is an educational record within the content of FERPA, the IEP is also a planning document that must be available to all interested parties in order to implement the plan. The confidentiality of IEPs is important but access cannot be restricted from legitimate service providers, especially the child's regular classroom teacher, under the guise of confidentiality. The regulations have clarified that the IEP is a planning document that must be "accessible to each regular education teacher, special education teacher, related service provider, and other service provider who is responsible for its implementation."[82] Parents "have the right to inspect and review any education records, including the IEP itself, relating to their children that are collected, maintained, or used by the agency."[83] If a parent believes that an education record contains inaccurate or misleading information, the parent can request that the school district amend the record. The school district, in turn, can either amend the record or refuse and inform the parents of their due process rights.

PL 93-112. The Rehabilitation Act of 1973 is a grant-in-aid program that began in 1920 (PL 66-236) for services relating to training, counseling, and placement. Section 102 of PL 93-122 (see also 29 USC 722) describes the elements of an individualized written rehabilitation program, and Section 504 (see also 29 USC 794) prohibits discrimination because of a person's disability.

A Section 504 plan or Section 504 accommodation is merely one way of avoiding discrimination so that an otherwise qualified child is not "excluded from the participation in, be denied benefits of, or be subjected to discrimination" because of his or her disability. Although *otherwise qualified* includes adults who can perform the essential job functions, all children eligible to receive FAPE are otherwise qualified. The surprisingly terse language of Section 504 states that

> No otherwise qualified individual with a disability in the United States, as defined in section 706(8) of this title shall, solely by reason of his or her disability, be excluded from the participation in, be denied benefits of, or be subjected to discrimination under any program or activity receiving Federal financial assistance.[85]

There is considerable overlap between the two sets of regulations for PL 93-112 (34 CFR 104) and PL 94-142 (34 CFR 300). The mandate for Section 504 is to ensure that special education and related aids and services . . . are designed to meet individual educational needs of handicapped persons as adequately as the needs of nonhandicapped persons are met" and that the "implementation of an individualized education program developed in accordance with the Education of the Handicapped Act is one means of meeting" this standard.[86] Because a disability under Section 504 does not require that a child need specially designed instruction, and because a disability under Section 504 is not confined to specific categories as previously discussed in the section entitled Section 504 Plan,[87] Section 504 can be used to provide special education, specific related services, supplementary aids and services, or specific program modifications and supports for children who have disabilities or who no longer have disabilities (e.g., declassified children).

PL 94-142. Public Law 94-142, Education for All Handicapped Children Act[88] (EAHCA) defined and outlined the IEP as a written statement for each handicapped child developed in any meeting involving the school, teacher, parents, and the child whenever appropriate. Most importantly, the statement was required to include the following five elements:

1. a statement of the present levels of educational performance of such child,
2. a statement of annual goals, including short-term instructional objectives,
3. a statement of the specific educational services to be provided to such child, and the extent to which such child will be able to participate in regular educational programs,
4. the projected date for initiation and antic-

ipated duration of such services,
5. appropriate objective criteria and evaluation procedures and schedules for determining, on at least an annual basis, whether instructional objectives are being achieved.[89]

PL 101-476. The next major modification to the IEP was the result of PL 101-476 or the Individuals with Disabilities Act (IDEA)[90] of 1990. These amendments not only changed "handicap" to "disability," but included the need for a statement of transition services by age fourteen or no later than age sixteen.[91] The purpose of this statement was for schools to develop "activities within an outcome-oriented process, thus enhancing a young adult's chances to achieve an adequate level of self-care, independence, self-sufficiency, and community integration."[92] The six required IDEA-1990 elements of an IEP are shown below with the added transition service requirement (#4) highlighted:

1. a statement of the present levels of educational performance of such child,
2. a statement of annual goals, including short-term instructional objectives,
3. a statement of the specific educational services to be provided to such child, and the extent to which such child will be able to participate in regular educational programs,
4. **a statement of the needed transition services for students beginning no later than age 16 and annually thereafter (and, when determined appropriate for the individual, beginning at age 14 or younger), including, when appropriate, a statement of the interagency responsibilities or linkages (or both) before the student leaves the school setting,**
5. the projected date for initiation and anticipated duration of such services,
6. appropriate objective criteria and evalua-

tion procedures and schedules for determining, on at least an annual basis, whether instructional objectives are being achieved.

PL 103-227. An important concern of IDEA-1997 is the participation of students with disabilities in districtwide and statewide assessment, the involvement of parents in the IEP process, and a new emphasis on high expectations for children with disabilities. Much of this emphasis can be traced to PL 103-227 (1994), Goals 2000: Educate America. A basic tenet of Goals 2000 is that "all students can learn and achieve to high standards and must realize their potential" and that "improvement strategies must provide all students with effective mechanisms and appropriate paths to the work force as well as to higher education." Of particular importance for children with disabilities is the belief that "all students are entitled to participate in a broad and challenging curriculum and to have access to resources sufficient to address other education needs."

The following Goals 2000 findings are especially important in establishing a philosophy that high standards and expectations should be for all children, including children with disabilities:[93]

> All students can learn and achieve to high standards and must realize their potential if the United States is to prosper;

> State and local systemic improvement strategies must provide all students with effective mechanisms and appropriate paths to the work force as well as to higher education;

> All students are entitled to participate in a broad and challenging curriculum and to have access to resources sufficient to address other education needs.

The goal is to "ensure that all students learn to use their minds well, so they may be prepared for responsible citizenship, further learning, and productive employment" and "every school will promote partnerships that will increase parental involvement and participation in promoting the social, emotional, and academic growth of children." This is also a primary goal of special education in that children with disabilities should become responsible and productive citizens to the maximum extent possible.

PUBLIC LAW 105-17 (IDEA-1997)

Public Law 105-17 or Individuals with Disabilities Education Act Amendments of 1997 (IDEA-1997), which was signed into law June 4, 1997, significantly modified IEP content so as to place special emphasis on the presumption that a child is entitled to participate in the general curriculum, modifying programs and assessments for inclusion in the general curriculum, and providing effective specially designed instruction. The IEP content requirements previously defined in the Code of Federal Regulations are now also incorporated in Section 614(d) of PL 105-17 and in 20 USC 1414(d).

The IDEA amendments of 1997 represent a well-articulated and focused philosophy concerning the role and purpose of special education which is intended to (1) improve educational results, (2) ensure equality of opportunity, promote full participation in regular education settings, (3) develop independent living and economic selfsufficiency,[94] and (4) require effective education of children with disabilities.[95]

These goals can be achieved by maintaining high expectations, strengthening the role of parent participation, supporting high-quality professional development, ensuring access in the general curriculum to the maximum extent possible, and encouraging wholeschool approaches and prereferral interventions to reduce the need to label children as disabled in order to address their learning needs.

The basic IEP content for IDEA-1997 has been substantially changed and increased from six to eight elements. These modifications include measurable annual goals, benchmarks and short-term objectives, supplementary aids and services to promote general curriculum participation, a statement of nonparticipation, test modifications, specifying the frequency and location of services, and reporting IEP progress to parents.

IEP Statutory Consolidation

Section 614(d) and 20 USC 1414(d) of IDEA-1997 provide a detailed explanation of evaluations, eligibility determinations, individualized education programs, and educational placements. Public Law 105-17 "consolidates in section 614 all interrelated provisions regarding the evaluation and reevaluation of children with disabilities and the development, review, and revision of individualized education programs (IEPs) for these children."[96] The purpose of this consolidation is to "reduce the burdens imposed by the interpretations of current law and make the requirements more understandable." In order to improve compliance with the IEP procedures, all IEP provisions were placed in Section 614(d) so that "the definition of the Individualized Education Program includes all of the required elements of an IEP, beginning with a statement of a child's present levels of educational performance, including how the child's disability affects the child's involvement and progress in the general education curriculum."[97]

The following is a list of PL 105-17 headings relating to the development and revision of IEPs contained in sections 20 USC 1414(d)(1)(A)(i)-(viii):

1414(d) Individualized Education Programs
(1) Definitions
  (A) Individualized Education Program
    (i) Present levels of educational performance
    (ii) Measurable annual goals, including benchmarks or short-term objectives
    (iii) Special education and related services and supplementary aids and services
    (iv) An explanation of the extent of nonparticipation
    (v) State and districtwide test modifications
    (vi) Beginning date, frequency, location, and duration of services
    (vii) Transition services and age of majority statement
    (viii) Progress evaluation method and reporting progress to parents
  (B) Individualized Education Program Team
(2) Requirement That Program Be In Effect
  (A) In General
  (B) Program for Child Aged 3

Through 5
(3) Development of IEP
   (A) In General
   (B) Consideration of Special Factors
   (C) Requirement With Respect to Regular Education Teacher
(4) Review and Revision of IEP
   (A) In General
   (B) Requirement With Respect to Regular Education Teacher
(5) Failure To Meet Transition Objectives
(6) Children With Disabilities in Adult Prisons
   (A) In General

(B) Additional Requirement

In addition to 1414(d), other important sections of IDEA-1997 relating to IEPs include individualized family service plan (IFSP) requirements in section 1436, state eligibility and evaluation requirements in Section 1412. In addition, the IEP team is also responsible for reviewing existing evaluation data,[98] and procedural safeguard responsibilities involving the development of behavioral functional assessment assessments,[99] determination of alternative settings,[100] and manifestation determination review.[101]

IEP-1997 Changes and Modifications

In an attempt to make the IEP a more dynamic document, the definition of an IEP was changed to mean "a written statement for each child with a disability that is developed, reviewed, and revised" and must include, when appropriate, eight elements. Depending on a child's needs and age, a child may or may not need a statement of nonparticipation, test modifications, or a statement of transition services.

1. PLEP. The statement of present levels of educational performance or PLEP has been expanded to emphasize the impact of the disability on regular curriculum participation.
   (i) a statement of the child's present levels of educational performance, including
      (I) how the child's disability affects the child's involvement and progress in the general curriculum; or
      (II) for preschool children, as appropriate, how the disability affects the child's participation in appropriate activities;

2. Goals. There are three key changes con-

cerning goals: First, goals must be "measurable"; second, the goals are measured by short-term objectives or benchmarks; and third, the focus of goals is regular curriculum involvement to the maximum extent appropriate.
   (ii) a statement of measurable annual goals, including benchmarks or short-term objectives, related to
      (I) meeting the child's needs that result from the child's disability to enable the child to be involved in and progress in the general curriculum; and
      (II) meeting each of the child's other educational needs that result from the child's disability;

3. Services. The statement of services has been expanded to include supplementary aids and services to promote regular classroom participation. As with PLEP and Goals, the emphasis of services is to promote general curriculum involvement and progress.
   (iii) a statement of the special education and related services and supplementary aids and services to be

provided to the child, or on behalf of the child, and a statement of the program modifications or supports for school personnel that will be provided for the child

(I) to advance appropriately toward attaining the annual goals;

(II) to be involved and progress in the general curriculum in accordance with clause (i) and to participate in extracurricular and other nonacademic activities; and

(III) to be educated and participate with other children with disabilities and nondisabled children in the activities described in this paragraph;

4. Nonparticipation. The statement of nonparticipation is new to IDEA-1997 and is the result of presumption that children with disabilities are to be educated in regular classes. If a regular class is not appropriate, the reason for the inappropriateness must be given. If a child cannot participate in several classes or activities, the reason for nonparticipation for each class and activity should be stated.

(iv) an explanation of the extent, if any, to which the child will not participate with nondisabled children in the regular class and in the activities described in clause (iii);

5. Modifications. Prior to IDEA-1997 many IEPs had a section concerning general test modifications. The statement of test modifications emphasizes the importance of regular curriculum assessment as a key to educational opportunities (e.g., a diploma, postsecondary opportunities). The IDEA-1997 requirement that an IEP include a statement of the individual modifications to state or districtwide assessments is also part of the mandate to maximize participation in the regular

educational programs.[102] This requirement highlights the importance of high-stakes standardized testing in the determination of academic competence and as a critical step in accessing other educational benefits (e.g., a regular education diploma). An additional requirement concerning test modifications is the need to signify "alternative assessments" if a state or districtwide assessment is inappropriate.

(v) (I) a statement of any individual modifications in the administration of state or districtwide assessments of student achievement that are needed in order for the child to participate in such assessment; and

(II) if the IEP Team determines that the child will not participate in a particular state or districtwide assessment of student achievement (or part of such an assessment), a statement of

(aa) why that assessment is not appropriate for the child; and

(bb) how the child will be assessed;

6. Conditions. In addition to the date indicating the beginning and duration of services, PL 105-17 also requires a listing of the frequency and location of services. For the most part IEPs should be implemented as soon as possible following the IEP meeting and the duration of services is generally up to 12 months. The addition of the *location* of services was added to further promote the union of special and regular education. For example, a related service might be provided in the regular classroom, thus precluding the need to choose between a needed service and regular classroom participation.[103] Likewise, the frequency of services

provides an index of the amount of "specifically designed instruction" and related services needed by a child.

(vi) the projected date for the beginning of the services and modifications described in clause (iii), and the anticipated frequency, location, and duration of those services and modifications;

The modifications cited in (vi) above include program modification and supports. For example, if an assistive technology device is required program modification, the date when this program support will be available should be specified.

7. Transition. The statement of transition services required at age sixteen (or earlier) has been augmented by a statement of transition services at age fourteen which focuses on planning a school program, classes and other school activities which will promote school-to-work transition. Beginning at age fourteen (or earlier if younger is appropriate) a statement of transition services is required relating to the student's course of study (e.g., a vocational program, specific academic program). Beginning at age sixteen (or younger if appropriate) the statement of transition services emphasizes "interagency responsibilities or any needed linkages."[104]

(vii) (I) beginning at age 14, and updated annually, a statement of the transition service needs of the child under the applicable components of the child's IEP that focuses on the child's courses of study (such as participation in advanced-placement courses or a vocational education program);

(II) beginning at age 16 (or younger, if determined appropriate by the IEP Team), a statement of needed transition services for the child, including, when appropriate, a statement of the interagency responsibilities or any needed linkages; and

(III) beginning at least one year before the child reaches the age of majority under state law, a statement that the child has been informed of his or her rights under this title, if any, that will transfer to the child on reaching the age of majority under section 615(m); and

As part of the transition services, a statement must also be provided when a student reaches the age of majority to inform the student of his or her rights, or appoint the parent or other responsible person to represent the interests of the child. The purpose of this statement is to ensure that the state develops "procedures for appointing the parent or another individual to represent the interests of the child" when the child is incapable of making educational decisions.[105] When a child with a disability reaches the age of majority under state law "all other rights accorded to parents under this part transfer to the child" unless the child "is determined not to have the ability to provide informed consent with respect to the educational program of the child." The age of majority varies from state to state. In Wisconsin when a child reaches the age of eighteen, unless the child has been determined to be incompetent, the local educational agency provides notice to both the individual and the individual's parents, and all other rights accorded to the individual's parents transfer to the individual. In New York State no transfer of rights is permissible and thus New York does not require a transfer of rights statement.

8. Evaluation. The statement on evaluation now requires not only an evaluation of progress toward annual goals, but informing parents on a regular basis or "as often as parents are informed of their nondisabled children's progress" toward achieving the annual goals. The previous requirement concerning progress had been to list criteria, procedures and schedules for evaluating goals on least an annual basis. This often resulted in an end-of-the-year evaluation by "teacher observation" with the venerable 80% accuracy criterion. Now progress must be reported on a periodic basis at least as often as parents of nondisabled children are informed of progress. If students in the regular curriculum receive report cards four times a year, annual goal progress should be reported at least four times a year.

(viii) a statement of

    (I) how the child's progress toward the annual goals described in clause (ii) will be measured; and

    (II) how the child's parents will be regularly informed (by such means as periodic report cards), at least as often as parents are informed of their nondisabled children's progress, of

        (aa) their child's progress toward the annual goals described in clause (ii); and

        (bb) the extent to which that progress is sufficient to enable the child to achieve the goals by the end of the year.

•

As will be discussed in the next chapter, the procedures for determining the need for an IEP and for developing IEP content is the first step for ensuring an appropriate IEP. If procedures for developing content have not been followed (e.g., parents were not given prior written notice) or IEP content is lacking, the IEP is not in compliance and the appropriateness of the IEP is problematic.

Of course, in addition to following the procedures and including all required IEP content, the IEP must be a serious plan that is designed to impart educational benefit. The IEP content described above must not only be addressed in the IEP, but the content must be a real plan (or a "reasonably calculated" plan) to meet a child's unique educational needs.

NOTES

[1] PL 91-230 (1970) and PL 93-380 (1974).

[2] Such as PARC v. Pennsylvania, 334 F.Supp. 1257 (ED Pa. 1971).

[3] As required by 34 CFR 300.194, every child must receive FAPE: "(a) All children with disabilities who are participating in programs and projects funded under Part B of the Act receive FAPE, and that those children and their parents are provided all the rights and procedural safeguards described in this part."

[4] Pennsylvania Association for Retarded Children (PARC) v. Commonwealth of Pennsylvania, 334 F.Supp. 1257 (1971).

[5] PL 94-142, Section 601(a)(18)(C).

[6] 34 CFR 300.347(a)(2)(i).

[7] The "general curriculum" means "the same

curriculum as for nondisabled children." The term "general curriculum," as defined in this section, relates to the content of the curriculum and not to the setting in which it is used. Thus, to the extent applicable to an individual child with a disability and consistent with the LRE provisions under Secs. 300.500–300.553, the general curriculum could be used in any educational environment along a continuum of alternative placements described under Sec. 300.551.

8 20 USC 1414(d)(1)(A)(ii).

9 PL 94-142, Section 602(a)(19) and 20 USC 1401(a)(19) of the United States Code.

10 The IEP is defined in 20 USC 1401(11) and detailed in 20 USC 1414(d) of PL 94-142.

11 PL 94-142, 20 USC 1414(a)(5) and 20 USC 1412(4).

12 IDEA-1990, Appendix C, I. Purpose of the IEP.

13 IDEA-1990, 34 CFR 300.352(b).

14 20 USC 1414(b)(4)(A).

15 Wyoming State Board of Education Rules and Regulations for Serving Children with Disabilities, Chapter 7, Section 14.

16 34 CFR 300, Appendix A, Question #1.

17 House Report 94-332.

18 Senate Report 94-168.

19 *Ibid.*, p. 1435.

20 Senate Conference Report 94-455.

21 34 CFR 300, Appendix A, Question #32.

22 *Ibid.*, Question #32.

23 *Ibid.*, Appendix A, Question #9.

24 *Ibid.*, Question #5.

25 Senate Report 105-17, p. 5.

26 34 CFR, Appendix A, Question #5.

27 34 CFR 300.345, Parent participation.

28 20 USC 1415(k).

29 Hudson v. Rowley, 458 U.S. 176 (1982).

30 898 F.2d 1186 (6th Cir. 1990).

31 458 U.S. 176 (1982).

32 Senate Report 94-168, p. 1435.

33 House Report 94-332 (which accompanied bill HR 7217 which became PL 94-142), p. 13.

34 34 CFR 300, Appendix A, Question #32.

35 34 CFR 300.344(a)(2).

36 34 CFR 300.344.

37 20 USC 1415(i)(3)(D).

38 Senate Report 105-17, p. 25.

39 20 USC 1414(d)(1)(A)(viii).

40 IDEA-1990, Appendix C, Question #57.

41 34 CFR 300.29(a)(1).

42 IDEA-1990, 34 CFR 300, Appendix C, Question #36.

43 Senate Report 105-17, p. 24.

44 State of Montana, IEP.

45 34 CFR 300.452(b).

46 Virginia Administrative Code, 12VAC30-130-540. Definitions.

47 Ministry of Education, British Columbia, Canada.

48 22-7-504 Pupil assessments – individual literacy plans.

49 20 USC 1436(d)(5).

50 20 USC 1436(d).

51 20 USC 1414(d)(2)(B).

52 IDEA-1990, 34 CFR 300.342, Note 3.

53 20 USC 1437(a)(8)(A)(ii)(II).

54 34 CFR 300.451.

55 34 CFR 300.452(2).

56 34 CFR 300.456(a). On-site services.

57 Senate Report 93-318, p. 2097 for the Rehabilitation Act of 1973 (PL 93-112).

58 *Ibid.*, p. 2098.

59 20 USC 1414(d)(1)(B)(vii).

60 34 CFR 300.344(b)(1) & (2).

61 Senate Bill 1579 and 29 USC 722(b)(1)(B).

62 Senate Report 105-17, p. 2.

63 29 USC 706(8)(B).

64 29 USC 794.

65 20 USC 1415(k)(1)(B).

66 Senate Report 105-17, p. 24.

67 Final regulations, Office of Special Education and Rehabilitative Services, Department of Education, *Federal Register*, March 12, 1999, Volume 64, Number 48, Rules and Regulations, p. 12406.

68 Federal involvement in special education began at the section level in 1930 with the Section of Exceptional Children in Youth which developed into the Division of Handicapped Children and Youth in 1963 (PL 88-164), and as the Bureau of Education for the

Handicapped (BEH) in 1966 (PL 89-750).

69 What had been previously designated Title VI under PL 89-10 was redesignated Title VII. The numbering for the new Title VI under 89-750 comprised Section 601 to Section 610.

70 PL 89-10, Title II—Financial Assistance to Local Educational Agencies for the Education of Children of Low-Income Families, Section 201. Declaration of Policy.

71 PL 89-750, Section 604(e).

72 Public Law 91-230 has been amended on several occasions by PL 93-380 (1974), PL 94-142 (1975), PL 98-199 (1983), PL 99-457 (1986), PL 100-630 (1988), PL 101-476 (1990), PL 102-73 (1991), PL 102-119 (1991), PL 103-382 (1994). For PL 105-17 the codification for this law states that the addition of PL 105-17 is made "without reference to such intervening amendments because of the extensive revision of Part A by" PL 105-17.

73 20 USC 1413(a)(12)(A).

74 PL 93-380, 20 USC 1413(a)(13).

75 Section 20 USC 1413(a)(13)(B).

76 Hartmann v. Loudoun, 118 F.3d 996 (4th Cir. 1997).

77 Oberti v. Board, 789 F.Supp 1322 (D.N.J. 1992), p. 1326.

78 Greer v. Rome, 950 F.2d 688 (11 Cir. 1991), p. 695.

79 See also 20 USC 1413 state plans (a)(11) for PL 94-142 that requires "procedures for evaluation at least annually of the effectiveness of programs in meeting the educational needs of handicapped children (including evaluation of individualized education programs)."

80 PL 93-380, Title V—Education Administration, Sec. 513. Protection of rights and privacy of parents and students.

81 20 USC 1232g and 34 CFR 99.3.

82 34 CFR 300.342(b)(2).

83 Also see 34 CFR Sec. 300.501: Parents have a right to "inspect and review all education records with respect to the identification, evaluation, and educational placement of the child."

84 34 CFR 300.567. Amendment of records at parent's request.

85 29 USC 794.

86 34 CFR 104.33.

87 As per 29 USC 706(8)(B) a disability under Section 504 is defined as (1) a physical or mental impairment which substantially limits one or more of such person's major life activities, (2) has a record of such an impairment, or (3) is regarded as having such an impairment.

88 20 USC 1400 et seq.

89 PL 94-142, Section 602(a)(19).

90 This changed the name of PL 94-142 (Education for All Handicapped Children Act).

91 IDEA-1990, 20 USC 1401(a)(20)(D).

92 House Report 202-544, p. 10.

93 Title III: State and Local Education Systemic Improvement, Sec. 301: Findings of Goals 2000.

94 20 USC 1400(c)(1).

95 20 USC 1400(c)(5).

96 Senate Report 105-17, p. 17.

97 *Ibid.*, p. 19.

98 20 USC 1414(c)(1).

99 20 USC 1415(k)(1)(B).

100 20 USC 1415(k)(3).

101 20 USC 1415(k)(4).

102 20 USC 1401(19)(C) "and the extent to which such child will be able to participate in regular education programs."

103 Senate Report 105-17, p. 21.

104 20 USC 1414(d)(1)(A)(vii).

105 Senate Report 105-17, p. 22.

106 State Education Department, NYS, Policy 97-09, p. 28, January 1998.

107 20 USC 1414(d)(1)(A)(viii)(II).

Chapter 2

AN APPROPRIATE EDUCATION

EQUAL EDUCATIONAL OPPORTUNITY

S PECIAL EDUCATION IS DIRECTLY LINKED TO THE CIVIL RIGHTS LITIGATION of the 1950s that established the need and right for all children to receive an appropriate education. In *Brown v. Board of Education*[1] of Topeka the Supreme Court stated that ". . . it is doubtful that any child may reasonably be expected to succeed in life if he is denied the opportunity of an education. Such an opportunity, where the state has undertaken to provide it, is a right which must be made available to all on equal terms." The essential question in *Brown* was whether segregation, regardless of the nature of the segregated facility, was appropriate. The court's determination of the inappropriateness of segregation laid the basis for a free appropriate public education for children with disabilities and participation in the regular curriculum mainstream to the maximum extent appropriate. In *Brown* the court resolved that "segregation of children in public schools solely on the basis of race, even though the physical facilities and other 'tangible' factors may be equal" does deprive equal educational opportunity.

The *Brown* decision mandated that *on equal terms* requires schools to provide equal educational opportunities for all children, and that this cannot be achieved by separate educational opportunities. For students with disabilities, this means that a child cannot be "excluded from the participation in, be denied benefits of, or be subjected to discrimination under any program or activity receiving Federal financial assistance."[2] The question for the Warren Court was whether segregation in schools deprived children of equal educational opportunities. The task for educators today (and one not infrequently undertaken by the courts) is to provide *full educational opportunities* to children with disabilities as described in the IDEA-1997.

One of the findings of Congress in IDEA-1997 is that more than one-half of the children with disabilities in the United States are not receiving appropriate educational services.[3] For children with disabilities, the goal of special education is not merely to provide equal educational opportunity, but to provide full educational opportunity by means of an appropriate educational program that will allow a child to participate in the regular curriculum to the maximum extent appropriate.

For a child with a disability, equal educational opportunity means that an educational program is developed that addresses the child's unique needs. *Brown* resulted in a simple and straightforward procedural dictate: segregation is wrong and it must not exist. For children with disabilities, the task is more complex because a program or service apart from the regular classroom might be necessary to provide an appropriate educational program. The many regulations and procedural safeguards provided by IDEA are designed to carefully balance the need for an appropriate education with the child's right to a public education. If a child is excluded from the regular curriculum because of a disability, when the child is able to participate in the regular curriculum to some extent, special education might actually serve to deny full educational opportunity. On the other hand, a child might be deprived of full educational opportunity because individual needs have not been addressed and special education not provided. A child who is capable of learning science but is not provided science by a qualified teacher because of a special education placement, is not being provided an opportunity to learn or an appropriate environment in which to learn. On a similar basis, a child might be in a regular science classroom, but if the child's unique needs are not met, the regular education experience might be inappropriate.

As is the case in *Brown* where segregation resulted in discrimination, for children with disabilities discrimination can occur in either a regular classroom or a segregated setting if individual learning needs are not considered. As stated in Section 504 of the Rehabilitation Act of 1973 a child with a disability cannot "be excluded from participation in, be denied the benefits of, or be subjected to discrimination under any program or activity receiving Federal financial assistance." Obviously, if a child is deprived of a program, either specially designed instruction or a regular education program, or a benefit thereof, the result might be discriminatory.

The reasoning for the *Brown* decision was exceedingly simple: segregation is "inherently unequal." Likewise, unnecessarily segregating a child because of a disability, a perceived disability, or a misconstrued disability is no less pernicious and inherently unequal. The dilemma in special education is that although education must be made available to all children on equal terms, equal terms for a child with a disability can mean a modified curriculum, a different curriculum, or a different curriculum setting. The solution to the problem of a providing full and equal educational opportunity for children with disabilities is to provide a program that is individualized, complies with the regulations, is reasonably calculated to provide educational benefit, and is provided in the least restrictive environment.

For *Brown*, the cornerstone for full and equal educational opportunity was a decree that segregation deprived children "of the equal protection of the laws guaranteed by the Fourteenth Amendment." For children with disabilities, the mechanism for providing an appropriate education is an individualized plan that explicates needs, defines specific annual goals and services, and provides children and parents with a variety of due process safeguards to serve as "the foundation for ensuring access to a free appropriate public education."[4]

FAPE

The word *appropriate* is used throughout IDEA-1997 and the regulations: appropriate special education and related services are necessary to provide effective educational programs;[5] an appropriate public education will prepare children with disabilities for employment and independent living;[6] children should be educated with children who are not disabled "to the maximum extent appropriate;"[7] and children with disabilities and their parents are guaranteed procedural safeguards so that they can receive a free appropriate public education.[8]

A free appropriate public education is defined in IDEA-1997 as special education and related services which

1. have been provided at public expense, under public supervision and direction, and without charge;
2. meet the standards of the State educational agency;
3. include an appropriate preschool, elementary, or secondary school education in the State involved; and
4. are provided in conformity with the individualized education program required under section 614(d).[9]

A free appropriate public education for a child with a disability is achieved by an appropriate education plan as defined in the child's IEP. For a child with a disability, the IEP provides the operational definition of what is appropriate for each child. By definition, if the IEP does not comply with IDEA (e.g., no present levels of performance, goals are not measurable and short-term objectives are not intermediate steps), the IEP is deficient and not in compliance with the law and regulations. An IEP can be procedurally inappropriate yet provide appropriate and effective services for a child. However, because the determination of what is educationally appropriate is subject to considerable disagreement, procedural appropriateness becomes the one standard, albeit a very minimal standard, that is clearly defined. If procedural appropriateness is ignored, the foundation for educational appropriateness no longer exists.

A free appropriate education under IDEA-1997 is not intended for all persons with disabilities, but is designed for children with disabilities, aged three through twenty-one, including children with disabilities who have been expelled from school.[10] For children ages three to five and eighteen to twenty-one, the provision for FAPE must be consistent with state law.[11] After reaching the age of twenty-one or upon graduation from high school with a regular high school diploma, a student is not entitled to FAPE. Before a student is determined to no longer have a disability and thereby not need FAPE, parents must be given prior written notice of this change in placement, a notice of procedural safeguards, and consent to a re-evaluation. This evaluation is not required if the student graduates with a regular high school diploma or exceeds the age eligibility requirement.[12] If a student receives an IEP diploma or a special diploma, the student remains eligible to receive FAPE.[13]

The IEP is the vehicle for providing a child with an education that is appropriate and nondiscriminatory, and the definition of FAPE in IDEA-1997 places a great deal of emphasis on the IEP for determining what is appropriate. If the IEP is developed in compliance with the regulations and the IEP team is in agreement with the content of the IEP, the IEP is appropriate. As noted in *Hudson v. Rowley*,[14] although the somewhat vague guideline that compliance and an agreed-upon document is the basis for determining what is appropriate, "like many statutory definitions, this one tends toward the cryptic rather than the comprehensive, but that is scarcely a reason for abandoning the quest for legislative intent."

As noted in *Hudson v. Rowley*, a free appropriate public education is "the principal substantive phrase used in the Act" so that even though the definition of the phrase might be lacking, the intent of FAPE must be considered. According to the court, "The Act's intent was more to open the door of public education to handicapped children by means of specialized educational services than to guarantee any particular substantive level of education once inside" and "to require the States to adopt procedures which would result in individualized consideration of and instruction for each child."[15]

In *Burlington v. Massachusetts* the court referred to the IEP as the *modus operandi* of the Act, and that the IEP is the primary method of operation for implementing PL 94-142. The IEP is considered the cornerstone of IDEA-1997, or, as described by the Supreme Court in *Honig v. Doe*,[17] "the centerpiece of the statue's educational delivery system for disabled children" (p. 699). The IEP is more than a document developed to show regulatory compliance, but a plan for an *appropriate* education designed to meet the unique needs of a child, a plan that recognizes "the importance and indeed the necessity of parental participation in both the development of the IEP and any subsequent assessments of its effectiveness."[18] For many children with disabilities a free appropriate public education can be achieved by participation in the regular school curriculum and through the participation of regular classroom teachers. The law recognizes the regular classroom teachers' "increasingly critical role in implementing, together with special education and related services personnel, the program of FAPE for most children with disabilities, as described in their IEPs."[19] To accommodate this need, the IEP team requires not only the child's teacher, but "at least one regular education teacher of the child, if the child is, or may be, participating in the regular education environment."

The right of a public education was asserted in *Pennsylvania Association for Retarded Children v. Commonwealth of Pennsylvania* (or *PARC v. Pennsylvania*)[20] and *Mills v. Board of Education of the District of*

Columbia.[21] These cases confirmed the need for appropriate educational services, guided by periodic review, and were the most prominent of the cases contributing to the enactment of the P.L. 94-142.

In *Mills*, the issue centered about the right of every child "to receive a free educational assessment and to be placed in a publicly supported educational program suited to his needs" and the need to develop a plan (by the defendants) to "describe the curriculum, educational objectives, teacher qualifications, and ancillary services for the publicly-supported educational programs to be provided to the class members."[22] The *Mills* decision admonished the defendants "to enroll . . . children in an appropriate educational program" and to accomplish this by means of a plan. This plan for an appropriate education would later become the IEP as defined in PL 94-142. Although *appropriate* was not defined in *Mills*, the court realized that what was being provided was inappropriate and must be changed. Operationally, the court understood that a comprehensive plan was needed involving "identification, notification, assessment, and placement of class members" and that the curriculum and educational objectives should be described for each class member. Both *PARC* and *Mills* drew initial attention to the need for an appropriate education. For *PARC*, the court directed school districts to provide every "retarded person . . . access to a free public program of education and training appropriate to his learning capacities" (p. 1258).

In *PARC* the court defined an appropriate program as one that met a child's needs and was provided in the least restrictive environment so that

each mentally retarded child in a free, public program of education and training appropriate to the child's capacity, within the context of a presumption that, among the alternative programs of education and training required by statute to be available, placement in a regular public school class is preferable to placement in a special school class and placement in a special school class is preferable to placement in any other type of program of education and training.[23]

The *PARC* decision directed the development of educational programs "appropriate to the child's capacity," and "within the context of a presumption" that the least restrictive educational placement is preferable. This presumption, of course, is the basis for the present-day concept of *least restrictive environment.* With respect to IDEA-1997, this has been taken one step further in that "the law and this bill contain a presumption that children with disabilities are to be educated in regular classes."[24]

THE COMPLIANCE CRITERION

Critics of existing IEP practice and implementation often point to the overemphasis on compliance rather than providing appropriate educational programs as the overriding problem. As explained in *Hudson v. Rowley*, procedural compliance is intended to ensure an appropriate education. The problem does not entail an overemphasis on compliance, but a blatant disregard for both the letter and the spirit of statutory and regulatory guidelines. If compliance is regarded as nothing more than producing an IEP document in which parents are uninvolved, needs are misidentified, and goals poorly defined and regular curriculum participation not considered, compliance is not only overemphasized but blatantly inappropriate. If, however, the law and the regulations are carefully considered, the type of compliance expected by IDEA and by the courts will provide the foundation for an appropriate education.

The concept is so obvious and so straightforward that few would question the need for an appropriate education. But determining an appropriate education is far more difficult than determining what is inappropriate. The determination of an appropriate education should always be made with parent involvement and participation, but the ultimate responsibility for providing each child with a free appropriate public education belongs to the school district. A parent might feel that appropriate is in the regular classroom, a school official might feel that appropriate for the same child is a self-contained classroom, and the child's teacher might believe that the child needs consultant teacher and/or resource room services. The law and the regulations provide guidance for IEP development and implementation, but the provision of *the most appropriate* education program cannot be legislated. As a result, statutory and regulatory compliance must serve as the foundation of an appropriate education, followed by a plan that is reasonably calculated to provide educational benefit.

When there is failure to agree among IEP team members as to the content or appropriateness of an IEP, a due process interpretation can be sought. This can occur either through mediation,[25] a due process hearing,[26] or a state-level appeal.[27] If an appropriate program cannot be agreed on by the school district and the parents or resolved by complaints, mediation, hearings, and state-level complaints, a judicial interpretation of appropriate can be sought in a state or district court.[28] The various court decisions discussed below are not intended to provide a definitive interpretation of *appropriate* in the context of IEP development, but to consider how *appropriate* is conceptualized in a judicial sense. Even for Supreme Court decisions there is often a high degree of case specificity regarding the meaning of an *appropriate education*, and a judicial interpretation of *appropriate* is not always easy to generalize to all situations. As explained in *Hudson v. Rowley*, the task is not to impose a judicial determination of what is educationally appropriate, and that reviewing courts should not have complete authority to determine what constitutes an appropriate education or what is included in an IEP. The Supreme Court opined that

> we find nothing in the Act to suggest that merely because Congress was rather sketchy in establishing substantive requirements, as opposed to procedural requirements for the preparation of an IEP, it intended that reviewing courts should have a free hand to impose substantive standards of review which cannot be derived from the Act itself. In short, the statutory authorization to grant "such relief as the court determines is appropriate" cannot be read without reference to the obligations, largely procedural in nature, which are imposed upon recipient States by Congress.[29]

Courts are obligated to give "due weight" to administrative hearings when determining the appropriateness of an IEP rather than to review a case *de novo*; that is, to review the case again but with little weight given to previous administrative hearings (e.g., a due process hearing). This is the point of the "due weight" provision in *Hudson* that a court does not have the sole responsibility for determining the appropriateness of an IEP, and that a court must acknowledge the procedures, if followed. As stated in *Hartmann v. Loudoun County Board of Education* "IDEA does not grant State courts a license to substitute their own notions of sound educational policy for those of local school authorities, or to disregard the findings developed in state administrative proceedings."[30]

The responsibility for developing an appropriate IEP belongs to the IEP team. In most instances, the court's task is not to determine what is appropriate, but rather which IEP is appropriate. For example, a school district proposes an IEP with vague goals and the parents want measurable goals; or the parents want an IEP that specifies mainstreaming while the school feels that a residential setting is most appropriate (or vice versa).

The Supreme Court's decision in *Hudson v. Rowley*[31] outlines a school district's basic responsibility for providing a child with a disability with an appropriate education. The issue concerned a child who is deaf and was denied the parents' request for a qualified sign language interpreter in all of her academic classes. A district court had found in favor of *Hudson* that, although the child was progressing easily from grade to grade, she was not performing up to her potential. "Because of this disparity between the child's achievement and her potential, the court held that she was not receiving a 'free appropriate public education,' which the court defined as 'an opportunity to achieve [her] full potential commensurate with the opportunity provided to other children.'" The Court of Appeals affirmed the District Court's decision.

The Supreme Court determined that when a suit is brought under the procedural safeguards rights of IDEA, a lower court must make a twofold determination:

> First, has the State complied with the procedures set forth in the Act? And

second, is the [458 U.S. 176, 207] individualized educational program developed through the Act's procedures reasonably calculated to enable the child to receive educational benefits? If these requirements are met, the State has complied with the obligations imposed by Congress and the courts can require no more.

In essence, the court defined *appropriate* as meaning that a school has complied with the regulations and a plan has been reasonably calculated to meet the child's needs. As stated in *Hudson* "it seems to us no exaggeration to say that Congress placed every bit as much emphasis upon compliance with procedures giving parents and guardians a large measure of participation at every stage of the administrative process . . . as it did upon the measurement of the resulting IEP against a substantive standard." By this reasoning, the court concluded that the "Court of Appeals erred in affirming the decision of the District Court. Neither the District Court nor the Court of Appeals found that petitioners had failed to comply with the procedures of the Act, and the findings of neither court would support a conclusion that Amy's educational program failed to comply with the substantive requirements of the Act."

Much of litigation involving IEPs refers to the *Hudson v. Rowley* two-prong test of compliance with IDEA and developing a reasonably calculated plan to provide educational benefit. The first test concerns procedural noncompliance. For example, there are regulations concerning parent participation, IEP development, and implementation. If a regulation is not complied with, then a determination must be made whether the procedural inadequacy rises to the level of denial of a free appropriate public education. In *W.G. v. Target Range School District*,[32] the Court of Appeals agreed that the Target Range School District had

presented the parents with a prepared IEP that did not comply with the regulations requiring parent participation and that "when a district fails to meet the procedural requirements of the Act by failing to develop an IEP in the manner specified, the purposes of the Act are not served, and the district may have failed to provide a FAPE" (p. 1484).

Simply failing to meet a regulatory procedure is not an automatic denial of an appropriate education but, as stated in *Target*, "procedural inadequacies that result in the loss of educational opportunity . . . or seriously infringe the parents' opportunity to participate in the IEP formulation process . . . clearly result in the denial of a FAPE." In *Bend-Lapine School District v. D.W.*,[33] the court found that the district's procedural violation of not providing all the services listed in an IEP "did not raise to the level of a denial of a FAPE." The reasoning for this decision was that the impact was not severe enough to deny FAPE, and because of other factors such as resistance to special education and school attendance. This is consistent with *Doe v. Defendant I*[34] where the school district was found not to be in violation of required criteria and schedules for evaluating IEPs for a student with a "dysgraphic disorder" even though the IEP document did not contain all the requisite data. The court reasoned that "to say that these technical deviations from section . . . render appellant's IEP invalid is to exalt form over substance" (p. 1190). This does not signify that an IEP need not contain all the required elements, but that in this situation "the parents and administrators had all of the information required . . . even though it was not contained within the four corners of the IEP" (p. 1190).

In most situations, an IEP should contain all the necessary information, within the four corners of the IEP, even if the information is contained in other documents (e.g., report cards). However, the important point in *Doe v. Defendant I* is that an IEP is not just a response to a list of technical requirements (and thereby exalt form), but a plan in which form is a necessary concern but substance is paramount.

There are occasions when the regulations regarding IEPs are not complied with because of misinformation or other concerns. For example, the active role of parents in the IEP process is not achieved because of a belief by the school district (or the parents) that the parents have nothing to contribute, or because of the demands or perceived demands of the parents. On the other hand, the importance of parent participation might be undermined by the refusal or disinterest of parents to actively participate in the planning process. The law does give "parents and guardians a large measure of participation at every stage of the adminis-trative process,"[35] but there is no legislative mandate that a parent must or will participate. School districts often assume a villainous mantel in the IEP process, but often, for whatever reason, the missing ingredient in the IEP planning process is a lack of parent involvement.

A complete IEP might not be appropriate, but an incomplete IEP is clearly inappropriate. In the first annual report to Congress on the implementation of PL 94-142[36] the bureau was enthusiastic by the level of teacher involvement caused by the IEP process, but also noted that "in some places, handicapped children were being educated in accordance with IEPs that were incomplete" and that "such deficits render the IEP ineffective as a tool for accountability, parental involvement, communication, and planning" (p. 106).

A REASONABLY CALCULATED PLAN

The second prong of the *Hudson v. Rowley* test to determine the adequacy of an IEP is the substantive requirement that an IEP is reasonably calculated to provide educational benefit. When PL 94-142 appeared in 1975, special education often entailed little more than a self-contained classroom where children were placed because of a perceived inability to participate in the regular curriculum and not to receive an appropriate education by following a reasonably calculated plan. Children were placed in special education classrooms to participate in a special education curriculum. The plan was not an appropriate education; the plan was removal from a regular to a special education classroom. The self-contained classroom was the plan, the program, and the curriculum. The other plan, the IEP plan required by PL 94-142, was a requirement to receive funding. This being the case, educational goals were vague and inappropriate, services were not provided, or services were provided that were inappropriate and did not address learning needs.

Although the 1990 regulations attempted to guide and focus planning, many IEPs were developed so that IEP entries under each IEP component were dutifully recorded but the IEP did not outline a calculated plan to address individual needs. For example, IDEA-1990 regulations define short-term instructional objectives as intermediate steps between present levels of educational performance and goals,[37] but IEP objectives were often annual goals or activities and not benchmarks or milestones to evaluate and report progress.

The problems with IEPs were noted shortly after the implementation of PL 94-

142 (1975) and continue to plague the implementation of PL 105-17 (1997). In a survey to evaluate the effectiveness of PL 94-142[38] "a significant proportion of IEPs did not contain all of the mandated information, or a direct link between areas of need and services" (p. 15). Also, "about 40 percent of the IEPs were informative and internally consistent" (9.8, p. 158) and "a significant percent of the IEPs either had statements of needs in functional/academic areas for which goals and/or objectives were not included, or they contained goals and/or objectives for areas in which a need statement was not included" (9.9, p. 159). More recently, Bateman offered a far more negative, albeit realistic, analysis of IEPs: "Most IEPs are useless or slightly worse, and too many teachers experience the IEP process as . . . a pointless bureaucratic requirement. The result is a quasi-legal document to be filed away with the expectation it won't be seen again except, heaven forbid, by a monitor or compliance officer."[39]

The amendments to IDEA have attempted to provide direction for developing reasonably calculated IEPs by stating the purpose of the plan, the direction of the plan, and how to plan. First, the IEP is a plan that is designed to meet the child's needs that result from the disability. Second, an IEP is a plan that enables children to be involved in and progress in the general curriculum. This does not mean that a child with a disability is required to perform at the same level as nondisabled children, but an opportunity to participate, to the maximum extent appropriate, in school and then in work with persons who are not disabled. Third, the plan contains measurable annual goals, each of which is composed of a logical series of intermediate steps, that plan progress over the course of a year. With the explicit guidelines contained in IDEA-1997, measurable annual goals and objectives are no longer vague statements and lists of classroom activities, but the essence of the calculated plan to provide educational benefit.

IEP Internal Consistency

The internal logic or consistency of an IEP indicates, to a large degree, the extent an individualized program has been thoughtfully planned. In a 1980 survey of IEPs, Pyecha and others found that approximately 40 percent of the IEPs were informative and internally consistent.[40] This report used the relationship between needs, goals and short-term objectives as a measure of internal consistency so that "the relationship between need statements, goals, and short-term objectives provides an indication of the student's special education needs and what is being done about them through educational programming."[41] The lack of consistency found in this study between

needs and goals is a problem that affects the IEP process today. Not only is there a lack of consistency between needs and goals, there is a lack of consistency between regular classroom performance and evaluation, evaluation and needs, needs and goals, goals and services, and goals and evaluation.

Referral/Evaluation. The reason why a child is referred should guide the conduct of an individualized evaluation and the development of an IEP. The referral process is an essential step in determining eligibility and need for special education. The task is not to *discover* a disability but rather to address one or more concerns raised by the teacher and/or parents.

Evaluation/PLEP. The statement of present levels of performance required for every IEP should be based on data, reports, test scores, curriculum-based assessments and observations collected during the evaluation and from existing test data. Often the evaluation provides data concerning general levels of educational test performance (e.g., IQ and standardized achievement test scores) but not specific information concerning classroom behavior or specific educational needs.

Disability/PLEP. The focus of an IEP is on needs that result from a child's disability. Levels of educational performance that are not affected by a child's disability are not addressed by measurable annual goals. If a child has a specific learning disability in written expression, there should be a relationship between this disability and significant levels of educational used to develop measurable annual goals.

PLEP/Goals. For each PLEP that signifies a need, there should be a goal. Goals are not determined for areas that are unaffected by the disability. If a child has a behavioral need, there should be a level of performance that represents this need and a goal to address the specific behavior and level of performance.

Goals/Objectives. Short-term objectives are intermediate steps or benchmarks for evaluating progress toward measurable annual goals. Not only are short-term objectives logically related to measurable annual goals in terms of increasing levels of performance, but the short-term objectives for each annual goal are logically and sequentially related to one another.

Goals/Services. Services are provided to achieve goals. If a child's educational performance is impacted by emotional disturbance, services are provided to meet the child's learning needs as defined by levels of performance and goals. The goal is

not to provide a service (e.g., to place a child in a segregated setting); the goal is to achieve measurable results that address individual needs that result from the service.

Services/Regular Classroom. What has been lost most in the special education process is the presumption that a child should be in the regular education classroom. Special education was not and is not intended to supplant this presumption, but to promote regular classroom participation. A special education placement or service should never be construed as an alternative to regular classroom participation but a tool to achieve regular classroom participation. The ultimate goal is not to provide special education or to list hundreds of tangential special education goals: the goal is to allow a child to function successfully, as much as possible, in the regular education classroom.

Goals/Regular Classroom. Special education requires specially designed instruction. This means that a child has educational needs that are not being met in the regular education classroom. The task is to build a network of goals that will lead to regular classroom participation. What occurs in the regular classroom (i.e., the curriculum) and what is required in the regular classroom (i.e., classroom behavior) are critical to the development of meaningful goals. More importantly, the regular classroom provides the ultimate test of special education effectiveness; that is, the ability to function independently in the regular classroom to the maximum extent possible is the real test of the effectiveness of special education.

IEP/Revision. Goals are evaluated, revised as necessary, and expanded to meet the changing learning needs of children. When all goals have been satisfactorily achieved, when the student no longer needs specially designed instruction, the special education process is complete. At least annually, goals and services must be reviewed to determine the process is complete or how the IEP should be revised.

Educational Benefit

In *Hudson v. Rowley* the Supreme Court found that the student was receiving educational benefit from a reasonably calculated plan, and that the Act did not require the state "to maximize the potential of each handicapped child commensurate with the opportunity provided nonhandicapped children." The concept of *receiving educational benefit* is critical in the determination of an *appropriate* education in that a child is not necessarily entitled to every conceivable benefit, or that the benefits offered must maximize the child's ability, but that *some* benefit must be conferred by a reasonably calculated plan. The Supreme Court recognized that the maximization of a child's potential is a "desirable" goal, but "it is not the standard that Congress imposed upon states which receive funding under the Act. Rather, Congress sought primarily to identify and evaluate handicapped children, and to provide them with access to a free public education. Implicit in the congressional purpose of providing FAPE is the requirement that the education to which access is provided be sufficient to confer some educational benefit upon the handicapped child." Procedural compliance that results in some educational benefit is the minimal substantive requirement set in *Hudson* when the court reasoned that an "adequate" education was a reasonable calculated plan.

Rather than interpreting the *Hudson* decision as a weakening of services for children with disabilities, the decision should be interpreted as a need to comply with the intent and sprit of the regulations, to develop plans that are designed to impart educational benefit. The basic problem with many IEPs is an emphasis on documentary compliance, but a disregard for developing individualized plans that are designed to impart even a modicum of real educational benefit.

The *Hudson* standard of an adequate, or some educational benefit, criterion applies to both federal and state IEP regulations. In *Logue v. Unified School District No. 512*[12] the parents of Noah, a hearing-impaired child, wanted an oral rather than a total communication approach used with their child. The parents asserted that Kansas statute required an IEP which "maximizes" a child's potential. This is not an unusual requirement in that the Senate report for PL 94-142 indicated that the legislation was intended to "result in maximum benefits to handicapped children and their families" (p. 6).[13] In response to the parents' belief that the legislative intent was "to set a higher standard" than that stated in *Hudson* (i.e., a *maximum* rather than a *some benefit* standard), the court affirmed that the school district was not required to develop an IEP that provides maximum educational benefit, and that "neither the language of the cited statute nor its amendments and related regulations indicate that the Kansas legislature intended to adopt an educational standard higher than the one established by *Rowley*." This was also the Supreme Court's response to the phrase "maximum potential" in *Hudson* where the court argued that even if this was the intent, "we could not hold that Congress had not successfully imposed that burden upon the States" (p. 205).

In *Logue* there was some question concerning the intent of the Kansas statute to maximize potential. In *David D. v. Dartmouth School Committee*[14] the maximum possible development standard of Massachusetts State Education law was interpreted within the context of IDEA. In this case the parents wanted a residential placement for David, a seventeen-year-old boy with Down's Syndrome, who exhibited "seriously inappropriate behavior" while a student at the Dartmouth school. The parents argued that because the IEP did not address these needs the school failed "to teach David self-control, rendering the IEP the town proposed for him fatally deficient" (p. 415).[45] Although David D. was receiving some educational benefit from the IEP, the state actually required a level of benefit higher than federal law because Massachusetts state law requires that programs assure the maximum possible development of disabled children. This is in contrast to the *Hudson* guideline that programs require only some educational benefit. For David D. the most appropriate program was one that would address his inappropriate behavior and thereby maximize his potential to develop independent living skills.

An important element in the *David D.* decision is the relation between Federal and state law. State law provides a floor of services, but not a ceiling. In other words, states must provide at least some educational benefit, but states are not restricted from exceeding this expectation. In other words, a state can require a greater level of benefit than mandated by Federal law. For David D,. the ability to develop appropriate sexual behavior was an overriding IEP concern. The fact that this need was not being addressed "showed that a change in David's IEP was warranted" (p. 423).

The *Hudson* decision does not mean that any gain, real or contrived, is viewed as a benefit. In *Hall v. Vance County Board of Education,*[46] the 4th Court of Appeals stated that "clearly, Congress did not intend that a school system could discharge its duty under the EAHCA by providing a program that produces some minimal academic advancement, no matter how trivial" (p. 636). Part of what the court found "trivial" was the schools' reputation for social promotions and minimal test score improvement. This is certainly the most common misinterpretation of *Hudson* that if a school is not required to provide a level of services that will allow a child to reach his or her full potential, then the only remaining obligation is to provide a minimal level of services. In *Hall* the Court of Appeals affirmed the district court's decision that the Vance County Board of Education made egregious procedural errors and failed to provide an appropriate education. The court responded to the school's contention that *Hudson* does not require the school to maximize potential and noted that "nowhere, however, does the District Court's opinion suggest that it held the defendants to that impermissible standard." Based on evidence introduced at trial, a determination was made that the plan in *Hall* was not reasonably calculated to provide educational benefit as required by the Act (p. 635).

Designing an IEP to provide educational benefit does not guarantee educational benefit. This is addressed by the accountability statement in the regulations that cautions that an IEP does not constitute "a guarantee by the public agency and the teacher that a child will progress at a specified rate"[47] although agencies and teachers are obligated to make a "good faith effort"[48] to help children achieve the specified goals and objectives. In *Bend-Lapine v. T.W.* the court found that although little progress was made during the school year, this was attributed more to the student than to the IEP. In other words, the IEP was designed to provide educational benefit and therefore this element of IEP appropriateness was met.

As important as the concept of educational benefit is to the development of a reasonably calculated IEP, there is a distinction between short- and long-term educational benefits. In *Poolaw v. Bishop*[49] the parents of a thirteen-year-old profoundly deaf student, Lionel, wanted their child to be mainstreamed. Because of the Lionel's communication problems, the school district recommended a placement at the Arizona School for the Deaf and Blind. This placement was found to be appropriate by a hearing officer, the District Court and the Court of Appeals. The 9th Circuit Court of Appeals agreed that Lionel "could receive some nonacademic benefits from continued mainstreaming," but that "IDEA is primarily concerned with the long term educational welfare of disabled students" and that Lionel would "receive no educational benefits from instruction in the regular classroom until he acquires greater communication skills." Possibly in deference to the "due weight" given the hearing officer, the Court of Appeals made the rather bold statement that Lionel would "receive no educational benefits" in a mainstreamed setting rather than stating that the educational benefits at the residential school substantially outweigh those in a regular classroom setting. In any case, *Poolaw v. Bishop* provides a more expansive view of an appropriate IEP so that even though there might be a variety of ways to design an IEP to provide educational benefit, the task is to design an IEP that provides the greatest "long-term educational" benefit.

Appropriate Due Process

One of the most controversial Supreme Court decisions relating to disabilities, *Honig v. Doe*, concerns the student's disruptive behavior which included "stealing, extorting money from fellow students, and making sexual comments to female classmates." As a result, the Student Placement Committee eventually suspended the student indefinitely "pending a final disposition in the matter." Smith sued in district court and the court ruled that an indefinite suspension because of Smith's behavior "attributable to their disabilities deprived them of their congressionally mandated right to a free appropriate public education" (*Honig v. Doe*, p. 702). The basic decision was affirmed by the Court of Appeals in that an indefinite suspension was a change in placement, and that the stay-put policy invalidated California law which allowed indefinite suspensions of a child with a disability. After a carefully worded interpretation of the case, the Supreme Court noted that school administrators were not powerless to deal with dangerous students (e.g., temporarily suspending students for up to ten days), and agreed with the lower courts that indefinite suspensions resulting from a student's disability prevents a child from receiving a free appropriate public education. An appropriate placement cannot be arrived at by a lack of due process or by ignoring procedural safeguards. For the students in *Honig v. Doe* an indefinite suspension or an alternative placement might have been appropriate if basic due process safeguards were not ignored. If a child has a disability and a change of placement is contemplated, decisions should not be arbitrary and should not be enforced until the child or the child's parents have had an opportunity to seek mediation or an impartial hearing to resolve the matter.

Effective IEPs

As explained in *Hudson* regarding the need to provide educational benefit, there is a difference between educational opportunity and providing, much less maximizing, a child's educational performance. An IEP is not intended to be a contract that guarantees the effectiveness of services. Even when a school district demonstrates a concerted and thoughtful effort to devise an effective educational plan, the plan might not be successful. Consistent with the accountability clause of the regulations[50] that teachers and schools are not accountable for progress toward goals, the *Hudson* decision requires a reasonably calculated plan that will enable a child to receive educational benefit and not a plan that, in fact, results in a child receiving educational benefit.

Effectiveness is certainly one factor for determining the appropriateness of an education, but an effective individual program cannot be provided at the expense of regulatory requirements. Consider a hypothetical situation in which a self-contained classroom might actually be more effective for meeting a child's needs than a regular classroom environment, but the child is able to function in a less restrictive setting. A desire to provide the most effective program cannot be at the expense of the concept of least restrictive environment or parent involvement in the planning process. If a child does not have a disability, a decision should not be made that the child has a disability in order to provide a special education service, regardless of how effective the service might be to improve the child's educational performance.

At the onset of IEP development best practice and proven methodology must guide the selection of services that will likely result in an effective IEP. In *Lachman v. Illinois State Board of Education* the parents of a deaf child wanted services in a neighborhood school using cued-speech while the school district proposed a self-contained classroom involving total communication. The court ruled in favor of the school because "it is clear that the IEP proposed by the school district is based upon an accepted, proven methodology, for facilitating the early primary education of profoundly hearing-impaired children." In this case, "accepted, proven methodology" is the basis for asserting that the IEP is reasonably calculated and therefore appropriate. Of course, parents have an opportunity through mediation, an impartial hearing, or the courts to present evidence that one approach is more effective than another, or to offer evidence that a certain approach is based on unaccepted or unproven methodology (e.g., perceptual-motor training).

Improving the effectiveness of an IEP is no less important than compliance and developing a reasonably calculated IEP. In *Florence County School District Four v. Carter*[52] a learning-disabled student was removed by her parents from a school because of IEP inadequacies (e.g., limited individualized instruction). The question was whether the parents should be reimbursed for tuition for the private school in which the student was subsequently enrolled. The Supreme Court, in agreeing that the parents were entitled to reimbursement, noted that the private school's deficiencies in terms of failing to meet state education standards (e.g., not developing IEPs) but that "the school district's emphasis on state standards is somewhat ironic. As the Court of Appeals noted, "it hardly seems consistent with the Act's goals to forbid parents from educating their child at a school that provides an appropriate education simply because that school lacks the stamp of approval of the same public school system that failed to meet the child's needs in the first place.'"

In *Florence v. Carter*, an appropriate education is more than a program that meets a set of regulatory requirements, and that a free appropriate public education does not necessarily require either intensive or difficult-to-supply services. In *Irving Independent School District v. Tatro*[53] Amber was born with spina bifida and a neurogenic bladder disorder that prevents her from emptying her bladder voluntarily. As a result she requires a procedure known as clean intermittent catheterization (CIC) that is easily performed with less than an hour's training. For Amber, "a free appropriate public education," entails "related services," that are defined to include "supportive services (including . . . medical . . . services, except that such medical services shall be for diagnostic and evaluation purposes only) as may be required to assist a handicapped child to benefit from special education." In *Tatro* the key to an appropriate education

was not an extensive special education program, carefully crafted goals, or a difficult to provide educational setting, but a relatively easy-to-provide related service (i.e., CIC).

Florence v. Carter demonstrates that an appropriate education can be provided, even if a private school does not meet state educational standards, if the public school has failed to provide an appropriate education. Not having the school district or state imprimatur does not preclude an appropriate education, and complying with minimal requirements does not automatically suggest an appropriate education. In *Gregory M. v. The State Board of Education of the State of Connecticut*[54] the parents of Gregory M. enrolled their child in a private school approved for special education and sought reimbursement for this education. The court found that Gregory "regressed socially and emotionally" and therefore the private school placement was not appropriate.

Appropriate Goals and Objectives

The judicial concept of *appropriate* often centers about meaningful goals and objectives; that is, goals and objectives that are specifically designed to address a child's needs, and objectives that can be measured and evaluated. In *Chris D. v. Montgomery County Board of Education*[55] the task was to provide services for a child who had serious behavior and academic difficulties. The court noted that after a new IEP had been written for the student, "the new plan included only broad, generic objectives and vague method's for monitoring . . . progress" (p. 925). The Court observed that the objectives were written using a standard form and then gave the following example: "One typical objective read simply: 'Student

will participate in reading activities in the regular classroom,'" and 'The student will maintain a/an_____% average in math on the 3rd grade level with '80' written in the blank space, and stated that . . . would be evaluated by reference to his 'Daily work' and 'Chapter tests.'" The opinion in *Chris D. v. Montogomery* was that gratuitous objectives, written more to complete a paper-work task than to provide educational benefit, are not appropriate.

Goals and objectives must not only be appropriate, they must be developed in a timely fashion. In *Brookheart v. Illinois State Board of Education*[56] fourteen secondary school students were not given high school diplomas because of an inability to pass the

Illinois Minimal Competency test. The court observed that the issue of passing the test was not included in the students' IEPs and thus there was insufficient time to prepare the students to take the test. Although there were a number of other issues raised in this case, a very important educational need, passing a competency test in order to graduate, was not considered and certainly not met. If IEP goals and objectives had been developed in a timely fashion to prepare the students, there is no guarantee that any or all of the students would have passed the test. The purpose of a goal and objectives is to address a need, but only stating a goal or objective does not ensure success. In this case, because no other remedy seemed reasonable, the plaintiffs were granted diplomas.

Generic and vague goals were also a focal point in *Evans v. the Board of Education of the Rhinebeck Central School District*[57] the court found (among other procedural violations) that "the IEPs include only broad, generic objectives and vague, subjective methods for monitoring . . . progress" and that "although the IEP repeatedly incants these phrases—'teacher observation,' 80% success'—because there is little indication . . . of success . . . when the IEP was written, it fails to specify strategies for adequately evaluating . . . academic progress and determining which teaching methods are effective and which need to be revised" (p. 97). Overall, the court declared that because of deficiencies, the IEP was not reasonably calculated to provide educational benefit. Here, "reasonably calculated" was interpreted to mean that an effort was made to provide real goals and

objectives rather than token statements that were included more for compliance than to provide legitimate educational benefit.

A contention could be made that every goal and objective is either too broad, too specific or otherwise does not address real educational needs. One of the objections of the IEP in *Logue v. Unified School District N. 512* was that the goals and objectives lacked specificity, but the court responded with an example of an objective that stated "Noah will produce verbs and prepositions at the sentence level in response to pictures with no clinician prompts with 90% accuracy over 2 consecutive sessions." This may or may not be an appropriate goal, the task might be too easy or too difficult, or the task might not reflect a real educational need, but the goal does not seem to lack specificity. Just as goals can be overly vague and generic, an overemphasis on day-to-day instructional activities can be just as inappropriate. An IEP is not a daily lesson plan[58] and when an IEP becomes bogged down in daily instructions by the inclusion of myriad goals and objectives, the primary purpose of an IEP to provide an overall educational plan is undermined. More often than not, excessive detail means that objectives are not short-term intermediate steps, and are not used to gauge progress toward measurable annual goals throughout the year. Not only does this approach compromise the overall planning process and make evaluation and reporting results to parents exceedingly difficult, but the attention to detail in the IEP can lessen the role of the teacher in the design and implementation of effective instruction.

Appropriate Placement

Underlying many of the disagreements between parents and school districts is the

issue of least restrictive environment (LRE), mainstreaming, and inclusion. The pivotal concept in IDEA-1997 is the LRE provision that "to the maximum extent appropriate, children with disabilities, including children in public or private institutions or other care facilities, are educated with children who are not disabled" and that separate schooling occurs only supplementary aids and services cannot be used satisfactorily in the regular classroom.[59]

Both mainstreaming and inclusion refer to the participation of children with disabilities in the regular education environment. Depending on who and how the terms are used, mainstreaming and inclusion may or may not be synonymous. The difference between mainstreaming and inclusion is more philosophical than statutory in that advocates of full inclusion believe that all children with disabilities should be included in the general education environment, while mainstreaming suggests the inclusion of students in the regular curriculum "to the maximum extent appropriate." In either case, there is no statutory or regulatory mandate that requires or even mentions mainstreaming or inclusion (although the LRE provision has been interpreted as indicating "a strong preference in favor of mainstreaming"[60]).

In *Hartmann v. Loudoun County Board of Education* the parents wanted their son to be educated in the least restrictive environment. The Hartmanns' son, a twelve-year-old autistic child, had developmental disorders disabilities involving communication, motor, and social skills. The parents rejected the IEP that proposed a class designed for autistic children in favor of a regular education classroom. The hearing officer described the child's various disruptive behaviors as including continual vocalizations, whining, screeching, hitting, pinching, kicking, biting, rolling on the floor, removing clothing. The district court found that the school district "simply did not take enough appropriate steps to include Mark in a regular class" and that "disruptive behavior should not be a significant factor in determining the appropriate educational placement." The 4th District Court of Appeals (1997) rejected this decision and chided the District Court by stating that "in rejecting reasonable pedagogical choices and disregarding well-supported administrative findings, the District Court assumed an educational mantle which IDEA did not confer." This was the same criticism in *Hudson v. Rowley* when the Supreme Court clarified PL 94-142 by explaining the statement that a court "shall grant such relief as the court determines is appropriate" does not mean that a court can ignore previous administrate procedures and findings.

In *Hartmann* the school district wanted a more restrictive environment and the parents a mainstreamed or less restrictive environment. The Court of Appeals stated that IDEA "explicitly states that mainstreaming is not appropriate . . . when the nature and severity of the disability is such that education in regular classes with the use of supplementary aids and services cannot be achieved satisfactorily." Although IDEA does not "explicitly" mention mainstreaming, there is a directive that the regular classroom may not be appropriate for all children with disabilities.

An appropriate placement is determined by individual need and not by philosophy or convenience. The most appropriate placement is not necessarily the most cost-effective or the placement that conforms to a philosophy of inclusion or exclusion. In *DeVries BeBlaay v. Fairfax County School Board*[61] the district court ruled that a regular high school placement was not appropriate for a seventeen-year-old autistic student, even with supplementary aids and services. The student had an IQ of 72 and academic skills at the fourth grade level. The school felt, and the court agreed, that the student would gain little from classes and that the appropriate setting was a vocational center thirteen miles further from the student's home. The Court of Appeals indicated that mainstreaming is not required when (1) the child would not receive educational benefits from mainstreaming, (2) "marginal" benefits of mainstreaming would be outweighed by a separate education, and (3) the child's behavior is a disruptive force in the regular classroom.

In *Seattle School District No. 1 v. B.S.* (parent of A.S.) the school district less wanted a more restrictive environment for a child classified as "seriously emotionally disturbed" who exhibited "physical and verbal aggression, lying, stealing, and oppositional behavior." The school district proposed a special education self-contained behavioral classroom, while the parents wanted a residential placement. The Court of Appeals agreed that the residential placement was appropriate and that "IDEA does not require A.S. to spend years in an educational environment likely to be inadequate and to impede her progress simply to permit the School District to try every option short of residential placement."

Appropriate "Public" Education

The *child find*[62] mandate requires that all children with disabilities are identified, located, and evaluated applies to both public and private schools. A child in a private school is entitled to a full and individual evaluation and, if the child is determined to have a disability, an IEP, special education and related services.[63] If a child is in a private school because this was determined to be an appropriate placement by the school district, the school district is required to provide a free and appropriate education. If the child is placed in the private school by the parents, and the school has made special education services available in the public school setting, whether the parents are reimbursed for the cost of schooling depends on a procedural determination as to the appropriateness of the private and public school programs.

The provision of *on the premises* services for children with disabilities can have a significant impact on the design and implementation of IEPs for children in private school environments. This does not mean that if a child in a private school is determined to have a disability that the public school must provide a special education teacher on the premises of the private school. The law does not mandate or prohibit on the premise services, but rather permits such services if deemed appropriate by the school district: "such services *may* be provided to children with disabilities on the premises of private, including parochial, schools, to the extent consistent with law."[64] This does not necessarily mean that a child with a disability in a private school will receive the same services as provided in a public school. A consultant or resource room teacher services could be a cost-effective and practical way to provide services to a child in a private school, but the school district is not required to provide this service.

The basis for the on the premises clause in IDEA-1997 is the Supreme Court *Zobrest v. Catalina Foothills School District* decision[65] where the court ruled that the establishment of religion clause of the First Amendment did not prevent a public school district from providing a sign language interpreter from accompanying a deaf student to classes at a

Catholic high school. The court explained that the provision of an interpreter by the public school district entailed a service which was (1) neutral and was "in no way skewed towards religion," (2) did not create a financial incentive for a student to attend a sectarian institution, and (3) did not result in an economic benefit for the sectarian school which relieved the school of "an otherwise necessary cost of performing their educational function."

The scope of on the premises services for children with disabilities was further expanded in *Russman v. Board of Education/ Watervliet*[66] when the court reversed an earlier decision that required the school district to provide a consultant teacher to a disabled student attending a Catholic school. After this judgment was vacated by the Supreme Court and remanded for further consideration,[67] the Court of Appeals upon reconsideration concluded that the language of IDEA "is permissive rather than mandatory" and that "IDEA cannot be read to require school districts to provide on-site services to disabled children voluntarily enrolled in public schools."

AN APPROPRIATE CLASSIFICATION

The determination of a child's disability, or lack thereof, is essential for the development of an appropriate IEP. The effectiveness of the IEP team is compromised when a disability is not determined or misinterpreted, or when a child is misidentified as disabled. An IEP that is designed for a child who does not have a disability, or does not need special education, is inherently flawed and can supplant a child's ability to be involved in and progress in the general curriculum.

An IEP is required for every student receiving special education where "special education means specially designed instruction, in the classroom, home, or other settings, at no cost to the parents, to meet the unique needs of a child with a disability."[68] Specially designed instruction requires adapting the content, methodology, or delivery of instruction to (1) address the unique needs of the child that result from the child's disability, and (2) ensure access of the child to the general curriculum, so that he or she can meet the educational standards within the jurisdiction of the public agency that apply to all children.[69]

For a child with a disability who is eligible under IDEA, an IEP outlines "the content, methodology, or delivery of instruction" to address these needs and to ensure access to the general curriculum. The purpose of determining eligibility is not categorization, but to determine the need for specially designed instruction. If a child does not have a disability, or does not require specially designed instruction, special education under IDEA is not the appropriate vehicle for providing educational services. As defined in the regulations,[70] there are thirteen categories of disabilities. Although much of the criticism concerning special education categorization is justified, especially from the standpoint of stigmatization (for instance, mental retardation), an essential role of having a framework for determining disability categories is to provide special education for children who actually have disabilities and special needs.

Regarding the development of an IEP, the definition of special education is extremely important. If a child does not need special education, the child does not have a disability under IDEA-1997, and therefore does not need an IEP. Likewise, for a child to receive related services, the child must need special education. If the child does not need special education, an IEP cannot be developed under IDEA-1997 to provide a related service but not special education. This, of course, is an important function of Section 504: to provide services that are not covered under IDEA.

In order to receive services under IDEA a child must have a disability and need specially designed instruction. If a child is determined to be a "child with a disability,"[71] the next step is to determine whether the child requires specially designed instruction and therefore an IEP, whether the appro-

priate program is the general curriculum with no specially designed instruction, or whether a Section 504 plan or accommodation is appropriate. The number of children identified under IDEA indicates the general need for specially designed instruction as well as the number of IEPs required to provide an appropriate education. As shown in Table III, specific learning disabilities account for over 50 percent of specially designed programs, and the high-incidence disabilities (learning disabilities, speech, mental retardation, and emotional disturbance) account for over 91 percent of programs and IEPs developed for students with disabilities.

Table III. Students Age Six to Twenty-one Served Under IDEA[72]

Disability	1987-88		1996-97		Percent Change
	Number	Percent	Number	Percent	
Specific learning disability	1,942,304	47.1	2,676,299	51.1	37.8
Speech/language impairments	953,568	23.1	1,050,975	20.1	10.2
Mental retardation	598,770	14.5	594,025	11.4	-.8
Emotional disturbance	372,380	9.0	447,426	8.6	20.2
Multiple disabilities	79,023	1.9	99,638	1.9	26.1
Hearing impairments	56,872	1.4	68,766	1.3	20.9
Orthopedic impairments	46,966	1.1	66,400	1.3	41.4
Other health impairments	46,056	1.1	160,824	3.1	249.2
Autism			34,101	.7	
Visual impairments	22,821	.6	25,834	.5	13.2
Traumatic brain injury			10,378	.2	
Deaf-blindness	1,454	<.1	1,286	<.1	-11.6
All disabilities	4,120,214	100	5,235,952	100	27.1

Classification and the IEP

When identifying children with disabilities, the task is not just to identify children who meet certain disability criteria but to find children with disabilities who also need specially designed instruction. A child might have reading or content area needs but not need specially designed instruction; or a child might exhibit certain behaviors in the classroom that are inappropriate, but not need specially designed instruction.

The consequences of a misclassification, whether unintentional or otherwise, can result in no services being provided to a child who is disabled, inappropriate special education services being provided to a child who is not disabled, or misdirected goals and services for children when the incorrect disability is identified. For example, if a child has an emotional disturbance but the IEP team determines that the child has a specific learning disability in basic reading, important and primary behavioral needs might be treated as secondary factors, or even ignored, in the child's IEP.

De facto segregation. In *Brown* the majority decision cited the Court of Appeal's acknowledgment that the impact of segregation "is greater when it has the sanction of the law" and "segregation with the sanction of law, therefore, has a tendency to [retard] the educational and mental development." For children with disabilities who do not need specially designed instruction and who are segregated from the regular curriculum *under the sanction of an IEP*, the result can retard educational and mental development and deprive them of benefits they would receive in the general curriculum. To provide specially designed instruction for children who do not have disabilities is likely discriminatory, can detract from an appropriate regular education and the school district's responsibility to provide an appro-

priate regular education, and can result in services not being provided or a diminished level of services to children who do in fact have disabilities under IDEA.

Overclassification that results from race, cultural, or socioeconomic factors is, in the words of the Supreme Court, inherently unequal. As with racial segregation, unnecessarily restrictive settings "are not 'equal' and cannot be made 'equal.'" The issue of overclassification is specifically addressed in IDEA-1997, especially with regard to minorities and students with LEP. Regarding minorities, the inappropriate use of special education, rather than a lack of special education, was identified as a major concern. The law identified problems relating to mislabeling and cautioned the following: (1) greater efforts are needed to prevent the intensification of problems connected with mislabeling; (2) more minority children continue to be served in special education than would be expected; and (3) poor African American children are 2.3 times more likely to be identified by their teacher as having mental retardation than their white counterparts.[73]

Unintentional misclassification. For every test and assessment there is an element of error, and this is certainly the case when determining whether or not a child has a disability. A child can be unintentionally misclassified because a disability is not determined, a nondisabled child is incorrectly identified as disabled, or because the disability is misidentified (e.g., an emotional impairment is thought to be a learning disability or vice versa).

Although there are reasonably defined selection criteria for low-incidence disabilities, this is not always so for high-incidence disabilities. For specific learning disabilities the appropriateness of the classification can be confounded by the definition of the disability. For example, a specific learning disability requires a severe discrepancy between achievement and intellectual ability[74] but there is little agreement as to what a severe discrepancy is or how to measure a discrepancy. For children suspected of being emotionally disturbed, the vagueness of the term (e.g., "inappropriate types of behavior or feelings under normal circumstances")[75] can easily result in a less than appropriate classification. For children suspected of having attention deficit disorders (ADD) the problems associated with specific learning disabilities and emotional disturbance are combined and magnified.

A child with ADD can be classified under the specific learning disability category if the criteria are met, or under the emotionally disturbed if the criteria for this classification are met. In the IDEA-1990 regulations, children in the ADD category could only be identified as Other Health Impaired if the ADD was "a chronic or acute health problem that results in limited alertness, which adversely affects educational performance."[76] The definition of Other Health Impairment was redefined in the IDEA-1997 regulations to mean "limited strength, vitality or alertness, including a heightened alertness to environmental stimuli, that results in limited alertness with respect to the educational environment." This can be the result of chronic health problems such as asthma or ADHD, diabetes, epilepsy, sickle cell anemia, etc. that affects educational performance.[77]

Exactly what "heightened alertness to environmental stimuli, that results in limited alertness" in an educational environment means is less than clear, but if this determination is made and educational performance is affected, an IEP must define a program to establish measurable annual goals and provide services. This, of course, is difficult to accomplish if the "heightened alertness to environmental stimuli" is the result of boredom, a lack of motivation, or an educational environment that is less than motivational.

The difficulty in determining an appropriate classification is readily acknowledged in IDEA-1997 by the use of the term *developmental delay* for children aged three through nine. This generic term can be used if the state permits this classification and the school district chooses to use the term. A developmental delay can entail physical, cognitive, communication, social or emotional, or adaptive development. The use of developmental delay allows for the provision of special education and related services without locking children into eligibility categories that may be inappropriate or incorrect, "and could actually reduce later referrals of children with disabilities to special education."[78]

Often the cause of misclassification is confusion between educational need and disability. The purpose of special education to provide services for children with disabilities who need specially designed instruction is either not understood or misunderstood. For children with limited English proficiency (LEP), "studies have documented apparent discrepancies in the levels of referral and placement of limited English proficient children in special education."[79] A teacher might correctly believe that a child with limited English proficiency requires extensive individualized but special education is inappropriate if the child does not have a disability. This is also the case if a child has LEP, and has had insufficient educational opportunities. As a result "services provided to limited English proficient students often do not respond primarily to the pupil's academic needs."[80]

Of paramount importance when determining an appropriate educational program for a child with LEP is differentiating limited English proficiency, lack of instruction, and a disability. For a child with LEP, a lack of instruction is not tantamount to disability,[81] and the IEP team must determine whether the child has a disability and needs special education "rather than measuring the child's English language skills."[82] A child with LEP might require no special education, special education in a language other than English, or special education in order to develop English skills. In addition, a child with LEP might require services

> for those aspects of the educational program which address the development of English language skills and other aspects of the student's educational program. For a LEP student with a disability, under paragraph (c) of this section, the IEP must address whether the special education and related services that the child needs will be provided in a language other than English.[83]

Not identifying a child as disabled because of environmental, cultural, economic disadvantage,[84] lack of instruction in reading or math, or limited English proficiency,[85] directly addresses the basic issue of overidentification. A child might have educational needs but not because of an underlying disability. When environmental factors are the cause of poor educational performance, special education in the form of specially designed instruction is not the solution. Indeed, special education might serve to mask needs and prevent participation and progress in the regular curriculum.

Intentional misclassification. Error is an inextricable part of the assessment, and error is certainly a part of the process used to determine the existence of a disability. Children will be misidentified as disabled or not disabled, or one disability will be confused with another, because of legitimate errors of relating to data, judgments, and overall decision making. The IEP team has an obvious responsibility to minimize the extent of these errors, but the team has an even greater responsibility to avoid intentional misclassification.

In certain instances, misclassification is intentional. If a child is known not to have a disability, or does not need special education, identifying the child to provide a service to appease a teacher or parents, is blatantly inappropriate. Special education is not intended to be a mechanism for providing individualized help, for appeasing teachers or parents, for providing specialized services, for removing problem children from the classroom, or providing children with an unfair advantage (e.g., having tests read) or accommodation. Special education is intended to address educational needs that are the result of, or affected by, a disability.

The foundation for an IEP is a good-faith effort to determine the child's eligibility in terms of disability and need. Of course, determining a disability is not always straightforward. A child might have specific learning and emotional problems so that a clear determination of a specific learning disability or emotional disturbance is not possible. Likewise, the interrelationship between intellectual ability, academic achievement, and classroom behavior might be such that a single classification is more conjecture than certainty. A good-faith effort means that a child with LEP is not labeled speech impaired to provide needed services when, in fact, there is no disability; that a child is not labeled mentally retarded because of socioeconomic and environmental factors rather than actual mental retardation; or that a child with an emotional impairment, with no corresponding specific learning disability, is labeled as having a specific learning disability because specific learning disability is an acceptable label to the parents.

Responsibility

The question of responsibility is essential for the development of an effective IEP. The basic responsibility of the state educational agency is to ensure that school districts develop and implement an IEP for each child with a disability,[86] and that procedural safeguards are established, maintained, and implemented.[87] In the all-important planning process, school districts are responsible for taking steps to ensure that parents are present at IEP meetings and "are afforded the opportunity to participate."[88] The specific requirements articulated in the law and the regulations are underscored by the basic responsibility to comply with the regulations which provide the basis for an appropriate education.

Often, the question is not whether a child has legitimate educational needs, but rather who is responsible for those needs. If a child does not have a disability, treating the child as disabled is discriminatory and irresponsible. If a child is having difficulty in school that can be attributed to environmental factors, this problem should be dealt with in the regular classroom. If such a child requires additional help, it should be provided but not under the guise of special education. Responsible special education entails addressing the unique needs of children with disabilities who need specially designed instruction, and not using special education to address needs that are the result of environmental or socioeconomic factors, lack of instruction, or limited English proficiency.

The criticisms of IEPs are many, disturbing, and often valid. Frequent IEP concerns include procedural deficiencies, lack of parent involvement, inadequate evaluation and assessment of needs, and document deficiencies such as incomplete IEP content or illogical IEP elements. Certainly the most remarkable criticism of IEPs, in view of the fact that the IEP is designed to provide an appropriate education, is the repeated complaint that goals, objectives, and services are often inappropriate. Between the judicial attempts to determine an appropriate education and the various deficiencies associated with IEPs, several basic guidelines can be developed for designing and implementing IEPs that provide an appropriate public education.

The basic requirements for IEPs are straightforward: IEPs should be written in compliance with the regulations, contain the prescribed content, are in effect at the beginning of the school year, and are reviewed at least annually. In addition to these requirements, emphasis must be placed on the developing IEPs that are "reasonably calculated" to provide educational benefit by (1) identifying real needs that are the result of a child's disability; (2) emphasizing involvement in and participation in the regular curriculum to the maximum extent appropriate; (3) developing goals that are linked to the child's needs; (4) developing measurable annual goals that are actually measured; (5) developing short-term objectives or benchmarks that represent a plan for achieving the goals; and (6) providing services, supports and modifications that promote the achievement of annual goals.

•

The effectiveness of IEPs is most affected by the IEP-accountability provision in the regulations[89] which requires a "good faith effort to assist the child to achieve the goals and objectives or benchmarks listed in the IEP." Regulatory compliance can be shown, but unless there is a good faith effort to develop meaningful and effective IEPs, and to implement IEPs, the concept of a free and appropriate education for children with disabilities will never be fully realized.

Regulations can be written, but an appropriate IEP will not be the result of regulatory enforcement; an appropriate IEP, an IEP that is in compliance and provides educational benefit, will be the result of a good-faith effort to develop real plans and real programs to meet real individual needs.

NOTES

[1] 347a U.S. 483 (1954).

[2] 29 USC 794(a).

[3] 20 USC 1400(c)(B).

[4] Senate Report 105-17, p. 25.

[5] 20 USC 1400(c)(5)(D).

[6] 20 USC 1400(d)(1)(A).

[7] 20 USC 1412(a)(5)(A).

[8] 20 USC 1415(a).

[9] 20 USC 1401(8); Section 614(d) of PL 105-17 corresponds to 20 USC 1414(d).

[10] 34 CFR 300.300 Provision of FAPE.

[11] 34 CFR 300.300(b).

[12] 34 CFR 300.534(b)(c)(2).

[13] 34 CFR 300.300 Provision of FAPE.

[14] Hendrick Hudson Dist. Bd. of Ed. V. Rowley, 458 U.S. 176 (1982). Board of Education, Argued March 23, 1982. Decided June 28, 1982.

[15] 458 U.S. 176 (1982).

[16] 471 US 359 (1985), Burlington School Commission v. Massachusetts Department of Education.

[17] 484 US 305 (1988) and 98 L Ed 2d 686 (1988).

[18] Honig v. Doe, 98 L 2d 305 686 (1988).

[19] 34 CFR 300, Appendix A, Question #1.

[20] 334 F. Supp. 1257 (ED Pa. 1971) and 343 F. Supp. 279 (ED Pa. 1972).

[21] 348 F. Supp. 866 (DC 1972).

[22] 348 F. Supp. 879 (DC 1972).

[23] 334 F. Supp. 1260 (ED Pa. 1971).

[24] Senate Report 105-17, p. 21.

[25] 20 USC 1415(e). Mediation.

[26] 20 USC 1415(f). Impartial Due Process Hearing.

[27] 20 USC 1415(d)(2)(K).

[28] 20 USC 1415(i)(2)(A). Although Section 1415(e)(3) prevents a change in placement during pendency (the stay-put provision), but for a student who is truly violent or not otherwise able to function in any type of school setting, 1415(e)(2) can seek relief as determined in either state or district court.

[29] Hudson v. Rowley 458 U.S. 176 (1982).

[30] 118 F.3d 998 (4th Cir. 1997).

[31] 458 U.S. 176 (1982).

[32] 960 F. 2d 1479 (9th Cir. 1992).

[33] 9th Circuit Court of Appeals, No. 97-35711, 1998.

[34] 898 F.2d 1186 (6th Cir, 1990).

[35] Doe v. Defendant I, 898 F.2d 1186 (6th Cir. 1990).

[36] Progress Toward a Free Appropriate Public Education: A Report to Congress on the Implementation of Public Law 94-142, Bureau of Education for the Handicapped, 1979, (ERIC #175 196).

[37] 34 CFR 300. Appendix C, Question #39.

[38] Pyecha, J. N., and others (1980). A National Survey of Individualized Education Programs (IEPs) for Handicapped Children. Volume I: Executive Summary. Final report. Research triangle Institute, Durham, N.C. (ERIC #199 970).

[39] Barbara D. Bateman, Writing Individualized Education Programs (IEPs) For Success, Secondary Education and Beyond, Learning Disabilities Association, 1995. Retrieved September 22, 2000 from the World Wide Web: http://www.ldonline.org/ld_indepth/iep/success_ieps.html.

[40] Pyecha, J. N., and others.

[41] Volume, III, Chapter 7, p. 126.

[42] 10th Circuit Court of Appeals, Nos. 97-3087, 973112, 1998.

[43] Senate Report 94-168.

[44] 775 F.2d 411 (1985) and 615 F.Supp. 639 (D.C. Mass. 1984).

[45] 775 F.2d 411 (1985).

[46] 774 F.2d 629 (4th Cir. 1985).

[47] IDEA-1990, 34 CFR 300.350.

[48] 34 CFR 300.350(a)(2).

[49] 67 F.3d 830 (9th Cir. 1995) 9th Circuit Court of Appeals, No. 9415324, 1995.

[50] 34 CFR 300.350.

[51] 852 F.2d 290 (7th Cir. 1988).

[52] 510 U.S. 7 (1993).

[53] 468 U.S. 883 (1984).

[54] 5-91-379 (WWE), 891 F. Supp 695, 1995, District Court.

[55] 753 F. Supp 922 (M.D. Ala. 1990).

[56] 697 F.2d 179 (7th Cir. 1983).

[57] 30 F. Supp. 83 (S.D.N.Y, 1996).

[58] IDEA-1990, 34 CFR 300, Appendix C, Question #37.

[59] 20 USC 1412(a)(5)(A).

[60] Daniel v. State, 874 F.2d 1036 (5th Cir. 1989).

[61] 882 F.2d 876 (4th Cir. 1989).

[62] 34 CFR 300.125.

[63] 20 USC 1412(a)(10).

[64] 20 USC 1412(a)(10)(B)(i)(II).

[65] 125 L. Ed. 2d 1 (1993).

[66] 150 F.3d 219 (2nd Cir. 1998) U.S. 2nd Circuit Court of Appeals.

[67] 117 S. Ct. 2502-03.

[68] 20 USC 1401(25).

[69] 34 CFR 300.26(b)(3) Special education.

[70] 34 CFR 300.7.

[71] As defined in 34 CFR 300.7.

[72] Twentieth Annual Report to Congress on the Implementation of the Individuals with Disabilities Education Act (1994), Washington, D.C., p. II-16.

[73] 20 USC 1400(c)(8).

[74] 34 CFR 300.541(a)(2).

[75] 34 CFR 300.7(c)(4)(C).

[76] United States Department of Education, Office of Special Education and Rehabilitative Services, (September, 16, 1991). Memorandum: Clarification of policy to address the needs of children with attention deficit disorders within general and/or special education.

[77] 34 CFR 300.7(b)(9).

[78] House Report No. 105-95, p. 86.

[79] 20 USC 1400(c)(7)(F).

[80] *Ibid*

[81] 34 CFR 300.534(b)(1).

[82] 34 CFR 300.532(a)(2).

[83] Proposed Regulations for IDEA-1997, Federal Register, October 22, 1997, Vol. 62, Number 204, p. 55090, 34 CFR 300.346 Development, review, and revision of IEP. Note 3.

[84] 34 CFR 300.541(b).

[85] 34 CFR 300.534(b).

[86] 34 CFR 300.341(a)(1).

[87] 34 CFR 300.500(a).

[88] 34 CFR 300.345.

[89] 34 CFR 300.350.

Chapter 3

THE IEP PROCESS

THE DEVELOPMENT AND IMPLEMENTA-
TION OF AN EFFECTIVE IEP requires a
system to identify children needing specially
designed instruction and related services, a
team of qualified individuals to evaluate the
need for special education and design an
IEP, an evaluation process, and a multifaceted system to fairly and efficiently
address complaints and disagreements. As
discussed in Chapter 1, the IEP is about
planning, and planning with parents is an
indispensable element of the IEP process.

The IEP process begins with regular
classroom behavior or performance. A
child's behavior educational performance in
the regular classroom provides a frame of
reference for determining the need for
special education. There is something that a
child does or does not do that is thought to
warrant the need for specially designed
instruction. A child has a problem with
expressive language, a hearing impairment
is detected, and the extent of the child's
language needs are examined. Or a child has
average or above average intelligence, is
three grade levels behind in reading, and a
determination is made that the child has a
specific learning disability in basic reading
and requires specially designed instruction
to develop the necessary reading skills.

Providing each child with a disability an
appropriate education is accomplished by
making accommodations, providing supports, and developing strategies that will
allow a child's needs to be met in the regular
classroom environment. When this is not
sufficient, the need for special education is
considered.

If a child has a disability and educational
needs that cannot be accommodated in the
regular classroom, a referral for a full and
individual evaluation is made to evaluate the
child in all areas of the suspected disability.
Before this evaluation is conducted, the
parents must be given prior written notice of
the evaluation and all procedural safeguards
(e.g., mediation, due process hearing)
available under IDEA.

The purpose of the full and individual
evaluation is twofold: to determine whether
the child is eligible to receive special
education and related services under IDEA,
and to determine the child's educational
needs. This evaluation is conducted by a
qualified team of professionals and the
parents. After a determination is made that a
child does have a disability and does have
educational needs, an IEP is developed and
implemented.

IEP Sequence

The sequence for developing an IEP is comprised of three basic components: (1) the determination of present levels of performance, (2) the development of measurable annual goals and short-term objectives or benchmarks, and (3) services.

PLEP. Present Levels of Educational Performance (PLEP) is the anchor statement of an IEP and provides the empirical basis for subsequent IEP components. There is no requirement for general and specific levels of performance, but both must be determined during the evaluation process to evaluate how a child's disability affects educational performance and to provide a basis for measurable annual goals. Each child's IEP must include a statement describing the child's educational needs and the affect the disability has on regular classroom involvement. In the development of measurable annual goals, the present level of performance for each goal is needed in order to anticipate yearly progress.

Goals. Following the determination of present levels of performance, measurable annual goals are developed to address these needs. Annual goals serve as the overall plan of instruction. Short-term objectives or benchmarks provide levels of anticipated progress that are used to monitor and report progress to parents throughout the year.

Services. After present levels of educational performance have been determined, and measurable annual goals to plan an appropriate program of instruction developed, services are designated to meet these needs, to enable the completion of goals, and to promote regular classroom participation to the maximum extent appropriate. New to IDEA-1997 is the requirement that the IEP include a statement as to why the child will not participate with nondisabled children in regular classroom activities. Throughout IDEA-1997 there is an emphasis on regular curriculum and regular class participation that highlights the importance of the presumption that a child will be educated in the regular classroom.[1] The reason for emphasizing regular curriculum participation is "intended to produce attention to the accommodations and adjustments necessary for disabled children to access the general education curriculum and the special services which may be necessary for appropriate participation in particular areas of the curriculum due to the nature of the disability."[2]

Because of the priority given to regular curriculum involvement, supplementary aids and services are always considered first to determine whether supports, specially designed instruction and modifications can be provided in the regular classroom or other settings to maximize education with nondisabled children. If a child is not able to be educated in a regular classroom environment, then the IEP team must consider a continuum of services that will result in the least restrictive environment; that is, the environment that will allow for maximum participation in the regular classroom.

Under IDEA, a child is eligible for related services only if the child needs special education services. Transition services are not required until age fourteen (or earlier if determined by the IEP team). Finally, extended school year services are determined on an individual basis in order to provide an appropriate education. The decision for extended school year services can be made when the IEP is first formulated, before the conclusion of a ten-month program, or during the development of IEPs other than the initial IEP.

IEP Timeline

The IEP process has several general federal time restraints[3] that are designed to ensure the development of an IEP as expeditiously as possible. As discussed below, individual states often have very specific and "reasonable, child-friendly timetables pertaining to the initial receipt of IEP services" (or parent consent for evaluation) to IEP implementation.[4] Figure I shows the federal timeline requirements for the development and implementation of IEPs.

There is no federal requirement concerning the period from initial referral to an individual evaluation. However, the time from referral to request for consent for an individual evaluation is not a time-consuming task and should not be used to delay the IEP process. For example, five to ten days is not an unreasonable period of time from when a child is first referred for services to the request for consent. In Wyoming when a referral is made though the Building Intervention Team, the school representative provides written notice to the parents within five days.[5] However, the time from referral to prior written notice and consent might be considerably longer if the school district and parents initiate pre-referral strategies or interventions.

After the parents consent to an individual evaluation, the school district is required to conduct an individual evaluation within a *reasonable period of time.* From consent to evaluation a reasonable period of time is generally within thirty days, as is the period of time from evaluation to the IEP meeting. Within 30 days of the individual evaluation, or when the determination is made that the child has a disability, the IEP team must meet to plan an individualized program.

Several states combine the period of time from consent to evaluation, or consent to IEP implementation. In Wyoming the evaluation must be completed within forty-five days after the receiving the parent written consent for evaluation,[6] while in Massachusetts the IEP must be sent to the parent within forty-five school working days after receipt of the parent's written consent for evaluation.[7] In California the evaluation and IEP meeting are completed within fifty days from the time of receipt of the written parental consent.[8] In New York State services must be provided within sixty days from the time of consent, or sixty days from the time of referral for a child who is already identified as disabled.[9]

Following the development of the IEP, the IEP must be implemented as soon as possible. If the IEP is developed during the summer and no summer services are need, this would result in an acceptable delay between development and implementation. Although a delay can occur (for example, because of transportation needs, difficulty finding a qualified service provider) there can be "no undue delay in providing special education and related services to the child."

The timeline from consent to services can be affected by procedural safeguard matters. If the parents refuse consent for a service offered by the school district, or the school district refuses a request for services by the parents, either party can either accept or refuse the action, propose a new action, or request a mediation or impartial due process hearing. Generally speaking, and in accordance with specific state timelines that might indicate otherwise, the time from the first referral for evaluation to providing services will be approximately ninety days or less.

Figure I. IEP Timeline

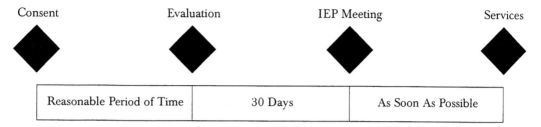

IEP Evaluations

The evaluation process consists of four stages: (1) initial evaluation, (2) goal progress evaluation, (3) annual evaluation, and (4) reevaluation. The initial evaluation is designed to determine whether a child has a disability, the present levels of educational performance and areas of need, and whether the child needs special education or additional modifications.

During the course of the year, parents must be periodically informed of their child's progress (which is one purpose of the short-term objectives or benchmarks). Progress toward goals is reported to parents as frequently as progress is reported to parents of nondisabled children, there must be periodic review of the IEP by the IEP team, at least annually, to determine whether goals are being achieved, whether the IEP should be revised, and to consider information resulting from a reevaluation or information provided by the parents.[10]

At least once every three years, or when requested by the parents or teacher, a re-evaluation is required to determine whether the child has a disability or whether the child should be declassified.[11] A major change from IDEA-1990 regulations is that existing evaluation data for a child is first reviewed, and based on that review a determination is made by the IEP team whether additional data is needed. The Senate report for IDEA-1997 considered this requirement one of the most "significant" changes in IDEA in that the triennial review has become "a highly paperwork-intensive process, driven as much by concern for compliance with the letter of the law, as by the need for additional evaluation information about a child." The purpose of the review of existing data requirement is to eliminate unnecessary testing, time, and expense. If the IEP team, with input from the parents, determines that additional information about continuing eligibility for special education is not necessary, the evaluation should focus on collecting information and data to improve instruction.[12]

The IEP Requirement

Each child with a disability must have an IEP before services are provided. Providing services without an IEP can mitigate planning, circumvent parent participation and minimize general curriculum participation. At the beginning of the school year each school district must "have in effect, for each child with a disability in its jurisdiction, an individualized education program"[13] as defined in the law and the regulations.[14] *In effect* means that the services and other provisions stipulated in the IEP are being provided. If IEP services are not being provided, the IEP is not in effect.

To phase in the IEP as defined in IDEA-1997, the March 12, 1999 final regulations state that "all IEPs developed, reviewed, or revised on or **after** July 1, 1998 must meet the requirements."[15] As a result of this rule, there will probably be IEPs circulating within school districts for many years based on IDEA-1990 requirements. Nonetheless, whenever an IEP is revised, the revision must adhere to IDEA-1997 requirements.

Non-IDEA IEPs

An IEP can be used to provide services to children who are not eligible for services under IDEA. For example, a child might have a disability, need a specific test or environmental accommodation, but not need specially designed instruction. Or a child might have been classified under IDEA, declassified because special education was no longer needed, but still receive IEP-related services in support of the declassification. For children who are considered disabled under Section 504 of the Rehabilitation Act of 1973 but not under IDEA, "regular or special education and related aids and services that are designed to meet individual educational needs of handicapped persons as adequately as the needs of nonhandicapped persons" must be provided. An IEP is one means for meeting this standard.

Under IDEA, a child must have a disability that meets one of the defined thirteen categories and need specially designed instruction. For Section 504, a disability means a physical or mental impairment which substantially limits one or more major life activities, a record of such an impairment, or when a child is regarded as having such an impairment.[16] By this definition a disability can be an impairment, or a record of an impairment, that limits a major life activity but the need for special education is not required. In contrast, IDEA requires that a child has a disability and needs specially designed instruction. For example, a child with a visual impairment might need a Braille translation service but not specially designed instruction or a special education teacher; or a child who is declassified under IDEA has a record of an impairment and is therefore entitled to support services under Section 504.

If an IEP is developed outside of IDEA (i.e., an IEP is developed for a child who does not have a disability under IDEA but does so under Section 504), there are no restrictions as to the content or structure of the IEP. However, if an IEP is developed under the auspices of IDEA, the child must have a disability, must need specially designed instruction, and the IEP must comply with the regulations.[17]

Interim IEPs. An IEP that has not been finalized can be used to provide services when a temporary placement is used to determine the suitability of a placement, or when the school district and parents agree upon an interim IEP when a child has transferred from another school. In the case of a temporary placement the guidelines caution "that it is essential that the temporary placement not become the final placement before the IEP is finalized." This can be accomplished by ensuring that (1) the interim IEP detail the specific timelines (e.g., 30 days) for the temporary placement; (2) the parents agree to the interim placement; and (3) the IEP team should schedule a meeting immediately following the trial period to finalize the IEP.[18]

Transfer IEPs. If a child transfers from one public school district to another within the same state, the new school district can adopt the old (or intrastate) IEP as written if the IEP meets the standards for the receiving state. If the IEP does not meet required standards or is deemed inappropriate by either the parents or school district, a new evaluation must be conducted and a new IEP developed. If the current IEP is inappropriate, and if the parents agree, the child can be placed in an interim placement until eligibility, placement, and services have been developed. If interim services cannot be agreed upon, the new school district must attempt to implement the old IEP until a new IEP is developed. However, if the parents disagree with the receiving district's placement, and request a due process hearing, the *stay put*[19] placement is the regular class if the parents do not agree to the interim placement.

Interstate IEPs. As is the case with intrastate IEPs, the receiving district can adopt the out-of-state IEP, treat the IEP as an interim IEP, or place the child in a regular education classroom and develop a new IEP following a careful review of the receiving IEP or conduct an entirely new individual evaluation. Because an interstate IEP might reflect requirements different than those of the receiving state, the IEP team and the parents should meet to evaluate every interstate IEP as soon as possible.

IFSP substitute. For infants or toddlers with disabilities under three years of age who need early intervention services,[20] a written individualized family service plan (IFSP) is developed by a multidisciplinary team, including the parents,[21] to provide the necessary services.

When a child moves from an early intervention program (Part C) to a preschool program for children aged three to five under Part B of IDEA,[22] the child can continue IFSP services or receive services via an IEP. In this case, an Individualized Family Service Plan "may serve as the IEP of the child if using that plan as the IEP is (i) consistent with State policy; and (ii) agreed to by the agency and the child's parents."[23] In order to use an IFSP in place of an IEP, the parents must be made aware of the difference between the IFSP and IEP, and give written informed consent.

Multiple IEPs. The IEP is "a written statement for each child with a disability."[24] Of particular importance in this definition is that the IEP is a single document and not a series of different plans, programs, or formats. If a child receives services from a private school placement or facility, the child's program is defined by one IEP and not a second individualized program developed by the private school or facility.[25] If a separate individualized transition program format is used to provide transition services, this is a part of the primary IEP. In other words, there should not be two sets of transition goals, two sets of services, etc. Without a single IEP to define a child's educational program, program continuity, revision and overall responsibility for program development and implementation can be affected.

A FRAME OF REFERENCE

The development of an IEP that provides educational benefit and is in compliance must be based on an assessment of regular curriculum and disability needs, pre-referral strategies and interventions, parent input, and team planning. The task prior to referral is to determine a child's regular curriculum needs, what can be done to meet these needs without special education, and whether the child requires an individual evaluation. The child's behavior and performance in the regular classroom, and the accommodation of these needs within the general curriculum, provide an essential frame of reference for special education referral, and for determining goals and services if the child is determined to need special education.

The assessment of regular classroom performance by the regular classroom teacher is especially important if a child is eventually referred for an individual evaluation. If a child is suspected of having a disability, there is some behavior or area of educational performance that the child exhibits that warrants this suspicion. Performance on teacher-made and standardized tests might be low, specific academic skills might be lacking, or the child might exhibit behaviors in the classroom that detract from regular curriculum participation. The regular classroom teacher must specify, as much as possible, exactly what the child does or does not do that seems to affect classroom performance. Because of the important IEP team role of the regular classroom teacher in IDEA, classroom observations and input should play a significant role in the direction and conduct of the overall individual evaluation.

The question of whether a classroom intervention is conducted prior to referral depends on the suspected disability and the severity of the disability. If a sensory disability is suspected, a referral should be made immediately. The severity of a child's problem or the existence of an obvious disability (e.g., blindness, physical disability) requires an immediate referral for a full and individual evaluation. The need to refer a child because of a low-incidence disabilities (i.e., visual or orthopedic impairments, autism, traumatic brain injury) is often obvious, but high-incidence disability referral (e.g., specific learning disabilities, speech impairments) is generally more problematic. For a child who is having difficulty with basic school or content skills, remedial resources should be exhausted before a referral for special education is made. At the very least, the appropriate remedial specialist should be given an opportunity to provide input and suggest remedial strategies before a referral is made. If a child is thought to have a reading problem, the remedial reading teacher should provide input and suggest possible pre-referral strategies and interventions. Not only can a specialist provide insight as to effective interventions, but also for determining the need for a special education referral. A child eligible for special education is also eligible to receive remedial services as would any other child, but a remedial service cannot be provided in lieu of special education.

The school district, with input from the parents, might try a variety of remedial strategies before a referral for an individual evaluation to determine the need for special education is made. Possible pre-referral interventions include parent-teacher or a child study team meeting (if available) to address specific problems, instruction from a remedial specialists, school counseling, special classroom grouping or projects within the regular classroom, in-classroom interventions, school-home coordinated activities, using paraprofessionals or volunteers, tutoring, peer-tutoring, small group teaching, curriculum modifications, test accommodations, or study groups. Pre-referral strategies and interventions provide an essential step in enabling a child to be involved in and progress in the general curriculum, and providing the direction for the individual evaluation if a referral for special education is made.

MAKING A REFERRAL

If regular classroom strategies and interventions are not successful, after consultation with the parents, a referral for an individual evaluation to determine eligibility for special education and the need for specially designed instruction is made. A referral for an individual evaluation might be made by the classroom teacher, school specialists, the school psychologist, other school personnel, and of course, the parents. If available, a child study team might first consider interventions in the regular curriculum, and, if unsuccessful, make a referral for an individual evaluation. In some instances nonschool personnel might be allowed to refer a child for special education such as a physician, officer of the court, or a representative of public agency. In the case of school personnel, the referral should indicate the specific reason for the referral (e.g., specific classroom behaviors, test scores), a list of attempted strategies and interventions, and input or attempts to solicit input from the parents (see p. 65). A self-referral is possible if the student is over eighteen, or an emancipated minor.[26]

Child Study Team

The special education process is driven by *Child Find*[27] that requires all children who need special education services in the state are identified, evaluated, and located. In order to identify all children, a multifaceted referral system is needed involving parents, school personnel, and other professionals so that

all children with disabilities residing in the State, including children with disabilities attending private schools, regardless of the severity of their disabilities, and who are in need of special education and related services, are identified, located, and evaluated and a practical method is developed and implemented to determine which children with disabilities are currently receiving needed special education and related services.[28]

Direct referral and screening are the primary methods used to identify children with disabilities needing special education services. A direct referral for an individual evaluation can be made by a parent, teacher, or other professional (e.g., school psychologist, physician) or an informal Child Study Team (CST). Many school districts attempt to resolve school problems by convening a small team of school personnel such as a Child Planning Team, Child Service Team, Child Assistance Team, Student Assistance Team, Student Study Committee, or Student Study Team. A CST is often a small group of professionals who "attempt to assist the teacher in modifying instruction or to determine if a referral for a comprehensive special education evaluation is warranted" (Smith et al., 1995, p. 41). Depending on the nature and severity of the school problem, the CST might first consider regular school strategies and interventions. If the CST is unsuccessful in resolving the problem, a referral is then made for an individual evaluation for special education.

The CST might be comprised of only three or four members such as the school principal, teacher, reading specialist, and the parent. Although the membership of the CST can vary, the parent of the child should either be a part of the team or have an opportunity to provide input just as the parents would provide input during the evaluation and IEP development process. The regular education teacher should always be on the CST, but the participation of a special education teacher depends on the severity of the problem. There is no federal requirement concerning the formation of a CST, but IDEA-1997 does recognize the need to provide "incentives for wholeschool approaches and prereferral intervention to reduce the need to label children as disabled in order to address their learning needs."[29] The CST is a very simple and effective approach for dealing with educational needs and classroom behavior, using available school resources, without the need for specially designed instruction.[30]

In contrast to an informally constituted team, a CST can also refer to multidisciplinary teams (as per IDEA-1990), or a group of qualified professionals and parents who determine whether or not the child has a disability and needs special education, or the IEP team. Salvia and Ysseldyke (1995) noted that the team of professionals who decides whether special education is warranted "is usually called a child study team, though in some states and districts

within states these teams go by other names such as IEP team or special education eligibility team" (p. 12). In New Jersey the CST is responsible for the identification of children needing services, the development and supervision of programs, and remedial instruction.[31] In New Jersey at least one CST team member is also one of the of the IEP team meeting participants.[32] In Montana the multidisciplinary child study team[33] completes a Child Study Team report that indicates the disability, the need for special education, and the implications for educational planning. An IEP team then develops the IEP.[34] Virginia also requires a CST to review records and performance, but the role of the CST is to consider options and the need for a referral rather than overseeing the evaluation and IEP process. Referrals are made to the principal (or designee), and the committee comprises at least three persons. If a child is suspected of having a disability, a referral is made to the special education administrator for formal assessment.[35]

The CST can play an important role in the special education process, especially in the collection of relevant classroom data and present levels of performance. In *Hacienda La Puente School District v. Honig*[36] the mother of a seventh-grade student requested a school evaluation for poor academic performance and school behavior. In response "the school convened an informal 'student study team'" and developed a homework contract and recommended counseling. The need for special education was eventually denied and the student was expelled for "frightening another student with a stolen starter pistol." However, a hearing officer concluded that the student was disabled, that the behavior was a manifestation of the disability, and the student was wrongly denied protection afforded by IDEA. In this case, the student study team began the process that first considered the problem, attempted interventions and should have provided the baseline data for the individual evaluation (which found that the student was not emotionally disturbed).

THE REFERRAL

A referral for special education is often made by the teacher or the parents. Also, as discussed above, a referral can be made by a CST if classroom strategies and interventions have been ineffective. For referrals made by teachers, school personnel, specialists, physicians, or other professionals, the referral should be in writing and contain, at the very minimum the following: (1) the reason for the referral, (2) attempts to address the problem in the regular classroom, and (3) parent contact or input. For a referral made by a parent, the referral can be in writing or simply an oral request. If the request is not in writing, an attempt should be made to ascertain, as much as possible, the reason for the referral and why attempts to deal with the problem have not been successful in the regular classroom.

Reason for referral. The referral should clearly indicate what exactly the child does or does not do that suggests the existence of a disability. The reason for the referral should be specific and should focus on classroom performance and not labels. The reason for a referral should not be a label such as ADD, ADHD, mentally retarded, or learning disabled because the disability is determined following the individual evaluation. The referral should indicate specific behaviors or levels of performance such as not completing assignments, low test scores, poor grades, not responding to teacher directions, poor reading skills, or specific classroom behaviors that affect classroom performance. If classroom behavior is a factor, labels should not be used to describe the problem such as "emotional distur-

bance" or "hyperactivity," but the referral should detail the type and frequency of the behavior as much as possible.

The reason for the referral provides the basis for the individual evaluation and development of the IEP. If a child has a severe reading problem as evidenced by both teacher observation and tests, this information is important in the determination of eligibility and developing an instructional plan. Likewise, if a referral cites specific classroom behavior (e.g., yelling, interrupting, biting, verbal abuse), the behavior cited in the referral should be addressed in the IEP.

Interventions. A record should be maintained of the classroom strategies and interventions attempted and the effectiveness of each. This information provides the rationale for referral for an individual evaluation by showing that attempts to deal with the problem in the regular curriculum have not been successful. Most important, attempted intervention data is extremely useful when deciding measurable annual goals, appropriate services and the extent of regular classroom participation if a child is determined to have a disability.

Parent input. If the referral is made by the teacher or school personnel, the parents should be consulted before the referral is made. Providing parents with an opportunity to participate in all aspects of the special education process includes the pre-referral stage and the initial referral for special education.

The referral for an individual evaluation is not the same as the information contained in the prior written notice. The referral includes basic information necessary to document and consider the need for an individual evaluation by the IEP team. The prior written notice, as described below, includes not only the information contained in the referral, but a listing of other data, options, and other relevant factors considered.

IEP Team Responsibilities

The IEP team has several mandated responsibilities. First, the IEP team must determine whether a child is a child with a disability if the IEP team is assigned this responsibility by state code, regulation, or guideline. The requirement for determining whether a child is a child with a disability "shall be made by a team of qualified professionals and the parent of the child.[37] Second, the IEP team must consider evaluation data and parent input before developing an IEP.[38] Third, following this evaluation, the IEP team must consider five special factors which are discussed in detail in Chapter 4 (p. 87):

1. Behavioral problems: behavioral interventions, strategies, and supports
2. Limited English proficiency: language needs
3. Visual impairments: Braille needs unless otherwise determined
4. Hearing impairments: language and communications needs[39]
5. Assistive technology requirements: the need for devices and/or services

Fourth, following the consideration data, parent and regular classroom teacher input and special factors, the IEP team develops an IEP comprised of the basic eight IEP elements (or seven if transition services are not required), and the need for extended school year (ESY) services[40] if necessary.

Fifth, the IEP team must review the IEP at least annually. The IEP must be reviewed periodically, but at least annually, to evaluate progress and goal achievement, and to make revisions in the IEP and/or in the general curriculum.[41] In addition to the annual review a re-evaluation must be conducted if service, placement, or eligibility needs change or if the parents request a re-evaluation. In contrast to a periodic or annual review, a reevaluation must be conducted at least once every three years.[42]

Finally, the IEP team has several special responsibilities regarding the removal of children with disabilities from a current placement for a violation of school rules. If school personnel remove a child with a disability from a placement for more than ten days because of a violation of school rules, the IEP team must conduct a functional behavioral assessment and then develop a behavioral intervention plan to address the behavior. If a plan already exists, the IEP team must review and revise the plan without an IEP team meeting unless a team member believes that the IEP must be modified.[43] If school personnel plan to remove a child with a disability because of a violation of school rules for more than ten days, the IEP team must conduct a review to determine whether the behavior is a manifestation of the child's disability. If one of the following conditions is met, the IEP team must determine that the behavior is a manifestation of the disability:

1. The IEP or placement is inappropriate to address the behavior.
2. IEP services, including behavior intervention strategies, are not provided.
3. The disability impaired the child's under-

standing of the consequences of the behavior.

4. The disability impaired the child's ability to control the behavior.

If the behavior is a manifestation of the disability, the IEP team must remedy the IEP, placement, or implementation of services. If the behavior is not a manifestation of the disability, "the relevant disciplinary procedures applicable to children without disabilities may be applied."[44] This means that if a child without a disability would receive a long-term suspension (or is expelled) because of a rule violation, a child with a disability could also receive a long-term suspension.[45] Services are not required for suspensions 10 days or less (if services are not provided for children without disabilities), but services must be provided for suspensions greater than ten days in order to allow the child to progress in the general curriculum and to achieve IEP goals.[46]

NOTICE, SAFEGUARDS, AND CONSENT

Following a referral for an individual evaluation, how the referral is processed and by whom varies from state to state. In Wyoming all referrals are made through the Building Intervention Team. If the team determines that pre-referral interventions have not been successful and a disability is suspected, parents are given prior written notice within five working days, and the child is referred for an individual evaluation.[47] In Kentucky the Admissions and Release Committee (ARC) reviews the referral to determine the need for an individual evaluation.[48] In all cases, the parents must be given prior written notice concerning the proposed action, a notice of the procedural safeguards that are available (e.g., mediation, due process hearing, etc.), and then give informed consent before an individual evaluation is conducted.

Prior Written Notice

Table IV lists the circumstances when parents must be given prior written notice,[49] a copy of procedural safeguards,[50] and when parental consent is required.[51] All actions regarding identification, evaluation or change of a child's educational placement, or the refusal to initiate or change, requires prior written notice. The procedural safeguards notice is required before evaluations, before each IEP meeting, and upon receipt of a request for a due process hearing. Parental consent is required before initial and reevaluations evaluations, and before the initial provision of services. Consent is not required for reevaluations if the school can show that an effort was made to obtain consent.[52]

The purpose of the prior written notice is to clearly explain what the school intends to do (e.g., conduct an individual evaluation) and why this is being proposed. The notice is designed to ensure that parents are involved, and that parents have a real voice in the IEP process. Prior written notice must be given to the parents in understandable language a reasonable period of time before the school district proposes (or refuses) to initiate or change the identification, evalua-

Table IV. Notice, Safeguards, and Consent Requirement

Parent Notice, Safeguards, and Consent

Action	Prior Written Notice	Procedural Safeguards	Parental Consent
Initial evaluation	✔	✔	✔
Re-evaluation	✔	✔	✔[53]
Initial services or placement	✔	✔[54]	✔
Change services or placement	✔	✔[55]	
IEP meeting notification	✔		
Due process request		✔	
10+ day suspension[56]		✔	

tion, or educational placement. Prior written notice is intended to include parents in the decision making process and not to overwhelm parents with a legal documentation. Table IV shows that prior written notice is required whenever an initial evaluation or re-evaluation is considered, or whenever a change in services is proposed by the school district. The regulatory wording for prior written notice is all-inclusive and is intended to include any and all actions proposed by the school district involving the initiation or change in identification, evaluation, or educational placement,[57] or if the school district refuses a similar action proposed by the parents. The prior written notice should consist of the following seven elements:[58]

1. Action. The notice must include a statement of the proposed action that the school district proposes to initiate. What exactly is it that the school is proposing, or what action does the school not want to do? For example, the school might want to conduct an individual evaluation, or make a substantial change in a child's IEP. Rather than initiating an action, a school might refuse a service thought necessary by the parents, or a placement requested by the parents. Although the notice must contain a description of the action proposed or refused

by the school district,[59] the action can be quite complex and involve a variety of services and accommodations so that understanding what the "action" is might require considerable explanation.

2. Reason. The reason for the proposed action should be clearly stated in the referral. For example, if individual evaluation is wanted because of a suspected learning disability, a hearing impairment, or multiple disability, the behavior and the suspected problem should be stated.

3. Options. The reason why the proposed action is necessary and what other options were considered and rejected should be stated.

4. Data. The notice should contain a description all information and/or data for an action (or not taking a certain action). Test scores or teacher reports might indicate a problem, or that a certain placement is no longer appropriate. As is the case when stating the reason for referral, all data relevant to an action should be given to the parents.

5. Relevant factors. The notice must list all factors that are relevant to a school district's proposed course of action. If a child is being referred and an incident concerning a physical threat made by the student is a factor, this information must be reported to the parents.

6. **Safeguards.** The notice must include a statement that parents have procedural safeguard rights, and how a copy of these rights can be obtained. A general rule of thumb is that whenever prior written notice is given, parents must be informed of their procedural safeguards rights. The requirement that if the notice is not an initial referral, "the means by which a copy . . . can be obtained"[60] suggests that the actual description is only required for initial evaluations. However, the regulations are also quite clear that the copy of the procedural safeguards must be given, at a minimum, upon initial referral, notification of each IEP meeting, re-evaluation and receipt of a due process request.[61]

7. **Help.** The notice should indicate who parents can contact in order to understand all of the above. Sources that can provide help include toll-free parent assistance lines,[62] local law centers, bar association resources, local university and college special education programs, and local chapters of professional and special education resource centers.

Additional material relating to the prior written notice can include a statement of special options considered such as classroom supports, remedial programs, or other types of strategies or interventions. If possible, the notice should be written in the native language of the parents or translated by other means.

Procedural Safeguards Notice[63]

A copy of the parents' procedural safeguards must be given to the parents upon (1) initial referral for evaluation or re-evaluation, (2) each notification of an IEP meeting, (3) each re-evaluation of the child, and (4) receipt of a request for an impartial due process hearing. In addition, parents must be provided the procedural safeguards notice when a decision is made to change a child's placement for more than ten days because of a rule violation.[65] The procedural safeguard notice must include "a full explanation of the procedural safeguards, written in the native language of the parents, unless it clearly is not feasible to do so, and written in an easily understandable manner."[66] The notice of procedural safeguards is more than informing parents of their rights, but should represent a good faith effort to help parents understand the rights that will assist in providing their child with an appropriate education, even when that is very different from what the school district is suggesting or

providing.

If necessary, a translator or reader might be necessary to explain each parental right or to read and review the various rights. So as not to bury parental rights in undecipherable text, certain rights should be emphasized when appropriate. For example, if the parent disagrees with a service, the parent should be made aware that a mediation process is available to resolve the dispute. If a child is enrolled in a private school by the parents, the parent should be aware that their child is entitled to an evaluation and an IEP but that services "may" be provide on-site. The explanation of rights is especially important for non-English speaking parents who might be completely unfamiliar with the legal and educational system. As is the case with prior written notice, a number of states provide a copy of the procedural safeguards in languages other than English.

The procedural safeguards notice is designed to convey "user-friendly information that the parents can understand"[67] although the terminology for a specific right might require further clarification or translation. The contents of the notice must fully explain each of the following safeguards (CFR or IDEA reference for each is in parentheses):

1. independent educational evaluation (34 CFR 300.502);
2. prior written notice (34 CFR 300.503);
3. parental consent (34 CFR 529(b)(1));
4. access to educational records (34 CFR 300.501(a)(1));
5. opportunity for a due process hearings (20 USC 1415(b)(6));
6. placement during pendency of due process proceedings (34 CFR 300.514&526);
7. interim alternative educational setting requirements (34 CFR 300.522);
8. requirements for unilateral placement by parents of children in private schools at public expense (34 CFR 300.454);
9. mediation (34 CFR 300.506);
10. due process hearings (34 CFR 300.507-09&511);
11. state-level appeals if applicable (34 CFR 300.510);
12. civil actions (34 CFR 300.512);
13. attorneys' fees (34 CFR 300.513); and
14. state complaint procedures (34 CFR 300.660-662).

Understanding the procedural safeguards outlined in IDEA can be a daunting task and several of the rights have a very specific application. Reimbursement for private school services when the school district has failed to provide FAPE is important when and if a parent considers private school services and whether or not a school is providing FAPE. Likewise, knowing that attorneys' fees can only be given for IEP meetings which are administrative or judicial actions, or as part of a mediation,[68] will not be of great importance to most parents.

Parents must not only be given a list of procedural safeguards but some inkling when a certain right is especially applicable (such as mediation).

Each procedural safeguard can have significant import for parents under the appropriate circumstances, but all parents should have a clear understanding that they can bring recommendations and complaints to the IEP team, and request a timely mediation conducted by a qualified mediator. In addition to the less formal mediation process parents can also request an impartial hearing and bring complaints directly to the state education department.

The procedural safeguards in IDEA-1997 have "historically provided the foundation for ensuring access to a free appropriate public education for children with disabilities."[69] The copy of procedural safeguards is for parents, but the IEP team plays an important role in addressing complaints, fulfilling certain rights (e.g., prior written notice), and participating in certain IEP team activities pursuant to specific rights (e.g., determining an interim alternative setting).

The mediation process added to the list of procedural safeguards by IDEA-1997 is considered an important innovation and must be available to resolve disputes. The mediation process must be voluntary, not used to delay the possibility of a due process hearing, and scheduled in a timely and convenient manner.[70] An agency may establish procedures, at a time and location convenient to the parents with a disinterested party, to encourage the use and explain the benefits of the mediation process. The mediation process is intended to become the primary vehicle for resolving disputes and developing a collaborative relationship between parents and schools that will engender the type of planning envisioned in PL 94-142. The Senate report asserts that in States where mediation is being used, litigation has been reduced, and parents and schools have resolved their differences amicably, making decisions with the child's best interest in mind. It is the Committee's strong preference that mediation become the norm for resolving disputes under IDEA. The Committee believes that the availability of mediation will ensure that far fewer conflicts will proceed to the next procedural steps, formal due process and litigation, outcomes that the Committee believes should be avoided when possible.[71]

Parental Consent

Parental consent, or "informed parental consent,"[72] is required before an evaluation (or re-evaluation), and before the provision of special education or a related service.[73] Parental consent means that the parent has been informed of all relevant information, agrees in writing to the action, and understands consent is voluntary and may be revoked at any time. Parental consent is not required for the IEP team to review existing data, or for every test given to a child with a disability, but is intended to ensure that consent is given for testing undertaken as part of an initial evaluation or re-evaluation.[74] For districtwide and state tests that are given to all children, parental consent is not required unless consent is required by all parents. The regulations require that "parental consent is not required before (1) reviewing existing data as part of an evaluation or a reevaluation, or (2) administering a test or other evaluation that is administered to all children unless, before administration of that test or evaluation, consent is required of parents of all children."[75] Also, parental consent is not required for re-evaluations if parents have not responded to reasonable attempts to obtain consent.

Although a signed IEP is not required, this could be used to indicate parent consent for initial services if parents are informed of all *relevant* information for which consent is sought, and the parents understand that the signed IEP is voluntary.

Parental consent for an individual evaluation does not mean that the parent agrees with the evaluation, the determination of eligibility, or consent for services. If a parent does not consent to an initial evaluation, the school district can seek mediation or a due process hearing.[76] Whether an impartial hearing is conducted to require an initial evaluation depends on state law. The IDEA-1997 regulation is permissive in that "the agency may pursue the need for an evaluation by using the due process or the mediation procedures.[77] In New York, if parents do not provide consent and request a conference, the board of education is required to initiate an impartial hearing to determine whether an evaluation will be conducted without parental consent.[78]

If the IEP requires change, an IEP meeting is required. If the change involves determining whether the child is no longer a child with a disability, a re-evaluation is required. A re-evaluation is not required for students graduating with a regular high school diploma or who exceed the age eligibility requirements of FAPE.[79] Parental consent is required before a change in services, placement, or eligibility. However, because the state is ultimately responsible for providing FAPE to a child,[80] a re-evaluation can be conducted if the school district "can demonstrate that it has taken reasonable measures to obtain that consent."[81] In this situation, the parents have the option of pursing an impartial hearing following the change that resulted in conjunction with the parent's failure to respond. The school district cannot conduct a re-evaluation without parent consent if the parents refuse a request for a re-evaluation. If parents disagree with a change (or a refuse a service), the school district can request an impartial hearing and the child remains in his or her educational placement unless the school district and parents agree otherwise.

A state can have additional areas in which consent is required. For example, Alabama requires consent when providing "temporary special education services." As is the case with prior written notice and procedural safeguards, the school district should attempt to ensure that the parents understand what is being proposed (e.g., an IEP) and not simply interpret a signature as informed consent.

Parents can respond to a request for consent by ignoring the request, revoking the consent if it has been given, or not giving consent for all or part of the action or activity requested.

No consent. If consent is not given because the parent ignores the request or chooses not to respond to the request (rather than refusing the request outright), the school district can conduct an evaluation if deemed necessary by an impartial hearing. If the failure to respond is for a re-evaluation, parent consent is not needed if reasonable efforts have been made to obtain consent.[82]

Refuse consent. If a parent refuses consent, an informal meeting can be conducted to resolve the dispute. If necessary, a school district can use the mediation or due process hearing to conduct an evaluation or provide services if parental consent is refused. If a mediation or due process hearing is used by the school district to initiate an evaluation or provide services, and the result is in favor of the school district, the parents can initiate a state complaint or civil action. If state law indicates that parental consent cannot be overridden, then the evaluation is not conducted and services are not provided or not changed. Of course, if parents refuse an action, and a mediation or due process hearing is either not possible or not pursued, the school can always reconsider the proposed action.

Partial consent. A parent might refuse one or two items that are being proposed in an IEP such as inclusion in a certain regular education classroom. Consent can be refused for a specific activity (e.g., speech therapy), but doing so does not affect services for which consent has been given. In other words, the parent's refusal to consent to a certain activity does not affect the responsibility of the school district to provide services that are not in dispute.

Revoke consent. A parent can revoke consent, but revocation is not retroactive; that is, actions taken prior to the action are not changed.

THE IEP TEAM PROCESS

A school district can have one team to oversee the individual evaluation and a second team to develop the IEP, or a single team to determine the existence of a disability and to develop the IEP. Whether one or two teams are responsible for determining eligibility and developing an IEP, parent participation is required. An effort must be made to include parents in all evaluation and/or IEP meetings by early notification and scheduling meetings at mutually agreed-on times. The notification of meetings should specify purpose, time, location, and who will be attending the meeting. If necessary, conference/telephone calls should be used to obtain parent input. An IEP meeting can be conducted without the parents if the parents refuse to participate, but detailed records must be kept of telephone calls, correspondence, and visits involving parent participation.

Evaluation Team

Previously, the task of determining eligibility was made by a multidisciplinary team or MDT, but as required by IDEA eligibility is now determined by a team of qualified professionals, including the parents, so that "the teams making these determinations include individuals with the knowledge and skills necessary to interpret the evaluation data and make an informed determination as to whether the child" has a disability and needs special education.[83]

Prior to IDEA-1997 IEP teams were often static in terms of composition so that one parent represented all parents, one teacher represented all regular classroom teachers, and the basic team membership rarely if ever changed. The IEP membership required by IDEA-1997 guidelines is intended to be responsive to each child's needs.

> The composition of the team will vary depending upon the nature of the child's suspected disability and other relevant factors. For example, if a student is suspected of having a learning disability, a professional whose sole expertise in visual impairments would be an inappropriate choice. If a student is limited English proficient, it will be important to include a person on the team of qualified professionals who is knowledgeable about the identification, assessment, and education of limited English proficient students.[84]

For IDEA-1997 the multidisciplinary team has been changed to a team comprised of qualified professionals and the parents of the child. This change is important for two reasons. First, parents are now part of the decision-making process that determines whether their child has a disability. Second, the group of qualified professionals is designed to create a team that is able to evaluate all of a child's needs rather than a fixed group of individuals who may or may not have the necessary expertise pertaining to all relevant needs.

The use of the term *qualified professionals* is intended to ensure that the teams include individuals with the knowledge and skills necessary to interpret the evaluation data and make informed eligibility decisions. By requiring a qualified team of professionals and the parents of each child when determining eligibility, team composition will be fluid and better meet the needs of the child but with some loss of scheduling efficiency. A person with expertise in the education of the hearing impaired is a necessary IEP team member if the child is suspected of having a hearing disorder, but not if the suspected disability is a visual impairment. A reading specialist might be eminently qualified to interpret a child's reading performance if the suspected specific learning disability is in reading comprehension, but might not be part of the team if the disability entails a speech impairment. Of course, if a student has limited English proficiency, a person with LEP expertise is an essential team member.

Although the team making the decision could be referred to as a multidisciplinary team, child study team, or evaluation team, in most instances the decision concerning eligibility is made by the IEP team, the parents, and other qualified professionals. A multidisciplinary team, comprising of a qualified group of professionals and the parents, could still serve to collect data, oversee and conduct necessary testing and evaluations, and determine what additional evaluations and assessments might be required.

Prior to IDEA-1997 when parent involvement on the multidisciplinary team was not mandated, separate multidisciplinary and IEP teams were often used to determine eligibility and develop IEPs. As a result of IDEA-1997 and because of the individualized composition of each team and the need for parent input, having one team to determine eligibility and develop the IEP is an efficient approach for meeting eligibility and IEP requirements. The regulations permit eligibility and IEP development decisions to be made at a single meeting providing that eligibility is made by a qualified group of professionals and the parents and the IEP is developed by a team composed of the required members.[85] If a single team or committee is used to make evaluations and IEP decisions, the IEP team might meet on separate occasions so that team members can consider the evaluation report and then determine eligibility, and develop an IEP. If one team is used to conduct the evaluation, eligibility and IEP development, all the rules regarding evaluation, parent notification and involvement, and IEP development must be followed.[86]

Differentiating eligibility determination and IEP development can enhance the consideration of evaluation data by IEP team members. In Ohio the evaluation team is referred to as the Intervention-Based Multifactored Evaluation (IBMFE)[87] and the

IEP meeting is conducted to review the IBMFE results and the current IEP, and to determine the learner's present level of performance. The task of evaluation and IEP development is also separated in Wisconsin so that an M-team (or multidisciplinary team) is responsible for the individual evaluation, and the IEP is developed at an IEP meeting in which the M-team report is considered.[88]

A single team to oversee both eligibility determination and IEP development can reduce meeting time and increase IEP team efficiency. In New York the Committee on Special Education (CSE) is responsible for initiating the individual evaluation and developing an IEP recommendation. In California[89] an individualized education program team is responsible for reviewing assessment results, determining eligibility, and the content of the individualized education program. The Case Conference Committee in Indiana[90] is responsible for determining a student's eligibility for special education and related services; developing, reviewing, or revising a student's individualized education program; and determining an appropriate educational placement. Kentucky uses an Admissions and Release Committee (ARC) to act on referrals; oversee the conduct of a full and complete evaluation; determine eligibility; develop a remedial plan if a child is not eligible for special education services; and develop, review, and revise IEPs.[91] In contrast to the comprehensive responsibilities of this type of committee, Virginia uses a four-tier process in which a child is first referred to a formally constituted child study team. A multidisciplinary team then conducts an evaluation, eligibility is determined by an eligibility committee, and an IEP committee develops an appropriate program.[92]

Individual Evaluation Report

Following the evaluation, an evaluation report documents the reasons for eligibility.[93] This report generally includes a summary of the standardized test scores, reports, evaluations, and work samples. Most importantly, the evaluation report includes the levels of performance that demonstrate how the child's disability impacts participation in the regular curriculum, and specific levels of performance that can be used as beginning benchmarks in the selection of measurable annual goals and short-term objectives. The parents must be provided with a copy of the evaluation report before the determination of eligibility. For parents (and many professionals) who are often bewildered by an abundance of tests and evaluations, an ample period of time should be provided to consider the data, needs, possible goals, and services. If the IEP team is responsible for both the evaluation and IEP development, and one meeting is used to determine both, the parents should have a copy of the evaluation report before the meeting.

The evaluation report should address general educational needs, specific instructional needs, and disability needs. Standardized test scores are often used to identify general educational needs, while curriculum-based assessments indicate specific instructional needs. For example, a child might have a percentile rank of 11 in mathematics computation or reading, and a curriculum-based assessment reveals that the child is able to identify 20 of 100 primary addition facts or read a grade-level passage with approximately 30 reading errors per 100 words. The data in the evaluation report are used to determine the impact of the disability on educational performance (e.g., a percentile rank of 11) and to indicate the beginning benchmarks for measurable annual goals. In this example, the general need is determined by the percentile rank of 11, the specific instructional need by the curriculum-based assessment, and the beginning benchmark is to increase performance from 20 to 60, 20 to 80 or whatever might be a realistic expectation of annual progress. In the case of reading performance, the benchmark might be to reduce oral reading errors from 30 to 20 or from 30 to 10 by the end of the year.

SLD report. Because of the large number of children identified as having specific learning disabilities, and because some of these children have instructional needs but are not disabled, specific guidelines have been developed for the determination of a specific learning disability. For a child suspected of having a learning disability, a *written report* is required by the IEP team that must include

1. whether the child has a specific learning disability,
2. the basis for making the determination,
3. the relevant behavior noted during the observation of the child,
4. the relationship of that behavior to the child's academic functioning,
5. educationally relevant medical findings, if any,
6. whether there is a severe discrepancy between achievement and ability that is not correctable without special education and related services, and
7. determining the effects of environmental, cultural, or economic disadvantage.

Following the determination of a specific learning disability, "each team member shall certify in writing whether the report reflects his or her conclusion. If it does not reflect his or her conclusion, the team member must submit a separate statement presenting his or her conclusions."[94]

IEP TEAM MEMBERSHIP

The term *individualized education program team* or *IEP team* means a group of individuals composed of the parents, teachers, school representatives, specialists, and the child (if appropriate) who are responsible for developing, reviewing, and revising IEPs for children with disabilities.[95] An IEP team has a flexible committee membership to meet the specific needs of each child. Because IEP team membership is fluid, IEP team composition will be different for each child. An IEP team with unchanging membership might facilitate scheduling, but often does not result in a team that is responsive to a child's individual needs.

The district representative for each IEP team is often the same for all teams, as is the individual who is able to interpret the instructional implications of the evaluation reports (e.g., the school psychologist). However, the parent member for each team is the parent of the child being considered, and the regular and special education teacher(s) members might be different.

Parents. The IEP team for a child includes the parents of the child with the disability rather than a parent representative. Prior to IDEA-1997, the law also required one or both of the parents but school districts frequently included a parent member to represent parents not able to attend. With a parent representative on the team, there is less of a need to encourage and arrange for the participation of the parent of the child being considered. In many instances, the parent representative became the primary source for IEP team parent participation.

Regular education teacher. The IEP team requires at least one regular education teacher of the child if the child is or may be in a regular classroom,[96] and not simply "the child's teacher" as required by the 1990 regulations. Depending on the situation, this might be more than one regular education teacher or even all of the child's regular education teachers. Because the focus of special education is on the regular curriculum, the role of the regular classroom teacher is essential in planning and implementing an IEP.

The 1990 regulations suggested that the regular classroom teacher should be provided with a copy of the IEP or informed of its contents,[97] but the regular classroom teacher was not obligated to participate in the development of goals and services, even when these goals and services were ostensibly designed to promote regular classroom participation.

If the child participates in the regular classroom to a very limited degree, the participation of the regular classroom teacher in IEP deliberations might also be limited. For a child with severe developmental disabilities, who might have limited regular classroom participation, the regular classroom teacher might not attend all meetings or only those meetings where some type of inclusion is contemplated. As noted in a memorandum to the Department of Education "Congress did not envision regular classroom teachers participating in all aspects of IEP-related activities and "the final regulations should also clarify that compliance . . . is not limited to the physical presence of regular education teachers in meetings to develop and revise IEPs." Most importantly, "participation by the regular education teacher in IEP-related activities should reflect flexibility,"[98] because the intent is to have an IEP team comprised of individuals who can make meaningful contributions to the child's education program.

The role of the regular education teacher includes assisting in the development of the IEP, helping formulate "appropriate positive behavioral interventions and strategies" when appropriate, and assisting in the "determination of supplementary aids and services, program modifications, and supports for school personnel." A major goal of IDEA-1997 is for a child to participate and progress in the regular classroom curriculum, and the regular education teacher is pivotal for determining necessary supports, strategies and interventions that will promote participation in the regular curriculum.

Special education teacher. The special education teacher is the teacher who is responsible for the implementation of the IEP and not an assigned IEP team member. If the student is to receive services in a resource room, the special education is the resource room teacher. If the student is to receive services in a regular education classroom, the special education teacher is the consultant teacher or the special education teacher overseeing specially designed instruction in the regular classroom (as well as the regular education teacher as noted above). If the primary impairment is a speech or language disability, the special education teacher is the speech specialist.

School representative. The representative of the local educational agency is someone who is both qualified and knowledgeable about special education, the general curriculum, and the availability of school and district resources. This could be a school administrator, the director of special education, or a special education teacher. A school administrator who is not able to supervise or provide special education could be an IEP member, but a representative of the school district must still be present who is qualified to supervise and provide special education, and who is knowledgeable about the general curriculum and school resources.

Evaluation specialist. The evaluation specialist is someone who can interpret the meaning and implications of evaluation results. This person could be a teacher, the LEA (Local Educational Agency) representative, school psychologist, or someone with specialized knowledge regarding assessment. For IDEA-1990 regulations many states included one or more members of the multidisciplinary team on the IEP team. For example, in New Jersey one or more Child Study Team members are IEP participants.[99]

Other Individuals. Other individuals who have knowledge or special expertise, at the discretion of the parent or school district, should attend team meetings when a particular service or aid is contemplated. Examples of specialists on the IEP team might include a person who has expertise in behavioral problems, ESL (English as a Second Language) specialist, reading teacher, social work, physical therapist, speech pathologist, school guidance counselor, or school nurse. The Senate Report encourages "to the greatest extent practicable and when appropriate, the participation of a licensed registered school nurse on the IEP team to help define and make decisions about how to safely address a child's educationally-related health needs."[100]

The regulations for IDEA-1997 has added "knowledge or special expertise" as a requirement for the IEP membership. If an aide has major responsibility for the implementation of a child's IEP, the aide might attend the IEP meeting to understand the overall scope and direction of the child's IEP. If the school district uses the *other* category to assign an administrator to the IEP team, this individual must have "knowledge or special expertise regarding the child." If the school district or the parent does invite a person under the *other* category, the determination of the invitee's knowledge or special expertise is made by the party who invited the individual.[101]

Child. If appropriate, the child with the

disability should attend the IEP meeting. The participation of the child at the IEP meeting often depends on the age of the child and the ability of the child to understand and contribute to IEP team proceedings. Rather than having the child attend the entire meeting, the IEP team might meet with the child for a brief period of time. In order to humanize the process and to provide the team with a clear picture of the child in question, a brief videotape might be useful to better understand the child and the child's educational setting.

The participation of older students at IEP meetings is important and the student must be invited to attend the meeting if transition services are being considered. If the student does not attend, the school district must "take other steps to ensure that the student's preferences and interests are considered."[102] Participation of the student in the development of transition services is consistent with a client-centered vocational philosophy in which the student must have a meaningful say in his or her vocational goals. This is in contrast to the traditional patient-centered approach used in the development of IEPs in which needs are determined and services provided on behalf of the child.

In all cases, the public agency must inform the parents who will be at the IEP meeting.[103]

For private schools, a representative of the private school should attend the IEP meeting or other methods should be used to ensure IEP meeting participation (e.g., conference telephone calls).[104] When the task of the IEP meeting is to develop transition services "representatives from all agencies which might be responsible for paying or providing services should be included in the development of the IEP."

Private School IEP Participation

If a child is placed in a private school or facility "any meetings to review and revise the child's IEP may be initiated and conducted by the private school or facility at the discretion of the public agency."[105] If the private school or facility conducts these meetings, the agency must ensure that the parents and a school representative attend the meetings, participate in making decisions, and agree to proposed IEP changes. Of particular importance is that the private school can review and revise the child's IEP but not create a second IEP. For instance, the IEP developed by the responsible school district is used to show compliance and a second IEP or goal plan is written to describe the educational plan of the private school. If a school develops an IEP that contains generic and meaningless goals, the private school or facility should not develop a second goal plan, but review and revise the existing IEP goals, at the discretion of the public agency, at a meeting attended by the parents and a representative of the public school. Although the private school can review and revise the IEP at the discretion of the public school agency, compliance with the law and regulations remains with the public school.[106]

SLD Team Members

If a child is suspected of having a specific learning disability, the IEP team must include the child's regular classroom teacher or a regular classroom teacher qualified to teach the child, and at least one person qualified to conduct an individual diagnostic examination of the child.

Regular education teacher. The 1997 regulations require that every IEP team include at least one regular education teacher if the child is, or may be, in a regular classroom setting. The SLD team must include the child's regular education teacher or a qualified regular education teacher if the child is not in a regular classroom who is best suited "to participate in the development, review, and revision of the child's IEP." If a child is not in an educational environment, then the regular classroom teacher could be someone who could teach the child.

Diagnostic specialist. The IEP team requires "an individual who can interpret the instructional implications of evaluation results," and the SLD team requires a diagnostic specialist "such as a school psychologist, speech-language pathologist, or remedial reading teacher" capable of conducting individual evaluations.[107] The diagnostic specialist should be someone who is able to interpret evaluation results and has expertise regarding the disability in question. For example, a speech-language pathologist might be less appropriate as a team member than a reading specialist or special education teacher if the suspected disability involves educational performance.

IEP Leadership and Decision Making

The IEP team will invariably have a coordinator or chairperson. Although this can be an administrator, teacher, school psychologist, or parent, the chairperson should be someone who is knowledgeable about evaluations, special education, and related services. In some states the chairperson of the IEP team is mandated by regulation. In Pennsylvania the chairperson of the IEP team is a representative of the district, other than the child's teacher. In Rhode Island the chairperson of the IEP team is the special education director (the agency representative) or his or her designee. As is the case for the Federal regulation governing the IEP team participation of a representative of the public agency,[108] this person "must be someone who is qualified to provide or supervise the provision of specially designed instruction to meet the unique needs of children with disabilities" (e.g., a special education teacher). In Rhode Island, school psychologists, social workers, occupational therapists, or physical therapists would not be qualified to serve as an IEP team chairperson since they provide related rather than special education services.[109]

An essential skill of the IEP team chairperson is the ability to collaborate with a variety of professionals, be responsible for arranging meetings and be familiar with the various procedural requirements such as conducting an IEP meeting without parents, dealing with IEP team disagreements, and providing IEP documentation. In addition to an IEP team coordinator or chairperson, an excellent practice is to assign each child a case manager. This could be the special education teacher or specialist who is primarily responsible for providing the specially designed instruction.

IEP team decisions. The only guidance

concerning IEP team decisions is that the IEP team should "work toward consensus" and that a majority vote is not "appropriate." There are, however, many avenues for reaching consensus. Overall, the decision-making process used by an IEP team is often a function of state guidelines, the general cohesiveness of the IEP team, and the general good intentions of the team members to develop appropriate IEPs.

Consensus is "an opinion held by most or all" or "general agreement." The Nebraska Department of Education defines consensus involving IEPs as an "agreement in which each side makes compromises." The steps for achieving IEP consensus include identifying areas of disagreement, listening, brainstorming, consideration, and discussion.[110] In Texas the IEP committee must develop the IEP by agreement of committee members, and a "majority vote may not be used to determine the individualized education program."[111] If the IEP is not developed by agreement, the IEP must include the basis for the disagreement. After the completion of the evaluation, the team of qualified professionals and the parents determine whether the child has a disability. In Wisconsin the director or his or her designee can approve a unanimous M-team report, a majority report, or even a minority report if the director or designee discusses the reason for doing so with the M-team.[112]

The IDEA-1997 regulations encourage consensus and resolving disputes informally and that the "IEP team should work toward consensus, but the public agency has ultimate responsibility to ensure that the IEP includes the services that the child needs in order to receive FAPE. It is not appropriate to make IEP decisions based upon a majority vote."[113] If consensus is not reached, the prior written notice must be given to parents concerning the action proposed by the school district.

The procedural safeguards provided in IDEA-1997 can suggest an adversarial relationship between schools and parents. Serious disagreements can be resolved by mediation, an impartial due process hearing, state administrative appeal, or civil action. The only provision concerning disagreement among IEP team members, other than school/parent disagreements, involves specific learning disabilities[114] in which "each team member shall certify in writing whether the report reflects his or her conclusion. If it does not reflect his or her conclusion, the team member must submit a separate statement presenting his or her conclusions."

There is no statutory or regulatory mandate as to how the IEP team reaches an agreed-upon plan, but if consensus cannot be reached, a vote could be taken to resolve the issues. Even if a majority vote is permissible under state law, voting is extremely problematic. If decisions are made by a majority vote, the parents might want their child to attend for this reason alone; or the addition of "other" professionals might skew the interpretation of a majority ballot. An IEP vote might be efficient but the net effect might be to detract from planning and an overall collaborative effort. Also, if a single team member were to veto all or part of a plan, this could interfere with school district's primary responsibility of providing a free and appropriate public education to children with disabilities.

Consensus should be the goal of the IEP team, and when this is not possible, when an issue is perceived by one or more team members as requiring resolution, there are built-in safeguards to accompany the IEP process for dealing with this possibility. In *Burlington v. Massachusetts Department of Education* the Supreme Court acknowledged the limitation of reaching IEP team consensus on all issues, but indicated that the solution was through available procedural safeguards: "Apparently recognizing that this cooperative approach would not always produce a consensus between the school officials and the parents, and that in any disputes the school officials would have a natural advantage, Congress incorporated an elaborate set of what it labeled 'procedural safeguards' to insure the full participation of the parents and proper resolution of substantive disagreements."[115]

If the school district and parents fail to agree, what is agreed upon can be implemented while those items in disagreement are resolved. If an interim IEP is agreed upon by all, this can be used until a complete IEP is finalized. If this decision cannot be resolved, mediation, due process hearing, State complaint or civil action can be used to resolve the disagreement.

Even if the IEP team does reach a consensus, and the parents agree with the IEP document, the parents need not consent or sign the IEP at the meeting but should take whatever amount of time is necessary to ensure that the goals and services proposed in the IEP are clearly understood. An IEP is often a complex and detailed document and parents should be given an opportunity to reflect on the provisions of the individualized program and to seek clarification if necessary.

•

The IEP process begins with a referral for an individual evaluation to determine the need for special education services. Following the referral, the parents are notified of the proposed evaluation and given a list of procedural safeguards. If the parents consent, an individual evaluation is conducted to determine whether the child has a disability and needs special education. If the child is determined to have a disability and needs special education, the IEP team documents present levels of performance, develops measurable annual goals and short-term objectives or benchmarks, and identifies services to best meet individual needs. The parents and classroom teacher play an invaluable role in the determination of the disability, the need for special education, and the development of the IEP. The goal of the entire IEP team is to reach a consensus as to what individualized program best meets a child's individual learning needs and thereby provide a free appropriate public education or FAPE.

NOTES

[1] Senate Report 105-17, p. 21.

[2] *Ibid.*, p. 20.

[3] 34 CFR 300.343(b).

[4] In a letter to Richard Riley, Department of Education (January 20, 1988) from Bill Goodling, Chairman, House Education and Workforce Committee, the importance of state timelines was emphatically stated in a request to remove a proposed regulation concerning the development of IEPs: "We object to the note following section 300.343 which requires that IEPs be developed within 60 days of receipt parental consent to an evaluation. Specifying that IEPs be developed in 60 days is not a reflection of the statute. In developing P.L 105-17 Congress was selective and specific when drafting provisions related to timelines. We chose not to set a timetable as specified in the note following section 300.343. Most States have set reasonable, child-friendly timetables pertaining to the initial receipt of IEP services. Federal guidance on this matter is not

necessary."

[5] Chapter 7, Wyoming State Board of Education Rules and Regulations for Serving Children with Disabilities, Section 13.

[6] *Ibid.*, Section 14(a)(iv).

[7] Massachusetts Department of Education, Question and Answer Guide on the New Special Education Individualized Educational Plan (IEP) and Related Chapter 766 regulations, January 1966.

[8] Guidelines for Individual Evaluation of California Students with Disabilities, Birth Through Age Twenty-One, October, 1998.

[9] New York State Education Department, Regulations of the Commissioner of Education, Part 200.4(d), January, 1998.

[10] 34 CFR 300.343(c).

[11] 34 CFR 300.536 and 34 CFR 300.534.

[12] Senate Report 105-17, p. 19.

[13] 20 USC 1414(d)(2)(A).

[14] 20 1414(d)(1)(A) and 34 CFR 300.347(a)&(b).

[15] 34 CFR 300.342(d). When IEPs must be in effect.

[16] 34 CFR 104.3(j)(1).

[17] 20 USC 1414(d).

[18] 34 CFR 300, Appendix A, Question #14.

[19] The *stay put* policy is based on the *Honig v. Doe* decision which states that school administrators are not powerless "to deal with dangerous students; it did, however, deny school officials their former right to 'self-help,' and directed that in the future the removal of disabled students could be accomplished only with the permission of the parents or, as a last resort, the courts" (98 L. Ed. 2d 686).

[20] 20 USC 1432(5).

[21] 20 USC 1436(a)(3).

[22] 20 USC 1419.

[23] 20 USC 1414(d)(2)(B).

[24] 20 USC 1401(11).

[25] 34 CFR 300.349. Private school placements by public agencies.

[26] See New York State Education Department, Regulations of the Commissioner of Education, Part 200, 200.4(a)(1)(vi), January, 1998.

[27] 20 USC 1412(a)(3)(A).

[28] *Ibid.*

[29] 20 USC 1400(c)(5)(F).

[30] New Jersey Permanent Statutes, 18A:46-3.

[31] *Ibid.*, 18A:46-3 and 18A:46-5.

[32] New Jersey Department of Education IEP form, 1999.

[33] ARM 10.16.114.

[34] ARM 10.16.2713.

[35] See 8VAC20-80-50.

[36] 976 F.2d 487.

[37] 20 USC 1414(b)(4)(A).

[38] 20 USC 1414(d)(3)(A).

[39] 34 CFR 300.346(a)(2)(iv). In addition to children who are deaf and hard of hearing, the IEP team must consider the communication needs of all children.

[40] 34 CFR 300.309.

[41] 20 USC 1414(d)(4)(A)(i).

[42] 34 CFR 300.536(b).

[43] 34 CFR 300.520(c).

[44] 34 CFR 300.524(a).

[45] The Final Regulations (*Federal Register*, Vol. 64, No. 48, Friday, March 12, 1999, pp. 12413–12416) contains a section clarifying regulations entitled "Discipline for Children with Disabilities."

[46] 34 CFR 300.121(d)(2).

[47] Chapter 7, Wyoming State Board of Education Rules and Regulations for Serving Children with Disabilities, Section 13. Referral for Multidisciplinary Evaluation.

[48] 707 KAR 1:190. Evaluation.

[49] 34 CFR 300.503.

[50] 34 CFR 300.504.

[51] 34 CFR 300.505.

[52] 34 CFR 300.505(c) and 34 CFR 300,345(d) Conducting an IEP meeting without a parent in attendance.

[53] As per 34 CFR 300.505(c) informed consent is not required if parents fail to respond to reasonable requests for a re-evaluation.

[54] Although a copy of procedural notice rights is not required, parents must be informed that they have these rights and where a copy can be obtained (see 34 CFR 300.503(b)(6)).

[55] *Ibid.*

[56] 20 USC 1415(k)(4)(A)(i).

[57] 34 CFR 300.300 Provision of FAPE.

[58] Section 615(c). Content of Prior Written Notice.

[59] 34 CFR 300.503(b)(1).

[60] 34 CFR 300.503(b)(6).

[61] 34 CFR 300.504(a).

[62] Bureau of Special Education Consultline (800-879-2301).

[63] 20 USC 1415(d).

[64] 34 CFR 300.507.

[65] 20 USC 1415(k)(4)(A)(i) and 34 CFR 300.523(a)(1).

[66] 20 USC 1415(d)(2).

[67] Senate Report 105-17, p. 25.

[68] 20 USC 1415(e). Mediation.

[69] *Ibid.*

[70] 20 USC 1415(e)(2)(A).

[71] Senate Report 105-17, p. 26.

[72] 20 USC 1413(c)(3).

[73] 34 CFR 300.504.

[74] 34 CFR 300.505(a)(3).

[75] 34 CFR 300.505(a)(3). Parental consent.

[76] Section 615 Procedural Safeguards, Section 15(e) Mediation and Section 615(f) Impartial Due Process Hearing.

[77] 34 CFR 300.505(b).

[78] New York State, The State Education Department, Updated Regulations of the Commissioner of Education, Part 200, Students with Disabilities, 200.5(b)(2).

[79] 34 CFR 300.534(b)(2).

[80] 34 CFR 300.300.

[81] 34 CFR 300.505(c).

[82] *Ibid.*

[83] Proposed Regulations for IDEA-1997, *Federal Register*, October 22, 1997, Vol. 62, Number 204, p. 55105, 34 CFR 300.533. Determination of needed evaluation data, Note.

[84] *Ibid.*

[85] 34 CFR 300, Appendix A, Question #19.

[86] *Ibid.*

[87] Ohio Administrative Code 3301-35-032.

[88] Wisconsin PDI, Model Special Education Policy Document, 1995, (IV).

[89] California Code 56342.

[90] 511 IAC 7-3-7.

[91] KAC 707.170-210.

[92] 8 VAC 20-80-50.

[93] 34 CFR 300.534(a)(2).

[94] 34 CFR 300.543(b).

[95] 34 CFR 300.16.

[96] 34 CFR 300.344(a)(2).

[97] IDEA-1990, Appendix C, Question #16.

[98] From Bill Frist (Chairman), House of Representatives, Subcommittee on Public Health and Safety, January 20, 1998, Richard Riley, United States Department of Education.

[99] New Jersey Department of Education, IEP form, 1999.

[100] Senate Report 105-17, p. 23.

[101] 34 CFR 300.344(c).

[102] 34 CFR 300.344(b).

[103] 34 CFR Appendix A, Question #7.

[104] 34 CFR 300.349(a)(2).

[105] 34 CFR 300.349(b).

[106] 34 CFR 300.349(c).

[107] 34 C.F.R. 300.540. Additional team members.

[108] 34 CFR 300.344(a)(4).

[109] Rhode Island Regulations of the Board of Regents Governing the Special Education of Children with Disabilities.

[110] Nebraska Department of Education, Steps to Building Consensus, Nebraska IEP Technical Assistance Guide, September, 1998, Lincoln, Nebraska.

[111] Texas Education Code, 29.005(c).

[112] Wisconsin DPI, 1995, Model Special Education policy document.

[113] 34 CFR 300, Appendix A, Question #9.

[114] 34 C.F.R. 300.543(b).

[115] 471 U.S. 359 (1985).

Chapter 4

DETERMINING NEEDS

THE IDEA-1997 MANDATE is to ensure that all children with disabilities have a free appropriate public education as defined in an IEP.[1] As cited in PL 105-17, these unique needs can take many forms including academic,[2] special education,[3] learning,[4] educational,[5] transition service,[6] language,[7] communication,[8] future[9] and anticipated needs.[10] Added to this list are a variety of disability needs (e.g., Braille instruction), related services (e.g., family counseling), supplementary aids and services (e.g., preferential seating in class), Section 504, instructional and curriculum-based needs.

Transition service needs are especially important in IDEA-1997 and are "designed within an outcomeoriented process, which promotes movement from school to postschool activities, including postsecondary education, vocational training, integrated employment (including supported employment), continuing and adult education, adult services, independent living, or community participation."[11] Transition needs represent the ultimate goal of special education: employment, independent living and community participation.

Instructional and Supportive Needs

A need is "a lack of something useful, required, or desired." Mehrens and Lehmann (1973) defined a need as "the discrepancy between an objective and the present level of performance" (p.18). In the context of an IEP, this definition of need can be restated as the discrepancy between present levels of educational performance and a measurable annual goal. The purpose of short-term objectives or benchmarks is to bridge the discrepancy between a present level of performance and the desired goal.

Figure II illustrates the relationship between a strength, a need, and a measurable annual goal. A strength indicates what a child can do or what has been achieved. The level of that strength is the present level of performance or the point beyond which performance is affected. The need is a weakness; deficiency; or lack of a required skill, behavior, or ability. An instructional need indicates that not only is an ability or skill lacking, but specially designed instruction can improve or increase the level of performance. In the IEP an instructional need is met by a measurable annual goal, and progress toward the goal is monitored by short-term objectives or benchmarks.

A child might also have noninstructional needs that require a service, aid, accommo-

Figure II. Strength/Need/Goal Relationship

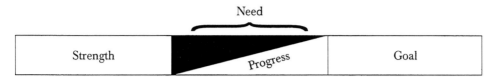

dation, or adaptation, but a goal is not required for these needs. These aids, services, and modifications can be referred to as supportive needs and include language translation, technological devices, magnification and amplification aids, transportation assistance, test accommodations, and adaptations to the physical environment (e.g., special equipment, enhanced lighting).

Providing the service, aid, or accommodation fulfills the supportive need without a measurable annual goal. For instance, a child might require physical assistance to access reading material in the regular classroom, but not a goal to improve reading. Noninstructional needs can range from a very simple classroom service (e.g., enhanced lighting) to extensive technological or physical accommodations. In *Cedar Rapids v. Garret* the Supreme Court required the school district to provide a nurse for a child who was wheelchair-bound and ventilator dependent during the school day,[12] but not a goal for the service.

For supportive service needs, providing the service is sufficient to impact performance without a progression of instructional steps. However, instructional and supportive needs are not mutually exclusive and often the IEP will contain both. A child might need an aide to provide physical assistance and a goal to improve reading; or a child might need a motorized wheelchair, and also instruction in using the chair. The IEP team

must be careful not to unintentionally ignore instructional needs because a supportive need has been provided. A child might need curriculum material and tests transcribed into Braille which is a supportive service, but also need instruction in using Braille. For a child receiving a test accommodation, more time might be given to complete tests or to take tests orally, but a goal might also be necessary to develop the ability to take tests orally. For an older student, work-related information or an opportunity to visit a junior college setting might be needed as part of the transition plan, but goals might be necessary to develop job interviewing or specific work-related skills.

For instructional needs, the extent of the need is based on the discrepancy between the present and desired level of performance. An instructional need cannot be defined if either of these benchmarks is lacking. If information is not available to indicate current level of performance, at what level to begin instruction or the desired level of performance (the goal) is not known. The purpose of specially designed instruction is to improve performance from a present to a desired level of performance. If the current level of performance has not been determined, there is no logical basis for evaluating the extent of the need, where to begin instruction, or the anticipated level of progress.

Disability Needs

Meyen and Skratic (1995) noted that "*disability* refers to a condition such as loss of a limb, whereas *handicap* describes the consequences of the disability. People are handicapped because of their disability" (p. 41). Public Law 101-476 (IDEA-1990) replaced *handicap* with *disability* but the distinction between disability and the consequences of the disability is nonetheless important. A child might have a disability, but require no services, accommodations, or specially designed instruction. In other words, the existence of a disability is not tantamount to a need. One child with a hearing impairment might only require an amplification device, while another child with a loss of the same magnitude might require speech services and specially designed instruction. For children with other health impairments (e.g., cancer, AIDS, asthma), the consequences of the disability might require no services other than a wait-and-see attitude, extensive curriculum modifications, or at-home instruction.

Educational Needs

For specific learning disabilities, the educational manifestation of the disability is necessary for the determination of the impairment. Before a child is identified as having a specific learning disability, the disorder must involve the ability to listen, think, speak, read, write, spell, or to do mathematical calculations.[13] A child cannot have a specific learning disability if there is not an educational manifestation of the disorder. If a child's specific learning disability involves basic reading, basic reading is therefore the disability and educational need. For specific learning disabilities the educational need defines the disability so that a child must have a need in one or more of the following areas: oral expression, listening comprehension, written expression, basic reading skill, reading comprehension, mathematical calculation, or mathematics reasoning.

For a child with a specific learning disability in basic reading, the disability and the educational need both involve basic reading. For autism, the characteristics associated with the disability (e.g., social and language needs) can impact educational performance. For a hearing impairment, the disability involves hearing acuity and the educational impact often centers about language (which can affect reading and written expression). For emotional disturbance the disability might involve inappropriate behavior that seriously affects participation in the regular classroom as manifested by classroom behavior and poor grades or classroom work. Needs that result either directly or indirectly from the disability must be addressed in the IEP "in order for the child to progress in the general education curriculum, such as the need of a blind child to read Braille, or of a cognitively disabled child to receive transportation training (i.e., how to use public transportation).[14]

For all disabilities, educational performance must be affected so that a child needs specially designed instruction. For a child to have an emotional disturbance under IDEA, the condition (e.g., maintaining interpersonal relationships) must affect educational performance. This criterion is the same for mental retardation[15] and autism,[16] both of which must *adversely* affect educational performance in order to be a disability under IDEA.

The IEP must not only address primary disability and educational needs, but meet needs that result from the child's disability to enable the child to be involved in and progress in the general curriculum.[17] For a child with a specific learning disability in basic reading, written expression might be impacted, or ability involving mathematical word problems. Or the disability in reading might affect classroom behavior which then must be addressed in the child's IEP.

Special IEP Needs

When developing an IEP, the IEP team is required to consider the strengths of the child and concerns of the parents, the results of the most recent evaluation, and state and districtwide assessments if appropriate.[18] The IEP team must also consider several special factors when developing an IEP because of the importance and/or neglect of these needs in the past. These special areas include (1) behavior, (2) limited English proficiency, (3) the Braille needs of visually impaired children, (4) the communication needs of deaf and hard of hearing children, and (5) the assistive technology needs of children.[19]

Behavior needs. If a child is classified as emotionally disturbed, the primary task is not necessarily to provide a more restrictive environment (although this might be necessary), but to consider strategies, positive behavioral interventions, and supports to address the behavior in the regular classroom if possible. All too often when classroom behavior is the primary concern, the focus of attention is where the behavior can be contained (viz., a special education class) rather than developing a plan to modify the behavior. When the disability centers about behavior in the regular classroom, the ultimate goal is to change the behavior in the regular classroom so that the child can participate in the regular education curriculum.

Input from the regular classroom teacher is critical for determining what behavioral interventions, modifications, supports, or other supplementary aids and services are necessary to promote regular classroom participation. One reason for having the child's regular classroom teacher on the IEP team, rather than a teacher representative, is to address specific behaviors and other needs that can be provided in the regular education class to enable the child to be educated with nondisabled children to the maximum extent appropriate.[20]

Limited English proficiency (LEP) special education needs. The IEP team must consider the language needs of a LEP child as those needs relate to the development of each IEP component.[21] If a LEP child is evaluated to determine the need for special education, the disability must be evaluated and not just the child's language skills. Observational data, existing records and data, and parent input are critical for determining a disability and differentiating the disability from limited English proficiency. For disabilities such as hearing impairments, mental retardation, multiple disabilities, orthopedic impairments, traumatic brain injury, and certain other health impairments (e.g., epilepsy, heart condition), lack of English proficiency is certainly a confounding variable but often one which can be circumvented by available evaluation techniques and existing data and reports. For all disabilities an evaluation of the child's disability and strengths in both the child's native language and English is important. For disabilities such as specific learning disabilities, emotional disturbance, and speech and language impairments, language is often the very essence of the disability and an evaluation of the child in his or her native language is critical. If an evaluation reveals that a behavioral problem occurs only in relation to the child's LEP, the behavior might be reflective of the child's LEP and not a disability. If a child does not have a disability in his or her native language, the child should be given an opportunity to demonstrate educational proficiency in English commensurate with other children with LEP.

School districts are required to provide LEP children with alternatives to meet bilingual, LEP, and English as a second language (ESL) needs.[22] If the school district does not have a sufficient number of children to develop a bilingual program, an ESL specialist, special language program, voluntary language program, transitional language program, native language proficient aide, or tutorial program might be an appropriate solution. However, if the child does not have a disability, special education should not be used to supplant the obligation of the public school to develop an appropriate program or provide necessary services.

Braille needs. For children who are blind or visually impaired, a determination must be made whether or not the child needs instruction in Braille. Not having personnel with expertise in Braille is not a reason for not providing Braille instruction. As noted by Barraga and Erin (1992) regarding reading

for students with low vision, "decisions must be made on an individual basis according to the physical and mental characteristics of each student, the age and grade level, and the stability or instability of the eye condition" (p. 85). Thus, a student might be able to develop literacy skills using Braille, large print, magnification, inkprint, or some combination thereof.

Communication needs. One of the most difficult areas of need to address are the communication needs of children who are deaf and hard of hearing. The IEP team must consider the child's language needs, opportunities for direct communication with peers, and opportunities for direct instruction in the child's language and communication mode.

Assistive technology needs. Assistive technology needs, involving both devices and services, must be considered. Because certain technological innovations or devices might require special expertise or are quite costly, the IEP team might not be aware of appropriate technological devices.[23] For all children who might have assistive communication needs, the IEP team should include or invite personnel with expertise in assistive technology to attend team meetings. A child might have cerebral palsy and require a single-switch device, but providing the technology without expertise in the use of the device might be ineffective and deprive the child of a necessary and important service.

Nonacademic Needs

The IEP team must address all of the child's nonacademic needs which can include transportation, recess periods, meals, clubs, recreational activities, athletics, intramural sports, and special interest groups. The need for physical education warrants special concern by the IEP team because

this is an area where children with disabilities are often excluded from participation. Not only must children with disabilities be given an opportunity to participate in regular physical education, but the IEP team must designate goals and special physical education if appropriate.[24]

Related-Service Needs

The distinction between instructional and supportive services, where the former indicates the development of an ability or skill and the latter an accommodation or aid, also applies to related services. As with disability and educational needs, a related service need might be dealt with by a goal or a service/aid. If a child requires speech pathology to profit from special education by improving language skills, there would be one or more measurable goals for this related service. If the related service need is a full- or part-time aide, equipment, or a transportation service, a goal would not be needed if there is no planned progression for improvement. If, in addition to providing transportation, there is a need to improve a transportation skill (e.g., getting on and off the bus), a measurable annual goal might be necessary to develop this ability.

In a policy letter from the Office of Special Education and Rehabilitative Services[25] the need for goals for supportive services was clarified so that if a supportive service "is not intended to increase the student's skills, no goals or objectives are necessary." For example, seating location, air conditioning, a dehumidifier, providing large print or Braille text, or using a reader, notetaker or interpreter, would not require measurable annual goals and objectives if the purpose is not to improve performance.

Accommodation Needs

The individual evaluation must include test accommodations when appropriate, and a determination of what accommodations are necessary to ensure that a child's ability rather than disability is assessed. The test accommodations described in the IEP are for activities and assessments used on a daily basis and for instructional purposes, or for "any individual modifications in the administration of State or districtwide assessments of student achievement that are needed in order for the child to participate in such assessment" or how the child will be assessed if participation in State or districtwide assessment is not possible.[26]

Often the determination of test accommodations is made at the IEP meeting without due consideration to actual needs, teacher or parent input, or factors that might result in the child's disability rather than ability being measured. Extended time might be appropriate for a child with a reading disorder or using a Braille format, but for a child with an attention deficit modularized testing (e.g., twenty-minute sessions) or individualized testing might be more effective accommodation.

Excluded Needs

Not all needs that a child has are addressed by an IEP. If a child has a disability, but does not need specially designed instruction, the school district must provide appropriate services under Section 504 and not IDEA. For all disabilities, and especially for specific learning disabilities, a child cannot be determined to have a disability because of lack of instruction in reading and math or limited English proficiency.[27] In cases involving lack of instruction, the remedy is to provide appropriate instruction but not specially defined instruction under IDEA. To determine that a child is disabled when the child has not been given a fair opportunity to succeed is discriminatory if the determination results in the child being excluded from participation in or is denied the benefits of the regular education program.

The needs of children with limited English proficiency exemplify the problem of differentiating between educational need resulting from lack of instruction and need resulting from a disability. For children with limited English proficiency who do not have disabilities, the appropriate educational program is defined within the context of regular and not special education. If a child has limited English proficiency and a disability is determined, the child might need specially designed instruction in English, instruction in the child's native language, and regular education services involving English acquisition available to all non-English speaking children.

In addition to educational needs that are the result of lack of instruction, several IDEA disability categories have specific requirements that can exclude certain types of needs. The term *emotional disturbance* excludes children who are socially maladjusted (unless they are determined to be emotionally disturbed). Specific learning disabilities excludes children who have learning discrepancies that are the result of sensory or motor impairments, mental retardation, emotional disturbance, or environmental, cultural, or economic disadvantage. Traumatic brain injury does not apply to congenital, degenerative, or birth trauma-induced injuries. Autism does not apply if educational performance is affected by emotional disturbance.

Strengths and Weaknesses

The IEP team is required to consider the strengths of the child in the development of the IEP[28] but the law and regulations say very little about strengths and virtually nothing about weaknesses. The only reference to strengths in IDEA-1997 and the regulations is the requirement that when developing an IEP the team consider "the strengths of the child and the concerns of the parents for enhancing the education of their child."[29]

When determining a child's needs, the essential task is to determine what specifically the child can (strength) and cannot (weakness) do. A national survey by Pyecha and others (1980) to evaluate the early effectiveness indicated that IEPs were more likely to emphasize weaknesses and that "the listing of both strengths and weaknesses is helpful both to those who review the IEPs and to those who carry out the student's program. By taking both strengths and weaknesses into account, goals and objectives can be focused more specifically on areas of need. Also, information about strengths can be used by teachers to determine strategies by which to work with the student" (p. 6.6).

Need correspondence. Identifying strengths is important insofar as the strength can help understand and address a need or weakness. Reading ten or fifty words might be a strength (ability achieved), and not reading forty of fifty (ability not achieved) words a weakness; receiving a score of 55 percent indicates a certain knowledge level, while not answering 45 percent signifies a potential deficit; or reading vocabulary is a strength and reading comprehension is a weakness. Levels of performance often imply both a strength and a weakness. If the stated strength is subtraction, an assumption might be made that the area of need is multiplication; or if auditory expression is a strength, auditory reception is not a weakness. There are exceptions to this linear interpretation of abilities (e.g., comprehension exceeds vocabulary), but not considering the correspondence between strengths and weaknesses can misdirect the determination of an appropriate beginning level of performance and instruction. Examples of this would be identifying a weakness in writing when basic reading is the problem, focusing remediation on regrouping or fractions when basic addition is the area of need, or attempting to reduce a behavior by a restrictive placement rather than actually identifying and reducing the occurrence of the behavior.

Instructional strategies. The concept of strength and weakness can be used to indicate areas of need, possible instructional strategies, or areas of interest or ability that can be used to promote success. If a child's rate of work is extremely slow (weakness), but the child is motivated (strength), activities might be designed that focus on completion and not timed performance. If a child is an excellent listener but poor reader, listening strengths can be used to convey important instructional information. An IEP will often include a checklist to indicate a child's learning style

Auditory Learner_____   Visual Learner_____
Tactual Learner _____   Kinesthetic Learner____

For the above scale, a child could be both an auditory learner and tactual learner or all the areas might be checked. If a child has a strong interest in sports, or the environment, or collecting stamps, these areas of interest could provide high-interest content for school-related activities such as reading. Instead of a checklist, a rating scale could be used to indicate needs in a variety of areas:

Rate each area in terms of the extent of individual needs:					
Area	Strength	Some Need	Moderate Need	High Need	Extensive Need
Reading					
Mathematics					
Written Expression					
Study Skills					
Speech and Language					
Self-Help Skills					
Socialization					
Classroom Management					
Other					

The above format can provide a useful summary of quantitative and qualitative data, and a simple means to visualize areas of need. The disadvantage of a rating scale is that ratings often lack specificity and can be highly subjective.

Incomplete Need Assessment

Knowing just a strength or weakness is not sufficient to determine an instructional need. Knowing only a strength requires a presumption that whatever is provided instructionally is a weakness. If a child can identify addition facts, and the goal is to identify subtraction facts, the appropriateness of this goal depends on the child's actual subtraction fact ability.

Knowing the level of strength but not the level of weakness prevents the determination educational need. On a similar basis, knowing just a weakness does not signify what a child can do or where instruction should begin. If a child is not able to identify division facts (e.g., $24 \div 8$, $10 \div 2$), the meaning of this weakness can only be interpreted if the child's other computational strengths are evaluated. If the child is unable to identify addition facts as well as division facts, the inability regarding division facts is obviously of less concern than the inability to identify addition facts. Likewise, stating that the child has a weakness in the area of writing is meaningless unless the child's ability to read is known. If the child is an average reader, the weakness in writing might indicate a writing disability; if the child is an extremely poor reader, the weakness in writing might reflect a more basic reading problem.

A statement of strengths or weaknesses, or strengths and needs or strengths and weaknesses is routinely required in IEP development but the purpose of the statement is not always clear. The area of strength and weakness must be educationally important, and used to develop measurable annual goals to improve performance. No matter how technically correct a goal might be, or how effective the short-term objectives are for monitoring and reporting progress, the strength and weakness must represent a significant area that is affected by the disability.

General Strengths and Weaknesses

If strengths and weakness or strengths and needs are listed in the IEP, the relationship between specific strengths and weakness should be indicated rather than recorded as two separate components. The following IEP statement might accurately reflect a child's strengths and weaknesses but the relationship between strengths and weaknesses is not specified. If classroom behavior is a strength and following directions a weakness, the intervention can focus on this specific weakness rather than a general intervention approach involving all classroom behavior. Furthermore, if classroom behavior is a strength, and not following directions and not completing tasks areas of weakness, not following directions might be the reason that tasks are not completed.

IEP Strengths and Weaknesses
Strengths: working with others, science, reading vocabulary, phonics, social studies, classroom behavior, basic computation
Weaknesses: written expression, following directions, word problems, language arts, fractions, reading comprehension, completing tasks

The question is not just a child's strengths and weaknesses, but the logical relationship between the two; that is, how does understanding a particular strength and weakness help to understand a child's level of educational functioning. Providing a disjointed series of strengths and weaknesses does nothing to define need or to help conceptualize the relationship between need, goals and services.

The separate lists of strengths and weaknesses shown above could be rearranged to show the relationship between each strength and each weakness:

Strengths	Weaknesses
Working with others, classroom behavior	Following directions, completing tasks
Science, social studies	Language arts
Basic computation	Word problems, fractions
Phonics, reading vocabulary	Reading comprehension, written expression

For every weakness there should be a corresponding level of strength. For the above list of strengths and weaknesses, ability in reading vocabulary and weakness in reading comprehension offers a frame of reference for interpreting educational need. If reading comprehension is a strength, specially designed instruction might be devoted entirely to written expression. However, knowing that a problem exists in reading comprehension would help understand written expression.

Focusing on strengths and weaknesses will also direct attention to needed data. All too often a child's strengths are underestimated, and too much emphasis is placed on weaknesses. For a child with a severe developmental disability, knowing that the child can intentionally move his or her hand or make a sound when distressed indicate important strengths. The emphasis should not be on all the child is unable to do, but to build on and expand existing strengths, abilities, and skills and "to tailor the education to the child; not tailor the child to the education"[30] (p. 24). If a child is an auditory learner, this strength could be used to develop content area knowledge. Behaviorally, strengths and areas of interest could be used to promote areas of weaknesses (e.g., reading high-interest material to develop on-task behavior).

Point of Instruction

Of the many ways a child's strengths and weaknesses can be used to identify and adapt instruction and content, identifying the level of ability (strength) and the point at which the task or content becomes too difficult (weakness) is the most important.

The point of instruction is the point between what a child can and cannot do, the point between a strength and a weakness, or the first step beyond the present level of performance. For very linear tasks, the point of instruction can be fairly clear. If a child can recognize ten sight words, the point of instruction might be to learn an additional five words. If a child can add, but not regroup, the point of instruction might be to teach this specific computational skill.

The point of instruction does not necessarily indicate a specific skill but often suggests an attainable level of performance. If a child in the fourth grade comprehends 50 percent of grade-level material read, the point of instruction is not necessarily third grade or even second grade-level reading difficulty, but one in which the instructional strategy is to raise comprehension to 60 percent or 70 percent. Also, the point of instruction might be different for each area of need so that the point of instruction might be different for word attack skills, reading vocabulary, and reading in content areas. Regarding classroom behavior, a child might have excellent interpersonal skills for the most part, but under certain circumstances the child exhibits temper tantrums or violent classroom behavior. In this situation the strengths (excellent interpersonal skills) are known and the need (temper tantrums and violent classroom behavior) is readily apparent, but exactly when excellent interpersonal skills are transformed into undesirable classroom behavior might be difficult to ascertain even after a functional behavioral analysis.

Specifying a need involves determining the next step that should be undertaken to allow a child to progress along a defined continuum of instruction. If a child is able to function in a regular classroom without incident for fifteen minutes, the next level might be to function in the same setting for thirty minutes. If a student is able to comprehend 50 percent of a basal reader, the next level might be to increase reading comprehension to 75 percent. If a child has limited receptive vocabulary, the next step might be to develop auditory receptive language skills. If a child has auditory receptive language skills, but no reading readiness skills (e.g., shape discrimination), readiness activities might be appropriate.

STANDARDIZED TEST NEEDS

Determining strengths and weaknesses involve both standardized and curriculum-based assessments. As shown in Table V, raw scores, frequencies, curriculum-based assessments, Statewide competency tests and standardized test scores can be used to indicate the appropriate level of instruction.

If the data is specific, the strength can indicate the level of the needed specially designed instruction. If a child can write single words, a goal might be to write three-word sentences or even phrases; if the child can write three-word sentences, the next goal might be to write five-word sentences an so on. For a statewide competency test, if a student receives a score of 50, and a score of 65 is required to pass, instruction should focus on areas in which the student has difficulty. For both standardized and nonstandardized tests, knowing what a child can and cannot do is used to determine the beginning level of instruction and for projecting anticipated levels of performance.

Standardized tests are especially important in determining general areas of educational need and the impact of a child's disability on educational performance. Although a standardized assessment is often used to denote a deficiency, implicit in every standardized score is a statement of both strength and weakness. For an eight-year-old child with an IQ score 70 and mental age of

Table V. Example of Strength and Weakness Correspondence

Strength	Need
knows 30 spelling words	needs to know 50 additional spelling words
2.5 grade level in reading	should be at the 5.0 grade level in reading
attentive in physical education	not attentive in the classroom
can do column addition	cannot regroup
can read words	has difficulty comprehending sentences
can understand directions	cannot express ideas verbally
good auditory language skills	poor reading skills
average IQ	below average reading
has good reading skills	has difficulty writing
able to write a 10-sentence paragraph	makes 30 errors when writing 10 sentences
received a score of 50 on state test	needs to receive a score of 65 to pass
has a vocabulary of 20 words	needs to increase vocabulary to 50 words
is able to write complete sentences	cannot take organized notes

5.6, one could say that the mental age of 5.6 is significantly below (a weakness) the chronological age of 8.0, or that the child has achieved a score (a strength) similar to that achieved by children in the 5.6 mental age range.

Standardized Test Scores

Standardized scores are based on tests and evaluations that are administered according to specific instructions, interpreted according to prescribed rules, and result in scores that are compared to a norm or standardization group. Standardized scores are important in determining the impact of a disability on educational performance, and in determining general areas of educational performance.

The mean and standard deviation for a standardized test indicates the extent a child's score on a test deviates from the test mean or average score. For an IQ test with a mean of 100 and a standard deviation of 15, a score of 85 is exactly one standard deviation below the mean, and a score of 70 is exactly two standard deviations below the mean.

The essential information provided by a standardized test is not the score but rather how far the score deviates from the mean or average score. Most IQ tests use a mean of 100 and standard deviation of 15; many achievement tests use stanine scores that have a mean of 5 and a standard deviation of 2; and advancement placement tests often use a mean of 500 and a standard deviation of 100. The standard deviation is an index that describes the percent of individuals within a sample above or below the mean at different points. If a child is one standard deviation below the mean on a test, 16 percent of the children in the normative sample are below this point and 84 percent above this point. If a child is two standard deviations below the mean, 2 percent of the children in the normative sample are below this score and 98 percent are above.

z scores. A *z* score is the basic unit for

determining most standardized test scores. A *z* score indicates the number of standard deviations a score is below or above the mean and is based on the mean and standard deviation of a test:

$$z = \frac{Score - MEAN}{STANDARD\ DEVIATION} = \frac{(X - X)}{SD}$$

An understanding of the mean and standard deviation provides a method for comparing different standard scores. If a student has an IQ score of 85 and a corresponding stanine score of 3, a comparison of these scores shows that both are one standard deviation below the mean. There are other statistical factors that can be taken into consideration when comparing scores but the basic interpretation for a standard score of 85 on a test with a mean of 100 and a standard deviation of 15, and a score on a test with a mean of 5 and a standard deviation of 2, is that both scores are one standard deviation below the mean.

Different tests use different means and standard deviations for historical reasons. Normal curve equivalents have a mean of 100 and standard deviation of 21.06 and offer a percentile-rank type score but with a set standard deviation; and stanine scores provide a single digit for interpreting academic achievement (important in the era of computer cards but less so now); IQ scores have long been associated with a mean of 100 and a standard deviation of 15 or 16 range. Table VI lists the various types of standardized test scores, and the relationship between scores, that are used with most educational and psychological tests. As shown, a percentile rank of 16 is equivalent to an IQ score of 85, and a stanine of 3, percentile rank of 16 and IQ of 85 are all one standard deviation below the mean

Table VI. Standard Score Equivalents

Standard Score	SD	- 1 SD	Average	+1 SD
Percentile Ranks		16	50	84
IQ (e.g., Stanford-Binet)	16	84	100	116
IQ (e.g., WISC)	15	85	100	115
Placement Tests (e.g., SAT)	100	400	500	600
Normal Curve Equivalent	21.06	29	50	71
Used with Subtests	3	7	10	13
Stanine Scores	2	3	5	7
z scores	1	-1	0	1

Standardized Test Need

Showing how a disability affects educational performance is often accomplished by means of standardized tests (e.g., total reading scores, complete battery score) and subtest scores (e.g., word attack skills, reading vocabulary, reading comprehension). Standardized scores can also serve as a safeguard to ensure that specially designed instruction is not provided to a child who does not need special education. If a child's behavior does not adversely affect academic performance, the child might have a disability, and might need services, but not special education. For specific test areas, standardized test scores provide direction concerning specific instructional needs. A low standardized score on a sentence reading subtest might indicate a need to develop instructional activities to increase sentence reading skills. Or a standardized test of computational skill might suggest the need to determine specific computational strengths and weaknesses.

Table VII illustrates the use of standardized scores for three different students. The first score for each student is a standard score (SS) with a mean of 100 and a standard deviation of 15. The second score for each student is a percentile rank where the median percentile rank is 50. As shown, Student A has an average IQ score, reading is significantly below average (two standard deviations), and language is at the one standard deviation cutoff value. As shown here, one of the disadvantages of percentile ranks is that differences toward the median (a score of 50) are more pronounced than differences that depart from the median. As a result, before a general statement of educational performance is made based on percentile ranks, consult Table VIII to interpret percentile ranks as standard scores.

Table VII. Interpreting General Standardized Scores

Test	Student A		Student B		Student C	
	SS	PR	SS	PR	SS	PR
IQ	100	50	66	1	107	68
Reading	70	2	76	5	101	54
Mathematics	92	29	89	22	77	6
Language	85	15	83	12	93	32

For Student B in Table VII the IQ score is low and achievement scores are higher but in the low range. For Student C, mathematics seems to be the primary area of concern. In the regular classroom this child's teacher might have observed difficulties in mathematics but the standardized score signifies that the student is significantly below the normative group. Of course, an individualized program cannot be based solely on one general index of test performance. However, a standardized test score can verify that the disability does impact educational performance, and can provide direction for curriculum-based assessment.

Because percentile ranks are easily misinterpreted, Table VIII can be used to interpret the correspondence between percentile ranks, z scores and standard scores. For example, a percentile rank of 22 (see column PR in Table VIII) is equivalent to a z score of -.8 (.8 standard deviations below the mean) and an IQ-type score of 89.

Table VIII. Percentile Rank, z Scores and IQ Correspondence

Percentile Ranks (PR), z Scores and Standard Scores

PR	z	SS	PR	z	SS
99	2.3	134	1	-2.3	66
98	2.0	130	2	-2.0	70
97	1.9	128	3	-1.9	72
96	1.8	126	4	-1.8	74
95	1.6	124	5	-1.6	76
94	1.6	123	6	-1.6	77
93	1.5	122	7	-1.5	78
92	1.4	121	8	-1.4	79
91	1.3	120	9	-1.3	80
90	1.3	119	10	-1.3	81
89	1.2	118	11	-1.2	82
88	1.2	117	12	-1.2	83
87	1.1	116	13	-1.1	84
86	1.1	116	14	-1.1	84
85	1.0	115	15	-1.0	85
84	1.0	114	16	-1.0	86
83	1.0	114	17	-1.0	86
82	.9	113	18	-.9	87
81	.9	113	19	-.9	87
80	.8	112	20	-.8	88
79	.8	112	21	-.8	88
78	.8	111	22	-.8	89
77	.7	111	23	-.7	89
76	.7	110	24	-.7	90
75	.7	110	25	-.7	90
74	.6	109	26	-.6	91
73	.6	109	27	-.6	91
72	.6	108	28	-.6	92
71	.6	108	29	-.6	92
70	.5	107	30	-.5	93
69	.5	107	31	-.5	93
68	.5	107	32	-.5	93
67	.4	106	33	-.4	94
66	.4	106	34	-.4	94

PR	z	SS	PR	z	SS
65	.4	105	35	-.4	95
64	.4	105	36	-.4	95
63	.3	104	37	-.3	96
62	.3	104	38	-.3	96
61	.3	104	39	-.3	96
60	.3	103	40	-.3	97
59	.2	103	41	-.2	97
58	.2	103	42	-.2	97
57	.2	102	43	-.2	98
56	.2	102	44	-.2	98
55	.1	101	45	-.1	99
54	.1	101	46	-.1	99
53	.1	101	47	-.1	99
52	.1	100	48	-.1	100
51	.0	100	49	-.0	100
50	.0	100	50	-.0	100

Standardized Need Criteria

For standardized tests the criterion for determining need is really an estimation rather than an exact determination. One standard deviation below the mean can indicate a problem, but the cutoff could be .9 or 1.1 standard deviations. A percentile rank below 16 might be used to indicate the need for remedial services, or that a child has not mastered the content being tested, but this cutoff point is arbitrary. Although there is no absolute guideline for determining below and above average standardized test performance, Table IX provides several cutoff values that are frequently used to interpret test scores.

Table IX. Interpreting Standard Score Need

Meaning	Percentile Rank	z score	Normalized Percentile Rank	Stanine Score	IQ-Type Score
Average	50	0	50	5	100
Low Average	23	-.75	34	3.5	89
Low	16	-1.00	29	3.0	85
Very Low	2	-2.00	8	1.0	70

For parents, and for many IEP members, a qualitative summary of standardized test performance can be very useful (and appreciated). The following example might be part of an IEP section entitled Educational Levels of Performance in which subtest areas are identified, followed by percentile ranks (or some other score), and then a word or statement concerning what the score means. As can be seen for math computation, a percentile rank of 25 is still within the average range. A percentile rank of 25 is .7 standard deviations below the mean and equivalent to an IQ-type score of 90.

Educational Area	PR	Performance
Reading Word Attack	32	Average
Reading Vocabulary	18	Low
Reading Comprehension	14	Very low
Math Computation	25	Average
Math Concepts	58	Above Average
Math Applications	32	Average
Spelling	11	Low
Writing	5	Very Low
Social Studies	20	Low
Science	40	Average
Language	19	Low

Subtest Interpretation

A standardized test might subdivide reading into a series of subtests such as reading vocabulary, word attack skills, and reading comprehension. Or the mathematics section might include subtests involving computation, applications, and problem solving. There are also a variety of individualized and specialized diagnostic test batteries to evaluate mathematics, receptive and expressive language, and written language. In the area of general academic achievement, individualized tests and subtests are routinely used in special education. The Peabody Individual Achievement Test–Revised (Markwardt, 1989) is comprised of mathematics, reading recognition, reading comprehension, spelling, general information, and written expression subtests; the Wide Range Achievement Test-3 (Wilkinson, 1993) consists of reading, spelling, and arithmetic subtests; and the Wechsler Individual Achievement Test (Psychological Corporation, 1992b) includes subtests that focus on specific learning disability areas: oral expression, listening comprehension, written expression, basic reading, reading comprehension, numerical operations, mathematics reasoning, and spelling.

Diagnostic standardized tests are similar to the individualized achievement tests described above, but the subtests generally focus on one area such as mathematics, reading or written expression. The KeyMath–Revised (Connolly, 1988) is comprised of thirteen subtests ranging from addition computation to assessing measurement.

The Woodcock Reading Mastery Tests–Revised (Woodcock, 1987) consists of the following subtests: visual-auditory learning, letter identification, word identification, word attack, word comprehension, and passage comprehension. The Test of Written Language-2 (Hammill & Larsen, 1988) entails subtests in such areas as vocabulary, spelling, style, and thematic maturity.

Standardized subtest performance can provide information concerning a child's general educational needs, and insights for assessing curriculum needs, but these tests will not necessarily indicate specific curriculum needs. On the Woodcock Reading Mastery Test a low letter identification subtest score might offer useful background information but would probably not represent an area that would be targeted for remediation. An IEP team can place a great deal of emphasis on subtest scores as a means for delineating specific needs. Wright and Wright suggest that if a "child has reading problems, the IEP should include reading subtest scores" or if a "child has problems in math calculation, the IEP should include the math calculation subtest scores."[31] Subtest scores can be very useful but the practitioner should be aware that the whole test is generally more reliable than subtests, and that subtest should not define or dictate intervention or remediation. Most important, standardized subtests are not as effective for identifying regular curriculum needs and levels of instructional performance as curriculum-based measures.

Grade Equivalent Need

There is an intuitive appeal to age and grade equivalents but both types of scores can be misleading. A grade equivalent of 2.5 does not indicate that a child is achieving at this level but only that the child received a raw score similar to the raw score received by a child at grade level 2.5.

Another problem with grade equivalents is that the standard deviation increases with increasing age and grade level. For a child in the third grade (grade level = 3.0) who receives a grade equivalent of 1.5 in reading the standard deviation might be 1.3; while for a child in the sixth grade who receives a grade equivalent of 4.5 the standard deviation might be 1.7. Both students are exactly 1.5 grade levels below average, but the first is more than one standard deviation below the mean while the second student is less than one standard deviation below the mean.

Determining grade equivalent need requires an increasingly larger grade equivalent with increasing grade level. For example in grades 1 to 3, a grade equivalent of 1.0 below average might indicate a difficulty; in grades 4 through 6 a grade equivalent of 1.5 below average would be required to indicate a problem; and in grades 7 through 9 a grade equivalent of 2.0 or more below average might be significant. A simple index of grade equivalent need that approximates the one standard deviation level is to multiply the child's age by .15 so that for a 10-year-old child, the estimated standard deviation is 1.5. All other factors being equal (which they rarely are), a grade-level deficiency of 1.5 would indicate an area of need.

Test History

Standardized testing is an extremely important facet of the individual evaluation, in spite of the fact that existing test data is often ignored. The standardized test history of a child can be invaluable in discerning trends in a child's educational performance. As shown in Table X, prior test scores might show a consistent lack of progress (Student A), a lack of progress beginning at a specific grade level (Student B), or even regression (Student C in reading). Although the standardized test score history might reveal little, this data should always be considered.

Table X. Evaluating Data Trends

Grade	Student A		Student B		Student C	
	Read	Math	Read	Math	Read	Math
3	1.2	2.3	3.0	3.3	3.2	3.5
4	1.8	2.6	4.2	4.0	2.6	3.5
5	2.0	3.0	3.9	4.1	2.2	3.6

SLD Need

The determination of a specific learning disability by the team of qualified professionals and the parents requires that (1) the child does not achieve at a level consistent with age and ability, (2) there is a severe discrepancy between achievement and intellectual ability, and (3) the discrepancy involves oral expression, listening comprehension, written expression, basic reading skill, reading comprehension, mathematics calculation, or mathematics reasoning.

The formula developed by Horn (1941) is often used to indicate a 50 percent discrepancy between achievement and intellectual ability (see Burns, 1982) is determined by:

$$\frac{2MA + CA}{3} - 5$$

For a student with an IQ of 90 and a CA of 12, MA is 10.8, or 90(12)/100=10.8, and expected achievement is (2(10.8)+12)/3 - 5 or 6.2. A 50 percent discrepancy is determined by multiplying 6.2 by .5 so that in this case an actual achievement score would need to be less than 6.2(.5) or 3.1.

Another frequently used method for determining a test score discrepancy entails the use of the reliability for each test and the standard deviation:

$$SE_{dif} = SD \sqrt{2 - r_{xx} - r_{yy}}$$

The state of Washington[32] relies on a regression approach to generate severe discrepancy criterion scores. When both IQ and achievement are expressed as having distribution means of 100 and standard deviations of 15, a student with an IQ of 100 would need an achievement score equal to or less than the criterion score of 82. The formula for determining discrepancy criterion scores is based on the SE_{est}:

$$Criterion\ score = r_{xy}\ (S_{IQ} - X_{IQ}) + X_{IQ} - (z)SD\sqrt{1 - r_{xy}^2}$$

so that for an IQ of 100 if a discrepancy is defined as a z of 1.5 and the correlation between IQ and achievement is .6, the score needed for a severe discrepancy (i.e., the criterion score) is 82. If IQ is 85 instead of 100, a discrepancy score of 73 is required.

Qualitative discrepancy. The Texas Education Agency provides two methods for determining a severe discrepancy.[33] The first method is based on a comparison of standardized intelligence and achievement test scores, while the second method is based on professional judgment (e.g., expected achievement is based on reports or observational data). For the test score method, when both tests have the same means (e.g., 100) and standard deviations, the achievement test score is subtracted from the IQ test score and if the difference is greater than one standard deviation the discrepancy is deemed severe. For example, if the IQ score is 90 and achievement is 70, then the difference of 20 points is greater than the one standard deviation criterion and is therefore a severe discrepancy. If a severe discrepancy cannot be determined using the standard deviation difference method because appropriate tests are lacking, a discrepancy can be determined based on information "obtained from standardized assessment instruments, reports from parents, observations of classroom performance, student work samples, and other items as needed." In Washington if a statistical determination of a discrepancy is not possible "the multidisciplinary team shall apply" professional judgment in order to determine the presence of a severe discrepancy."

Considering that many students are identified as having a learning disability who do not demonstrate a test score discrepancy, there must be some indication that the child has the ability to profit from specially designed instruction. A teacher or parent's belief that a student has the ability to perform (e.g., read at grade level) might be the result of compelling anecdotal evidence such as the ability to perform similar tasks when given special instruction, or high interest/motivation on the part of the student.

CURRICULUM NEEDS

After standardized testing has been considered to determine general educational needs and the impact of the child's disability on educational performance, specific educational needs must be determined. What exactly is it about the curriculum that presents a problem for a child with a disability? Or what is it about the child's behavior that affects the child's ability to be involved in and progress in the general curriculum? Special education means specially designed instruction, and this signifies that existing instructional methodology or content is not working or must be modified.

Instructional data can be gathered from regular and special education teachers and other specialists as appropriate. If a general assessment is made that a child exhibits inappropriate classroom behavior, the specific behavior and frequency should be determined before the IEP team meeting so that this data can be used to develop appropriate measurable annual goals and short-term objectives or benchmarks. If the child is significantly below average in mathematics on a standardized test, specific strengths and weaknesses in mathematics should be identified before goals and objectives are developed.

The ability of a "child to be involved in and progress in the general curriculum (i.e., the same curriculum as for nondisabled children)"[34] is a reoccurring theme throughout IDEA-1997 and the regulations. In order to meet this obligation, the curriculum expectations within the classroom or the school must be examined so that reasons why, when, and in what areas the child cannot participate in the curriculum are understood. This requires an evaluation of the entire curriculum and includes behavioral expectations, academic standards, workbooks, textbooks, activities, extracurricular activities, quizzes, classroom tests, statewide competency tests, districtwide tests, basic skills, teaching strategies, teaching philosophy, and learning expectations. In short, everything that occurs in the school and the classroom, and not just what is formally adopted by the school district, requires consideration to determine how a child with a disability can be involved in and progress in the area of the general curriculum affected by the disability.

Curriculum-based Assessment

Choate et al. (1995) defined curriculum-based assessment (CBA) as "the process of determining students' instructional needs within a curriculum by directly assessing specific curriculum areas" (p. 17). A curriculum-based assessment can involve whatever task or content is used in the curriculum. Word lists, flash cards, letter identification, key word identification, knowledge of compound words, pointing to blends, sight vocabulary, visual and auditory discrimination, letter naming, word relationships, and content-area reading comprehension can all be a source of a curriculum-based assessment if the task is used in the curriculum. If spelling is a part of the curriculum, how spelling is assessed in the curriculum determines the nature of the curriculum-based assessment. If writing is taught and measured by a creative writing task, a similar task should be used to develop the assessment. If there is a high emphasis on word problems in mathematics, a word problem assessment should be used to evaluate performance. The purpose of special education is to design instruction that will allow the child to be involved in and progress in the general curriculum, and not to create a new curriculum that further segregates the child from the mainstream.

Curriculum-based assessments provide the primary data for determining specific, beginning or instructional levels of performance. Whether a child needs assistance involving reading, mathematics, classroom behavior or self-help skills, what exactly the child can and cannot do in the curriculum is best determined by a curriculum-based assessment. If the problem involves oral reading, a passage from reading curriculum material is used to evaluate oral reading. If classroom behavior is a problem, when and how frequently the behavior occurs in the classroom is observed and recorded.

Often assessments, tests, rating scales, or evaluations must be created during the initial evaluation to determine appropriate beginning levels of performance. A series of passages from different textbooks and classroom materials might be used to assess reading comprehension, a nonsense word task to evaluate phonics skills, or a student might to asked to take notes from dictation to evaluate note-taking skills. Existing data and standardized testing indicate a child's general educational needs, and tasks and curriculum-based assessments must identify specific instructional needs. A standardized test might indicate a problem in reading vocabulary, while a curriculum-based assessment is constructed to assess the child's current level of performance involving the ability to read content words.

A curriculum-based assessment is a bridge between a standardized assessment and the measurable annual goal. If the standardized test indicates a need in reading vocabulary, and a goal is developed "to improve reading content vocabulary to 80% using a teacher-made test," the present level of performance prior to specially designed instruction to achieve this goal must be determined; that is, what percent content words the child can read prior to instruction using the teacher-made test. To provide this information, a curriculum-based test must be constructed and administered to determine the initial level of performance.

Teacher-made tests. Teacher-made tests can include curriculum-based assessments, classroom tests and quizzes, diagnostic tests, practice tests, test simulations, rating scales, checklists, and observational data collection. A teacher might construct a test comprised of a series of questions that are typical of those used in a high-stakes state competency test, or develop a list of nonsense words to evaluate different phonics skills. As is the case with all curriculum-based assessments, tests and evaluations constructed by teachers and specialists are invaluable in determining specific or instructional levels of performance. Whether the purpose of the assessment is to evaluate basic sight words, oral reading, reading comprehension, spelling, word attack skills, writing, note taking, computational skills, mathematical word problems, or content-area knowledge, teacher-made tests often provide the beginning

benchmark or level of performance for constructing meaningful measurable annual goals and corresponding short-term objectives or benchmarks.

The importance of teacher-made tests in the determination of beginning levels of performance is readily acknowledged, but teacher-made testing has also been used to suggest assessment rather than to actually to assess performance. This is often seen in goals and objectives when the method of evaluation is said to be a *teacher-made test.* Generally speaking, if a teacher-made test has not been developed to measure an initial level of performance, there is a good likelihood that a teacher-made test will not be used to measure short-term objective performance.

Work samples. If at all possible, samples of a child's work in the areas that are affected by the disability should be obtained. This might include workbook exercises, classroom tasks, homework, classroom tests and quizzes, papers, reports, writing samples, basal exercises, and other information that will provide insight as to the type of performance thought to necessitate specially designed education. Actual classroom tests and quizzes can provide very compelling data in the determination of a child's level of performance, but often this data is not considered. A good practice is to append a sampling of several classroom tests or work samples to the evaluation report or to the IEP to give a concrete example of actual curriculum achievement.

Grade History

Of all the tests and assessments that are included in the individual evaluation, a year-to-year profile of school grades is often lacking. School grades are not necessarily an accurate reflection of educational performance, especially when social promotion and grade inflation are prominent factors, but yearly grade profiles can suggest when and in what areas a child's educational performance has been affected. From a historical standpoint, an attempt should also be made to determine whether the educational manifestation of the child's difficulties occurs across all subject areas, and whether the problem is recent or can be traced to a specific point in time or grade level. Grades will not always indicate specific areas affected by the child's disability, but the historical circumstances surrounding an educational problem should be considered in terms of records, anecdotal information from parents and teachers, assessments, and school grades.

Observed Needs

Observational data is an important facet of every individual evaluation. Sources for observational data include the classroom teacher, parents, and other specialists. As part of the manifestation determination review, the IEP team must observe the child before a determination is made that the behavior is a manifestation of the child's disability.[35] During the development, review, or revision of an IEP, the consideration of special factors (e.g., behavior which impedes learning) "must include a review of valid evaluation data and the observed needs of the child resulting from the evaluation process."[36] In Ohio, the assessment of the effect of the learner's environment(s) on his or her learning, structured observations, and interview with a person knowledgeable about a child's functioning is required.[37]

When reviewing existing evaluation data for either an initial or reevaluation, the IEP team must review information provided by parents, current classroombased assessments, and observations by teachers and related service providers.[38] For children suspected of having a specific learning disability observational data involving a child's academic performance in the regular classroom is required by "at least one team member other than the child's regular teacher."[39] The relevant behavior of these observations is included in the written report required for a child having a specific learning disability.[40] As much as possible, an IEP member should attempt to observe the child during a time period when the disability is manifested. If necessary, several observational periods might be required to reliably determine the frequency and severity of behavior, and to cross-validate the behaviors with those of another observer.

Observational data is an extremely important source of data, and for students suspected of emotional disturbance, observational data might well be the single most important element of the individual evaluation when determining need. If goals are developed to improve behavior, the behavior must be specified, how the behavior is measured must be identified, and the circumstances surrounding the behavior must be delineated. If a child cannot participate in the regular classroom because of inappropriate behavior, exactly what that inappropriate behavior is must be identified. If the child disrupts the class, exactly how the child disrupts the class must be described.

Functional Needs

IDEA-1997 refers to functional skills, capabilities,[41] and evaluations in several contexts, all of which are intended to allow "the child to be involved in and progress in the general curriculum."[42] A functional vocational evaluation[43] is part of the definition of transition services in IDEA-1997, and the general need to assess functional skills is a basic requirement of the individual evaluation that includes "a variety of assessment tools and strategies to gather relevant functional and developmental information, including information provided by the parent"[44] to assist in determining the existence of a disability and IEP content.

The need for a functional behavioral assessment has received attention in the development of IEPs because of its inclusion as a procedural safeguard in IDEA-1997[45] that requires "either before or not later than 10 days after taking a disciplinary action" an IEP meeting must be convened to conduct a functional behavioral assessment and then develop a behavioral intervention plan to address the behavior.[46]

A functional behavioral assessment is an attempt to understand the function of the behavior that is the cause of concern. Tilly et al. (1998) defined a functional behavioral assessment as "the process of coming to an understanding of why a student engages in challenging behavior and how student behavior relates to the environment . . . in order to better understand the specific reasons for the student's problem behavior" (p. 1). Haynes and O'Brien (1990) defined a functional behavioral assessment as identifying "controllable, casual functional relationships" relating to specific target behaviors.

In one of the seminal studies relating to functional assessment, Iwata et al. (1982) identified the functional properties of self-injury by considering four different circum-stances or conditions: academic, alone, social disapproval, and play. Carr (1994) has summarized four major categories when determining functional behavioral needs: attention seeking, escape from tasks, the generation of sensory reinforcement, and access to tangible items or events. Miller, Tansy, and Hughes (1998) described a problem-solving approach for conducting a functional behavioral analysis that includes how data should be collected, describing the behavior (e.g., setting, frequency, duration, intensity), generating hypotheses about the causes or *function* of the behavior, and then developing a behavioral intervention plan.

The overall approach for a functional behavior assessment requires a careful description of the behavior, and how frequently, where, when, and with whom the behavior is most likely to occur. Understanding this antecedent information provides an opportunity to generate hypotheses as to the function of the behavior and why it occurs. The function of the behavior can include the general behavioral functions described by Carr (1994) such as attention seeking, escape from tasks, sensory reinforcement, and access to tangible items or events, but other factors can also play an important role such as family, substance abuse, and emotional disturbance.

If a child's disability is emotional disturbance, there should be a behavioral assessment that includes a description of the type, frequency, intensity, duration of behavior, and the setting in which the behavior occurred. However, the behavior of a child with a disability (and not necessarily a child classified as emotionally disturbed) might not have been identified during the initial evaluation and additional behavioral assessment data might be necessary in order to develop a behavioral intervention plan to address the behavior.

If classroom behavior is an area of need, there should be specific information available concerning classroom behavior. The reason for requiring a functional behavioral assessment[47] is to develop goals and strategies that deal with specific behavior, where the behavior occurs, and the function or purpose of the behavior. If the function of the behavior is to avoid certain tasks in certain classes, strategies can be implemented to deal with this behavior.

The exact data for a functional behavioral analysis can vary but the overall intent of the analysis is to clearly identify the behavior, develop hypotheses that might explain the reason for the behavior, and then develop appropriate behavioral strategies. The following are the type of concerns that can be considered when determining a child's functional behavioral and intervention needs:

1. What exactly is the behavior?
2. Where did the behavior occur?
3. What time did it happen and in what setting (e.g., classroom)?
4. Who was involved?
5. What happened before the behavior?
6. What might have caused the behavior?
7. What happened immediately after the behavior?
8. How frequently has this behavior occurred?
9. Have similar behaviors occurred?
10. Describe the intensity and duration of these behaviors.
11. Describe the circumstances when the behavior is most likely to occur.
12. What does the student think of the behavior that occurred?
13. What is the function of the behavior (e.g., attention, avoidance, reinforcement)?
14. What seems to decrease the occurrence of the behavior?

The strategies that result from a functional behavioral analysis can be defined in a behavioral intervention plan, can be a part of the statement defining special education and related services and supplementary aids and services,[48] or can be addressed by specific measurable annual goals and short-term objectives or benchmarks. The advantage of appending a behavioral intervention plan to the IEP is that the behavior (where, when, how frequently, etc.), causes and hypotheses for the behavior, strategies and interventions, and measurable annual goals and short-term objectives or benchmarks can be developed and presented in a reasonably sequential plan.

Referral Needs

The referral for special education is an extremely important source of data in the determination of IEP needs; that is, needs that must be addressed by measurable annual goals. The referral indicates the behavior or area of performance that is causing the concern, and the various attempts to address these needs indicate appropriate special education, related and supplementary aids and services. Kentucky requires that "referral information" is used to examine the child's status in physical, communication and cognitive functioning, social competence, academic performance, vocational functioning, recreation and leisure functioning and environmental, family and cultural factors.[49] Alabama's Student Referral Form includes a listing of attempted teaching strategies (e.g., modeling, slower pace, paraprofessionals), task requirements (e.g., provide prompts, break into smaller steps), and behavior techniques (e.g., student contract, behavior management) that have been used as pre-referral interventions in the regular classroom.[50] Because this information also includes the number of days each has been attempted, and the degree to which the intervention changed the problem, these data provide useful information for determining areas of need, services, and general instructional strategies for achieving measurable annual goals.

Evaluation Needs

Before special education services are provided, every child must have a full and individual initial evaluation.[51] The individual evaluation provides an overall or comprehensive assessment and review of a child's disability needs and educational performance. A major purpose of the evaluation is the assessment of disability and educational needs in order to determine whether the child is a child with a disability and whether there is a need for special education. Disability and educational needs are determined by providing an "evaluation that is sufficiently comprehensive to identify all of the child's special education and related service needs"[52] and to assess the child "in all areas related to the suspected disability, including, if appropriate, health, vision, hearing, social and emotional status, general intelligence, academic performance, communicative status, and motor abilities."[53]

The individual evaluation can include standardized testing, diagnostic tests, ecological assessments, curriculum-based assessments, classroom tests and quizzes, work samples, observational data, interviews, rating scales, records and reports, physical examinations, hearing and vision screening, vocational/employability assessments, and other forms of data and data collection techniques. Many states have specific evaluation requirements such as

1. physical examination to preclude sensory or physiological factors;
2. a social history to determine the impact of environmental, cultural, or economic disadvantage;
3. educational history to determine if educational performance is the result of lack of instruction in reading or mathematics, or because of limited English proficiency;[54] and
4. intellectual functioning as determined by an individualized test of intelligence.

The theme that binds these various areas, and the emphasis individual states give to each area, is that the child is evaluated in all areas affected by the suspected disability.

There are considerable differences from state to state regarding what needs must be assessed in an individual evaluation. New York State has four criteria: (1) physical examination, (2) individual psychological examination (unless determined to be unnecessary), (3) social history, and (4) "other appropriate assessments or evaluations as necessary to ascertain the physical, mental and emotional factors which contribute to the suspected disability." Wyoming includes information relating to adaptive behavior, career/vocational status, information from the parent and the child's regular classroom or environment performance as part of the evaluation.[55] Washington requires a review of "all available existing school, medical, and other records pertinent to the suspected disabling condition(s) . . . including previous screening and evaluation reports, health reports, relevant cumulative records and recommendations of related service providers."[56]

In addition to determining the existence

of a disability and the need for special education, a third function of the individual evaluation, one that is sometimes deemphasized, is the determination of the child's instructional levels of educational performance. When the IEP team develops, reviews or considers measurable annual goals and short-term objectives or benchmarks, the beginning level of performance for each goal must be known. Evaluation data must include "current classroom-based assessments and observations,"[57] and must be obtained that "provide relevant information that directly assists persons in determining the educational needs of the child."[58] If a standardized test reveals that a child has difficulty in reading comprehension, an instructional assessment in reading comprehension should be conducted to determine how this need is manifested in the general curriculum. If a child has poor verbal skills, how this need is reflected in the general curriculum should be determined during the individual evaluation. If a child's performance in school is adversely affected by "heightened alertness to environmental stimuli,"[59] the specific educational needs and levels of performance should be specified. This might involve the evaluation of the frequency of off-task behavior (such as noise making, interruptions, inappropriate comments, excessive comments, or talking), or observational reports detailing organizational skills, motivation, types of classroom work, etc.

The individual evaluation also provides data and information to determine whether the child needs, or continues to need, special education and related services. A child might have a disability but no longer needs specially designed instruction. In this situation, the child is entitled to all related services and modifications necessary to participate in and progress in the general curriculum, but these services are provided under Section 504 and not IDEA.

Finally, the individual evaluation is used to determine test accommodations and additions to the special education program so that the child can "meet the measurable annual goals set out in the IEP of the child to participate, as appropriate, in the general curriculum."[60] Test accommodations can include needed format changes (e.g., Braille tests, large print, having the test read), test adaptations (e.g., where the test is taken, preferential seating), presentation modifications (e.g., extended time, scheduling changes) and response accommodations (e.g., giving answers orally).

The individual evaluation must be viewed as a dynamic and comprehensive process that requires extensive collaboration among the various qualified professionals and the parents participating in the evaluation. The evaluation is not a single test or assessment conducted by one individual, but involves gathering all information relating to a child's suspected disability, identifying and collecting additional data that might be needed, and determining eligibility and educational needs. The evaluation must build on existing assessment and referral information, and must be closely articulated with the development of goals and services. The purpose of the individual evaluation is not to discover a disability, unrelated to past educational performance, but to explain why existing educational performance is affected by the disability. The need to determine how a child's disability affects the child's involvement and progress in the general curriculum highlights the importance of regular educational performance and what it is about that performance, caused by the child's disability, that requires specially designed instruction.

Evaluating Needs

The individual evaluation requires that a child is evaluated in all areas of the suspected disability, and that the different evaluation procedures used are not discriminatory. For standardized assessments the tests should be valid, given by trained personnel, and administered in accordance with the test instructions.[61] Overall, a variety of assessments should be used to evaluate performance, the assessments should be fair and all the data should be carefully considered in the determination of a child's suspected disability and educational needs.

Data for an individual evaluation must be obtained from different sources, including the parents, that indicate how the child can participate in the regular curriculum or other appropriate activities. The evaluations should "assess the relative contribution of cognitive and behavioral factors, in addition to physical or developmental factors," and should include evaluations and strategies that help to determine education need.

When the IEP team and/or the qualified group of professionals is determining the need for special education, the team must recognize the need for additional expertise. If possible, tests and other evaluation should be administered in the child's native language. If it is not feasible to test a child in his or her native language, the school district "still needs to obtain and consider accurate and reliable information that will enable the

agency to make an informed decision as to whether the child has a disability and the effects of the disability on the child's educational needs."[62]

Because of the dearth of standardized tests available in languages other than English (with the exception of Spanish), evaluating a student in his or her native language might require expertise from a local college or university, or using community resources. Needless to say, these informal evaluations require careful scrutiny to ensure that the data provide reasonably valid measures for evaluating a child's needs.

The individual evaluation should assess a child's ability rather than disability, "unless those skills are the factors that the test purports to measure."[63] If a child is assessed in science and has a reading disorder, the assessment might be modified to evaluate the child's ability in science rather than the reading disability. However, if the child has a visual or hearing impairment, the extent of the child's impairment would need to be determined. Likewise, if the child has a specific learning disability in reading, a reading assessment without modifications would be necessary to determine the extent of the reading disorder. Of course, if the child is visually impaired or has a physical disability, an alternative task might be necessary to evaluate performance.

Documented Needs

If the IEP team and other qualified professionals determine that no additional data are needed, the parents should be notified of the reasons for the determination and informed of the right to request an assessment to determine the continued existence

of the disability.[64] A careful review and consideration of existing data is essential for a meaningful and thoughtful evaluation of a child's needs. The requirement that the IEP team review existing evaluation data was included in IDEA-1997 so that children are not subjected to unnecessary tests and evaluations.[65]

For students who have an IEP, the re-evaluation must always consider previous IEP needs. The extent that previous goals and objectives have been achieved provides essential information for determining and/or modifying needed goals and objectives. If previous goals were not achieved, this should be reflected in determining new or modified goals. If goals were partly achieved, objectives require modification. If goals were achieved, this data would provide the basis for determining present levels of educational performance for the next IEP.

If available, statewide tests can be a useful source of information concerning curriculum ability. If there is a statewide curriculum, and a corresponding statewide assessment available to determine competency in the curriculum, a statewide test can provide a valid standardized assessment of curriculum performance. Because the content, task, and overall format of nationally standardized tests might differ from the actual curriculum, statewide tests often provide a more direct assessment of a school's actual academic curriculum.

Statewide tests can provide very useful curriculum information, but there are several potential drawbacks. First, many states do not have statewide tests at each grade level so that a year-to-year comparison is not possible. Second, there is no assurance that the content or the task of the statewide assessment is similar to what is used in the classroom. If a school relies heavily on language experience, or phonics, etc., and a statewide test employs a unique task and/or content to measure reading, the assessment task might be quite different from what is actually used to teach reading in the classroom.

•

A successful individual evaluation is one that identifies all of a child's academic and nonacademic needs, and then links these needs to measurable annual goals and services. The evaluation question is never what one test or even a series of tests indicate, but rather what tests, assessments, reports, and observations are best for understanding and identifying unique individual needs so that goals can be developed and services provid- ed. When this is accomplished, when "the evaluation is sufficiently comprehensive to identify all of the child's special education and related service needs,"[66] and when the evaluation identifies the impact of the disability and specific levels of performance, then the full and individual evaluation will provide the basis for a logical and effective IEP.

NOTES

[1] 20 USC 1400(d)(1)(A).
[2] 20 USC 1400(c)(7)(A)(F).
[3] 20 USC 1400(c)(2)(A).
[4] 20 USC 1400(c)(5)(F).
[5] 20 USC 1400(a)(1)(B)(ii).
[6] 20 USC 1414(d)(1)(A)(vii)(I).
[7] 20 USC 1414(d)(3)(B)(ii).

[8] 20 USC 1414(d)(3)(B)(iv).
[9] 20 USC 1414(d)(3)(B)(iii).
[10] 20 USC 1414(d)(4)(A)(ii)(IV).
[11] 20 USC 1401(30)(A).
[12] Supreme Court (No. 96-1793).
[13] 34 CFR 307.7(b)(10).
[14] Senate Report 105-17, p. 20.

[15] 34 CFR 300.7(b)(5).

[16] 34 CFR 300.7(b)(1).

[17] 34 CFR 347(a)(2)(i).

[18] The first two factors are required by 20 USC 1414(d)(3)(A) and the consideration of state and districtwide tests was added by 34 CFR 300.346(a)(1)(iii).

[19] 20 USC 1414(d)(3)(B)(i)-(iv).

[20] Which is the purpose of supplementary aids and services as discussed in 34 CFR 300.28.

[21] 34 CFR 300.346(a)(2)(ii).

[22] Title VI of the Civil Rights Act of 1964 (PL 88-352) states that "no person in the United States shall, on the ground of race, color, or national origin, be excluded from participation in, be denied the benefits of, or be subjected to discrimination under any program or activity receiving Federal financial assistance." This was the essence of the opinion in Lau v. Nichols 414 U.S. 563 (1974) in which the "failure of the San Francisco school system to provide English language instruction to approximately 1,800 students of Chinese ancestry who do not speak English, or to provide them with adequate instructional procedures, denies them a meaningful opportunity to participate in the public educational program and thus violates 601 of the Civil Rights Act of 1964."

[23] See 20 USC 1401(1) and 20 USC 1401(2).

[24] 34 CFR 300.307. Physical education.

[25] October 3, 1994.

[26] 20 USC 1414(d)(1)(A)(v).

[27] 20 USC 1414(b)(5) Special Rule for Eligibility Determination.

[28] 20 USC 1414(d)(3)(A)(i).

[29] *Ibid.*

[30] Senate Report 105-17, p. 24.

[31] Practical and Legal Guidance for Parents, Pamela Darr Wright, M.A., M.S.W. Licensed Clinical Social worker and Peter W. D. Wright, Esq. Retrieved September 22, 2000 from the World Wide Web: http://www.wrightslaw.com/advoc/articles/iep_guidance.html.

[32] Washington Administrative Code (WAC), 392-172-132, 1995.

[33] Texas Education Agency, (1997), Eligibility Report: Learning Disability.

[34] 34 CFR 300.347(a)(2)(i).

[35] 34 CFR 300.523.

[36] 34 CFR 300.346(a)(2), Note.

[37] Rule 3301-35-032 Standards for Ohio Schools.

[38] 34 CFR 300.533.

[39] 34 CFR 300.542(a).

[40] 34 CFR 300.543.

[41] 20 USC 1401(1).

[42] 20 USC 1414(b)(2)(A).

[43] 20 USC 1401(2)(A) and 20 USC 1401(30)(C).

[44] 20 USC 1414(b)(2)(A).

[45] 20 USC 1415.

[46] 20 USC 1415(k)(1)(B)(i).

[47] *Ibid.*

[48] 20 USC 1414(d)(1)(A)(iii).

[49] 707 KSAT 1:190, Section 4(2).

[50] Alabama State Department of Education, Student Referral Form, Montgomery, April 7, 1994.

[51] 20 USC 1414(a)(1)(A).

[52] 34 CFR 300.532(h).

[53] 34 CFR 300.532(g).

[54] 34 CFR 300.534(b)(1).

[55] Wyoming State Board of Education Rules, Chapter 7, Section 15.

[56] WAC 392-172-108(11).

[57] 34 CFR 300.533(a)(1)(ii).

[58] 34 CFR 300.532(j).

[59] 34 CFR 300.7(a)(9).

[60] 34 CFR 300.533(a)(2)(iv).

[61] 34 CFR 300.532(c).

[62] IDEA-1997, Proposed Regulations, *Federal Register*, Volume 62, Number 204, October 22, 1997, pp. 55104-55105, 34 CFR 300.532, Note #2.

[63] 34 CFR 300.532(e).

[64] 20 USC 1414(c)(4). Requirements if additional data are not needed.

[65] 20 USC 1414(c)(1)(A).

[66] 34 CFR 300.532(h).

Chapter 5

PRESENT LEVELS OF EDUCATIONAL PERFORMANCE (PLEP)

DETERMINING PERFORMANCE LEVELS

PRESENT LEVELS OF EDUCATIONAL PERFORMANCE (PLEP) is the first required element addressed in the development of an IEP.[1] The PLEP indicates a child's general and specific levels of educational performance, including

1. how the child's disability affects the child's involvement and progress in the general curriculum; or

2. for preschool children, as appropriate, how the disability affects the child's participation in appropriate activities.

The PLEP is a score, rating, frequency, report, or description of what a child has achieved in academic and nonacademic areas. The PLEP is not a subjective statement or a label "such as 'mentally retarded' or 'deaf'" which "may not be used as a substitute for the description of present levels of educational performance."[2]

In addition to PLEP, present levels of educational performance are also referred to as PLOP (Present Levels Of Performance), PLP (Present Levels of Performance), Current Levels of Performance (CLP), Current Level of Functioning (CLF), simply Levels of Performance (LP), beginning levels of performance, or beginning benchmarks when used in conjunction with measurable annual goals. The various names for PLEP are not necessarily interchangeable and the meaning of each depends on whether the levels of performance refer to general or instructional levels of performance or both. In this book PLEP refers to the general statement required by IDEA-1997 (which can include both general and specific levels of performance), and present level of performance (PLP) for a specific score, rating or level of behavior that is used as the beginning level of performance or beginning benchmark for each measurable annual goal (e.g., completed assignments = 0, reading comprehension = 40 percent).

The PLEP statement indicates the impact of the disability on educational performance, and specific or instructional levels of performance that signify the level of performance prior to beginning specially designed instruction to achieve a goal. If the goal is to decrease the occurrence of a behavior to 0, there must be a determination of the frequency of the behavior before the plan to achieve the goal is implemented; if the goal is to increase word attack skills on a curriculum-based assessment to 70 percent, there should be a beginning level of performance.

How the child's disability affects involvement and progress in the general curriculum is a primary consideration in the development of the PLEP statement. A variety of assessment techniques can be used to determine regular curriculum progress and involvement, including both standardized and nonstandardized tests.[3] This interpretation of the PLEP is more inclusive than that given in the 1990 regulations where "objective measurable terms" were required, test scores permitted, but raw scores were considered insufficient.[4]

Standardized test scores are useful for determining the impact of the disability on educational performance, while nonstandardized evaluations (e.g., teacher-made or curriculum-based tests) identify specific instructional levels of performance. A standardized test score might show that a child is significantly below average in reading comprehension, and a nonstandardized assessment indicates that the child is able to answer 1 out of 10 literal questions from a third grade basal reader. The standardized score indicates the impact of the disability, and the nonstandardized score signifies that the beginning level of performance for the goal to answer literal reading comprehension questions is 1 out of 10 or 10 percent.

In order to develop an effective IEP, the IEP team must consider the twofold role of the PLEP statement: First, the PLEP indicates general areas of educational need that should be addressed by special education, a related service, or a supplementary aid or service. Second, the PLEP statement provides the foundation for measurable annual goals and short-term objectives or benchmarks for evaluating progress. This is achieved by identifying beginning levels of performance, which relate to specific educational strengths and needs, recording this beginning level of instruction in the IEP, and then developing a series of short-term objectives that bridge the gap from this beginning level of instruction to the annual level of performance (i.e., the measurable annual goal).

Without a beginning level of performance, there is no frame of reference for projecting annual performance. A standardized test might indicate that a significantly low area of performance is the result of a child's disability. The IEP team decides that this need can be addressed by increasing (or decreasing) performance on some measure. The anticipated level of academic performance or goal only has meaning within the context of the beginning level of performance.

The levels of performance described in the PLEP statement involve disability needs (e.g., hearing or visual acuity, assistive technology needs), levels of academic performance and nonacademic performance (e.g., physical education, mobility needs), and areas affected by the disability such as when a learning disability causes a behavior problem or vice versa.

A major deficiency of IEPs is a lack of educational data pertaining to specific or beginning levels of educational performance. General educational performance data are often sufficient to determine educational need, but this information usually does not indicate specific skill or behavior levels that can be used as beginning benchmarks for annual goals.

PLEP Progression

A PLEP need is the result of the progression of evaluation from general to specific instructional needs. If an eight-year-old child is reading at a grade level of 1.0 and a curriculum-based assessment reveals a comprehension level of 20 percent, the child's general level of performance is a grade level of 1.0 and the specific level of performance in reading is a comprehension level of 20 percent. This data might be further supported by observational reports that the child has a difficult time remembering what was read, paying attention while reading, remembering and sequencing details.

The general PLEP statement is not just a listing of scores, but a progression of evaluation and assessment data that logically links general areas of need to specific instructional needs and to specific measurable annual goals. The general area of educational need might be a low standard score, poor grades or not completing classroom work, and the specific area of educational need might be reading vocabulary, completed homework assignments, or off-task behavior.

If the IEP is the linchpin of FAPE, the PLEP is the linchpin of the IEP. The referral and individual evaluation are intended to identify levels of performance affected by the child's disability, and the resulting PLEP statement indicates the impact of the disability on educational performance, and provides the beginning benchmarks for the development of measurable annual goals.

Because the effect of a child's disability on academic performance is readily depicted by standardized scores, the IDEA-1990 regulations linked the PLEP to standardized scores rather than curriculum-based measures that would serve as beginning benchmarks for annual goals. By emphasizing test results that "reflect the impact of the disability on the child's performance" rather than curriculum-based measures ("raw scores would not usually be sufficient"), the need to include beginning levels of performance in the PLEP statement was eliminated.[5] The 1990 regulations encouraged standardized test results while at the same time requiring that

"scores should be (1) self-explanatory (i.e., they can be interpreted by all participants without the use of test manuals or other aids), or (2) an explanation should be included."[6] In essence, the 1990 regulations wanted the psychometric benefits of standardized scores and the simplicity of curriculum-based data. Unfortunately, this cannot be achieved by standardized scores alone.

The stipulation in the 1990 regulations that the PLEP statement should be written in objective measurable terms, but that test scores "might be included, where appropriate" and "raw scores would usually not be sufficient," had the effect of restricting the PLEP statement to general standardized levels of performance. The intent of the 1990 regulations was probably not to use standardized scores as the beginning level of performance for annual goals, but to show the *impact* of a child's disability on educational performance. After the impact of the child's disability was determined, the PLEP statement was then linked to goals and objectives: "Thus, if the statement describes a problem with the child's reading level and points to a deficiency in a specific reading skill, this problem should be addressed under both (1) goals and objectives, and (2) specific special education and related services to be provided to the child."[7] The short-term instructional objectives would then provide "measurable, intermediate steps between the present levels educational performance" and annual goals.[8] The fault of this reasoning is that the short-term objectives should bridge the gap between a beginning level of performance and the annual goal, and not necessarily between a general level of performance and the annual goal. For example, a standard score significantly below the mean indicates a general area of need, but this score is probably not suitable as a beginning benchmark so that the first short-term objective or benchmark would be to increase this standard score (e.g., 70 to 80).

The emphasis on general levels of performance was rectified in IDEA-1997 by measurable annual goals that are defined by short-term objectives or benchmarks. In order to develop a sequence of short-term objectives or benchmarks to accomplish a goal, a beginning level of performance or beginning benchmark is now required. Thus, the general level of performance in the PLEP statement points to a specific need; this specific need is then measured and serves as the beginning benchmark for the annual goal.

The IDEA-1997 regulations recognize the need to use a variety of assessments when determining the PLEP "such as criterion-referenced tests, standard achievement tests, diagnostic tests, other tests, or any combination of the above." The purpose is to determine levels of performance and areas of need arising from the child's disability, and not just "the effect of the child's disability on the child's performance"[9] as described in the 1990 regulations. Most important, the PLEP must be linked to specific instructional strategies and interventions to ensure involvement and progress in the general curriculum, and so that "needed adaptations or modifications to that curriculum can be identified."[10]

The PLEP indicates the impact of the child's disability on educational performance and specific areas of need resulting from a child's disability as measured by beginning levels of performance. If reading is a general area of need as determined by a standardized test, the PLEP should indicate both the general level of performance as measured by a standardized test and the specific reading skill level which will serve as the beginning benchmark for achieving an annual reading goal. If a child has a behavioral impairment, there should be general

data to show the impact of the child's disability on educational performance and specific behavior data to provide a beginning benchmark for an annual goal.

By considering strengths and weaknesses in defined areas, the IEP provides a framework for identifying important areas of need. In New York "the IEP must describe the student's levels of educational performance, including the student's abilities and needs" (p. 2)[11] relating to academic or educational achievement, learning characteristics, social development, physical development, and management needs.[12] In Kentucky the PLEP includes "the performance level or status for each of the following: physical functioning, communication functioning, cognitive functioning, social competence, academic performance, vocational functioning, and recreation and leisure functioning."[13]

In Pennsylvania the PLEP statement must include strengths (what the child's does relatively well) and needs,[14] where needs are interpreted to mean "skills and knowledge areas where the student cannot demonstrate competency." In addition, the needs "identified must be addressed in the rest of the IEP under goals, objectives, and specially-designed instruction."

Smith et al. (1995) described the PLEP as comprising "functional summary statements of an individual's strengths and weaknesses" that "draw on information from a variety of sources rather than relying on any one form of description" (p. 54) so that the PLEP might include both formal and informal assessments. This is similar to the Massachusetts IEP where "a current level of performance must be written for <u>each area of need</u>. The information recorded should be a distillation of assessment reports, which contain the more in-depth information" (p. 12).[15] Friend and Bursuck (1996) described the present level of functioning as a way of highlighting information collected from the individual evaluation, including individualized achievement test scores, teacher ratings, and assessments by specialists. These authors do not link present level of functioning to measurable annual goals, but interpret the present level of functioning "as a baseline and makes it possible to judge student progress from year to year" (p. 62). As will be discussed, this is so to the extent that the standardized test measures instruction and is sensitive to instructional gains.

McLoughlin and Lewis (1990) referred to bridging the gap between current performance levels and goals with short-term objectives and "task analysis breaks down the annual goals into teachable subcomponents or objectives" (p. 30). By this interpretation, the beginning or instructional level of performance is that point in the task sequence in which the child is able to perform. For example, each skill in a sequence (e.g., *locate coat, put on coat, button coat*) could be a separate short-term objective.

Although task analysis can provide a sequence of short-term objectives for achieving a goal, the task must be conceptualized as an annual series of steps.

Bateman interpreted PLEP to mean an area of need "that is readily understandable and is precise enough to allow us to measure progress." She regarded the present level of performance (or PLOP) as what is occurring now or the "quantification of the characteristic or need," and the goal shows where the child is heading.[16] This interpretation of the initial level of performance for objectives is similar to that used in Oregon where the relationship between present levels of educational performance (PLOP), short-term objectives (STO) and LTG (long-term goals) is described as follows: "The PLOP establishes baseline levels, the LTG establishes end levels, and the STO simply is calculated as the difference between them divided by time (in days, weeks or months)."[17] The Oregon IEP PLEP statement links measurable annual goals and short-term instructional objectives/criteria using the following format:[18]

Present Level of Educational Performance (Including how the student's disability affects involvement in the general curriculum):
Measurable Annual Goal (Including how progress toward the annual goal will be measured):

Short-Term Instructional Objectives/Criteria	**Evaluation**	**Schedule**
1.		
2.		
3.		

The PLEP Benchmark

There should be a direct relationship between general PLEP items and measurable annual goals and benchmarks. If the beginning level of performance is documented in the PLEP statement and as the beginning benchmark for a goal, the link between the PLEP statement is direct and obvious. If a child receives a below-average score on a test of expressive vocabulary, and a goal is developed to increase auditory receptive vocabulary, an inappropriate benchmark might be to identify sight words. The effectiveness of an instructional activity increases the closer the task is to the PLEP need. If a child has a deficiency in reading as determined by a cloze task to evaluate reading, then the most direct reading task would use this technique. If an overall deficit in auditory receptive vocabulary is detected, then a task that measures this ability should provide the basis for a measurable annual goal.

As with all components of an IEP, when the IEP development task is compliance rather than individualized planning, the IEP components are often unrelated. This problem is eliminated by including explicit beginning levels of performance in the PLEP statement and in each measurable annual goal. Often the reason for not having a direct link between PLEP and goals is an inability to interpret normative data in terms of beginning benchmarks for goals. This can occur because the normative scores are not understood, there is no relationship between normative performance and curriculum content, or the normative test content is unrelated to actual curriculum needs.

The need for relatively vague guidelines for the PLEP statement is necessary in order to meet the diverse needs of children with disabilities. As explained in the 1990 regulations, "the statement of present levels of educational performance will be different for each handicapped child" and "determinations about the content of the statement for an individual child are matters that are left to the discretion of participants in the IEP meetings."[19] Nonetheless, this vagueness is not insignificant and is cited in *Bend-Lapine School District v. TW*[20] as the reason why the inclusion of year-old data in a child's IEP was not a procedural violation when "the Federal Regulations explains that there are no specific requirements for what information should be contained in a PLP statement . . . thus, there is no procedural violation here."

The use of the PLEP statement to establish a logical relationship between general and specific instructional needs is similar to the logical relationship between measurable annual goals and short-term objectives or benchmarks. The general need should lead to a specific and measurable instructional need; the instructional need, once measured, will indicate the beginning level of performance for the goal; each subsequent measurement (i.e., short-term objective or benchmark) will indicate progress toward the final goal. No matter how the PLEP statement is interpreted, whether the statement includes general or instructional data or both, the PLEP must be inextricable related to measurable annual goals and objectives. For example, the PLEP statement might indicate a standard score of 70 in reading comprehension and an oral reading error rate of 25 percent based on grade level reading material.

> PLEP: Reading standard score = 70
> Specific reading level = 25% oral reading errors

An initial benchmark or beginning present level of performance (PLP) is needed in order to have a logical basis for anticipating end-of-the-year performance. If the instructional PLEP is 25% oral reading errors for grade level material, this beginning benchmark provides the basis for anticipating end-of-the-year performance.

> PLEP: Reading standard score = 70
>   Specific reading level = 25% oral
>   reading errors
> PLP   = 25% oral reading errors
> Goal   = <5%

Without beginning levels of performance data, several instructional problems can occur. First, without beginning data there is no way to determine whether the beginning level of content is instructionally appropriate (i.e., too easy or too difficult). Second, if there is no beginning data or benchmark, there is no way to assess and monitor progress throughout the year toward goal achievement. If after three months of instruction a child exhibits a 20 percent error rate, the meaning of this can only be interpreted in the context of the beginning level of performance. Third, without specific beginning ability information, the annual goal might over- or underestimate the child's annual anticipated level of performance.

Fourth, if there is no beginning level of performance, overall annual performance cannot be assessed, goals cannot be revised, and the result is a static IEP in which goals and objectives are repeated from one year to the next with little or no change.

IEP progression. When the IEP was first defined in PL 94-142, the sequencing of the required elements was very important. As described in the House Report for PL 94-142[21] "the plan should include statements of the present level of educational performance, the instructional objectives, the specific services to be provided, and the extent to which the child will be able to participate in regular educational programs" (p. 27). The PLP provides a basis for the goals and objectives, and the goals and objectives signify what services are to be provided. The steps required to complete an IEP follow a logical order. The determination of need must precede the determination of goals and services, and not vice versa. In Ohio the IEP team must complete the following, in sequence:[22] review of the evaluation, determine the area(s) of the learner's needs, develop goals, determine services, and determine the least restrictive environment.

General PLEP Data

The PLEP statement is based on referral information, all available data, parent and teacher input and observations, the results of the individual evaluation, standardized and districtwide tests if available, diagnostic and curriculum-based measures, rating scales, observations, checklists, and all other data that will describe a child's disability and educational needs.

The general PLEP statement indicates the extent of the disability, and how the disability affects educational performance. If a child has a hearing loss or a visual impairment, the extent of the loss or impairment, and how it affects educational performance, is described. If a child is identified as autistic, verbal and nonverbal communication and level of social interaction is described to show how these areas affect educational performance. If a child is emotionally disturbed, the behavior that resulted in this determination is specified as part of the general statement of levels of performance to show the affects of the disability on educational performance.

The general level of performance shows the impact of the disability on educational performance, but also the need for specific instructional strategies, and the need for supplementary aides and services. If a child has a severe hearing loss, the levels of performance relating to hearing help determine residual hearing and general educational strategies (e.g., communication mode, amplification). Likewise, a child's functional vision would help in the selection of the appropriate reading media.

The general level of performance might indicate the need for additional instructional data. If the child's general level of classroom performance is judged by the teacher as disinterested, unmotivated and easily distracted, specific behavior would need to be identified in order to develop a measurable annual goal. For a child with a specific learning disability in mathematics reasoning which is reflected by very low standardized test scores in mathematics problem solving and applications, these scores would indicate the need to assess specific mathematics reasoning skills in the curriculum.

General levels of performance are also important for identifying related services, supplementary aids and services, program supports, and accommodations. A general evaluation of a child's level of performance might be that the child needs a one-to-one aide, a translator, or a part-time aide to help with specific tasks such as transportation or meals. For children with other health impairments, the disability might indicate certain restrictions (e.g., excessive activity), classroom accommodations (e.g., seating arrangement, lighting), or environmental concerns (e.g., the need for an air purifier).

Observations and ratings. In addition to test scores, general levels of performance can be based on observational data, ratings, and subjective evaluations. The IEP might have a section for a general evaluation or rating of language skills (in contrast to the language skills measured by standardized achievement tests), social behavior, management needs, learning style, physical development, self-help skills, and intellectual functioning.
Classroom work: good
Homework assignments: frequently late
On-task behavior: has difficulty
Comprehension: good
Self-concept: fair
Social interaction: has difficulty
Intellectual ability: above average
Reading: average
Mathematics: below average

The above areas provide general descriptions of educational performance but insufficient specificity to evaluate and monitor progress. If homework assignments are frequently late, a goal to improve this level of performance should be based on how frequently homework assignments are not completed. Without this beginning data, there would be no way to determine whether the goal or objective is a realistic estimate of anticipated progress. The above ratings also show how ratings can be used to identify academic strengths and weaknesses. The "average" rating in reading could be based on a standardized test score (e.g., the child is near the mean in reading) or the teacher's subjective evaluation of overall reading performance.

General PLEP ratings can be based on standardized tests (e.g., intellectual ability, academic achievement), observational data (e.g., study skills, work habits, learning style, learning rate), developmental or screening data (e.g., physical development, hearing, vision), or diagnostic evaluations (e.g., articulation, fluency, decoding skill), surveys (e.g., motor development, self-help skills, language), and reports and anecdotal information from parents and teachers (e.g., enjoyment of reading, relationships with peers). For certain traits or abilities, a general PLEP rating might suffice as a specific level of performance. For example, if a child indicates a strong dislike of reading, the goal might be to improve the child's self-reported interest in reading. Although a reading inter-est scale could be developed that results in a summated score across several categories (interest in action stories, biographies, science fiction), a simple goal to improve interest in reading from *dislike* to *like* might be sufficient.

Standardized PLEP Benchmarks

A beginning benchmark of performance is necessary for planning goals and developing short-term objectives or benchmarks. When a beginning level of performance is absent, there is no way to anticipate what the next level of instruction or behavior should or could be. When this occurs, anticipated levels of performance must be based on little or no data.

A standardized test score is often used as the beginning level of performance because specific curriculum needs have not been assessed. There is an intuitive appeal to using a standard score, but the score is more likely to indicate instructional need than a specific instructional level of performance that can be used as a beginning goal benchmark. For instance, a standardized test is given and a resulting score is listed as the PLP, followed by a series of activities. The logical goal for this beginning level of performance would be a higher end-of-the-year standard score on the same test. If the beginning grade equivalent is 2.0, the goal might be a grade equivalent of 4.0. More often than not, when a standard score is used as a beginning benchmark, there is no explicit corresponding goal such as increasing grade equivalent from 2.0 to 4.0, but only an implication that the annual objectives will have an impact on grade level but to an unknown and unmeasured degree.

PLP	Reading: 2.0
Goal	Increase computational skill
Objective #1	Improve addition
Objective #2	Improve subtraction
Objective #3	Improve multiplication

Standard test scores show the impact of the disability on educational performance, but are often inappropriate as beginning performance benchmarks. First, the relationship between standardized test content and remedial activities is often not considered; second, the standardized test cannot be administered throughout the year; and third, test scores might be insensitive to actual progress.

Standardized test content. Short-term objectives are designed to plan a progression of performance progress; standardized tests are designed to evaluate the comparative needs of children. A standardized test will measure what is achieved by specially designed instruction, areas that are not a part of instruction, areas specific to the test and test error. The result is that the gain on a standardized test will not necessarily reflect actual instructional gain. The best measure of the affects of instruction is to measure actual instructional activities or tasks. In the extreme example, if a child is determined to have a need in reading based on a standardized test score, but the remediation consists of activities other than reading (e.g., perceptual motor training activities), the impact of remediation on reading will probably be minimal or, to be more exact, will depend on the extent the test measures these types of instructional activities.

If the measure of the beginning level of performance is not a valid measure of the specially designed instruction, the sensitivity of the measure to gauge progress will decrease as the relationship between the measure and instruction decreases. If, instead of noting the number of verbal outbursts, a self-concept rating scale is used to measure the beginning level of performance, self-concept might not be a suitable measure of the effectiveness of an intervention designed to decreasing verbal outbursts. Or if a multiple-choice test is used to assess specific grammatical skills (e.g., *They _____ not here. a) be b) are c) is d) am*) and the remedial task is to increase the quantity of writing and not grammar or mechanics, the measure might be insensitive to the actual progress toward increasing writing quantity (or however writing is measured).

In addition to content, the standardized test might be insensitive to subtle content changes because of limited items or because the items must cover a wide difficulty range. Wide-range achievement tests are extremely useful in special education because of the wide range of content and difficulty covered and are therefore excellent for evaluating the educational needs of children with very diverse age and ability levels. However, this attribute might make a test insensitive to subtle but important increases in content ability. For instance, a child's sight vocabulary might increase from 100 to 200 words, but this might result in a minimal standard score increase, depending on the test, the number of items, and the range of difficulty of the items. A standard score can be used as a beginning benchmark for an instructional

goal but only if there is a logical content relationship between the test and the activities designed to improve performance.

Competency tests. Statewide competency tests are often a major improvement over achievement tests because these usually reflect the overall curriculum used by a school or school district, although even a state-mandated curriculum might be considerably different than the curriculum used by a school or school district. If a statewide test is a high-stakes assessment (e.g., passing is required for graduation), passing the test might be an important goal. If the goal is to pass a statewide test, old tests or practice tests should be used to indicate a probable beginning level of performance and content areas that should be addressed by specific objectives. If a test requires several attempts to pass, each testing provides invaluable information for gauging progress and determining instructional needs to pass the test.

If a competency test in mathematics has subsections relating to computation, applications, measurement, geometry, and problem solving, a goal to pass the test would be comprised of short-term objectives that addresses each of the subtest areas, or the areas where the student has specific needs. There is little logic in setting a goal to pass a state competency test by stating short-term objectives that are unrelated to skills measured by the test.

Problems with repeated testing (also see page 164). Using the same test on several occasions is a problem when evaluating instructional performance throughout the year. In most situations, because a standardized test cannot be used repeatedly during the year, the evaluation progress toward the goal must be based on teacher-made tests, curriculum-based assessments and other informal ratings and assessments. The problems with using the same test more than once include practice and memory effects, both of which are further confounded by boredom and disinterest.

When instructional levels of performance are used as beginning benchmarks, repeated assessment becomes less of a problem because the assessment need not be a structured list of test items as is found on standardized tests. Instead of using the same passage to measure oral reading skills, a sampling of different passages having similar content and difficulty might be used. Or the same passages might be used as the beginning and final benchmark, but different passages are used to monitor and report progress during the year. If appropriate, randomization techniques can be used when presenting items.

If a standardized test is used as the beginning benchmark, the test should not be used more than twice. When reporting progress to parents, teacher-made tests and work samples should be used to provide empirical evidence of performance. If teacher ratings are used to report progress, the ratings should concentrate performance toward achieving the goal.

Many assessments of instructional performance fall into the category of before and after assessment rather than a strict preposttest evaluation where the exact same test is used for both pretest and posttest. For example, the beginning benchmark could be the amount of work completed, number of errors, number, rating, frequency, unit of time, index, report, or whatever else represents the focus of the measurable annual goal. If the goal is to increase weekly test grades, end-of-the-chapter quizzes, or quarterly classroom test grades, the test, quiz, etc. provides the benchmark data. In this case, the data is not in the form of traditional pretest-posttest data in which the same test, comprised of a structured set of items, is administered on two or more occasions in order to determine whether there has been a change in performance.

Measured PLP

A *level* of performance indicates that the PLP is a measured level of performance. Stating that a child cannot read because of mental retardation is meaningless from the standpoint of what the child can or cannot do. Likewise, stating that content is too difficult for a child might be a factual statement, but it does not indicate a specific level of performance. The question is not that the material is too difficult, but what material is too difficult and how much of the material is too difficult. From an intervention standpoint there is a difference between understanding nothing, to understanding 25 percent, 50 percent, or 75 percent. If a goal is measurable, the measurements must be made before, during, and at the completion of the specially designed instruction.

The IDEA-1990 regulations described the role of PLEP in the context of measuring progress by a statement that is "written in objective measurable terms, to the extent possible."[23] These regulations also described IEP short-term instructional objectives as "measurable, intermediate steps between a handicapped child's present levels of educational performance and the annual goals that are established for the child. The objectives are developed based on a logical breakdown of the major components of the annual goals, and can serve as milestones for measuring progress toward meeting the goals."[24] Compare this to the interpretation of short-term objectives or benchmarks in the IDEA-1997 regulations that are intended "to gauge, at intermediate times during the year, how well the child is progressing toward achievement of the annual goal."[25]

Figure III. The Relation between PLP and Benchmarks

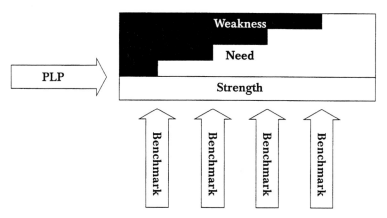

Figure III shows the relationship between PLEP, an area of weakness and strength, the resulting need, benchmarks, and the goal. As can be seen, the beginning level of performance is the initial point for planning progress toward the completion of a goal. The benchmarks provide a plan for improving performance or skill level over the course of the year. The PLP is the first of a series of benchmarks, and each subsequent benchmark provides a standard for evaluating progress toward the annual goal (the last benchmark). Each objective or benchmark represents an anticipated level of performance, measured at periodic intervals, that are used to monitor and report progress to parents; the goal is the anticipated level of performance at the end of the year. The area of need is defined by the strength and weakness and bridges the gap between PLP and the goal.

THE PLEP STATEMENT

PLEP Documentation

An IEP requires "a statement of the child's present levels of educational performance" and not a section in the IEP that specifically identifies Present Levels of Educational Performance. Because an IEP need not "include information under one component of a child's IEP that is already contained under another component of the child's IEP,"[26] general and instructional data could be described under a section entitled Student Profile, PLEP, Educational Achievement, Evaluation Report, Management Needs, Individual Needs, IEP Levels of Performance, Educational Development, Assessment, Testing Information, Individual Evaluation Report, or Individual Evaluation Summary. In Minnesota the PLEP consists of summary statements for each area of need, and an Assessment Summary Statement may be attached to the PLEP to substantiate the PLEP. With respect to specific PLEP benchmarks, this information could be in one of the aforementioned sections or listed in conjunction with specific measurable annual goals.

The IEP must have general and instructional PLEP data but where the data is included in the IEP depends on how the IEP form is developed and how the IEP process

conceptualized. The PLEP section shown below follows the basic IEP regulations for developing, reviewing, and revising IEP content:

Present Levels of Educational Performance

Student Strengths_____

Parent Concerns_____

Evaluation Summary_____
_____
_____
_____

General Curriculum
Involvement_____
_____

Special Factor Needs:
_____ Behavior _____ LEP _____ Braille _____ Communication _____ Assistive Technology

---

Of the many scores and grades noted in the evaluation summary, significant areas of need should be highlighted. If reading vocabulary is an area of need that is addressed by a measurable annual goal, there should be standardized score data to substantiate this need. The evaluation report could also include specific curriculum-based data to determine specific instructional needs. The classroom or special education teacher might discern, based on reports and test performance, an area of need and develop a curriculum-based assessment to indicate a beginning level of performance for a measurable annual goal. If a child receives a standard score of 70 in reading and a score of 25 percent on a curriculum-based reading assessment, both scores could be included in the PLEP, and both would provide a logical frame of reference for the measurable annual goal.

PLP: Reading score = 70
Curriculum-based vocabulary score = 25%

Measurable Annual Goal:
Curriculum-based vocabulary score = 85%

In this example the general and instructional data (the present level of performance or specific score) are both included in the PLEP statement, and the instructional data serves as the beginning benchmark for the measurable annual goal. Rather than including both general and instructional data in the PLEP statement, the statement might only indicate the impact of the disability on reading, and the instructional data is reserved for the measurable annual goal. This generally occurs when the evaluation report contains only standard scores and the IEP team then develops measurable annual goals with limited instructional curriculum-based data. For example, a child receives a standard score in reading of 70 (or two standard deviations below the mean) and a goal is developed to increase curriculum-based vocabulary to 70, 80, or 85 percent or whatever seems to be an appropriate level of performance. The problem with this plan is the indirect correspondence between the standard score and curriculum-based expected level of performance. The actual beginning curriculum-based vocabulary level could be 0 percent or 70 percent so that the goal might not reflect a reasonable anticipated level of performance. In the example below, the relationship between the PLP and the goal is minimal because there is no simple way to determine the relationship between a score two standard deviations below the mean on one test and a percentage of 85 on a curriculum-based assessment.

PLP: Reading Score = 70

Measurable Annual Goal:
 Curriculum-based vocabulary score = 85%

Another approach is to begin the IEP with a general report of the individual evaluation and resulting needs, and then link the PLEP with specific measurable annual goals. In this case, the general PLEP information is contained in the evaluation summary, student profile, or whatever is used to explain the child's overall assessments and needs.

Present Level of Performance

Academic Needs

Reading vocabulary standard score = 70
Curriculum-based vocabulary score = 25%

Measurable Annual Goal = 85%

Short-term Objectives or Benchmarks
1 = 40%
2 = 55%
3 = 70%

A variation of this approach is to include the general and instructional levels of performance in the PLEP statement, and then specify the PLEP as the first benchmark and the goal as the last benchmark:

Present Level of Performance

Academic Needs

Reading vocabulary standard score = 70
Curriculum-based vocabulary score = 25%

Measurable Annual Goal = 85%

Short-term Objectives or Benchmarks

Benchmark #1 = 25% (PLP)
Benchmark #2 = 40%
Benchmark #3 = 55%
Benchmark #4 = 70%
Benchmark #5 = 85% (Goal)

The individual evaluation frequently centers about standardized test scores so that when the data is discussed at the IEP meeting specific instructional data has not been collected. This presents an obvious problem when developing IEP goals because often little or no thought has been given to the child's level of performance for each annual goal. When this occurs, the goals that are developed must be vague and judgmental because there is scant data to construct meaningful annual measurable goals with specific beginning levels of performance.

There is not a single format for developing a PLEP statement other than the child's level of functioning should proceed from the general to the specific. With this basic rule in mind, the simplest approach for developing a PLEP statement is to provide a completely open-ended section with no instructions or guidelines. This method offers little structure (which can result in idiosyncratic PLEP statements), but an open-ended PLEP statement does require a *consideration* of levels of performance and not merely restating existing achievement test data or ratings of performance.

Present Levels of Educational Performance

An open-ended PLEP statement can result in test scores, overall ratings, or curriculum-based assessments. In Montana the PLEP statement requires that "test scores alone are insufficient" for indicating levels of performance, while in New York "standardized test results that are pertinent to the impact of the disability on the child's performance may be listed on the IEP. If test scores are listed, they must be self-explanatory or clearly explained."[27]

The PLEP statement is a method for highlighting a student's educational needs, both academic and nonacademic. The PLEP gives purpose to the IEP and provides the foundation for developing a reasonably calculated individualized plan of instruction. There is no list of test scores, observational information or areas of educational performance that should be included in the PLEP,

or information that should be excluded, other than all information that indicates the unique needs of the child and the direction for meeting these needs. For one child, subtest scores might be appropriate; for a second child with behavior management needs, a concise statement concerning the frequency of specific types of behaviors might be appropriate; while for a student at the secondary level who is seeking a regular high school diploma, performance on statewide tests or an advanced placement test might be critical, especially if acceptable statewide test performance is required to receive a regular high-school diploma.

The instructions for the PLEP statement can emphasize the importance of showing how levels of performance affects regular curriculum involvement:

> **Present Level of Performance**: State the child's present levels of educational performance, and how the disability affects involvement and progress in the general curriculum, or for preschool children, involvement in appropriate activities.

In New Jersey the PLEP instructions follow IDEA-1997 guidelines for IEP development by requiring consideration of the initial or most recent evaluation, a listing of evaluation data such as teacher reports, classroom observations), the strengths of the child, and parent concerns. The PLEP instruction in the Georgia IEP highlights several regulatory guidelines[28] which essentially restate the IDEA requirement to "consider (i) the strengths of the child and the concerns of the parents for enhancing the education of their child; and (ii) the results of the initial evaluation or most recent evaluation of the child."[29]

> **Present Level of Performance**: (Include, as appropriate, a description of the disability and its effect on educational performance; results of the most recent evaluation; strengths/weaknesses; how the disability affects the student's involvement and progress in the general curriculum; for preschool children, how the disability affects participation in appropriate activities; concerns of the parent for the education of the child.)

The PLEP statement can summarize the individual evaluation, while emphasizing significant elements of the individual evaluation (e.g., intellectual functioning and standardized achievement score data), and then consolidating levels of performance into predetermined areas:

> **Present Levels of Educational Performance**
>
> Academic Development:
>
> Social Development:
>
> Physical Development:
>
> Intellectual Development:

Many IEPs structure the PLEP statement around strengths and weaknesses or strengths and needs. Just as the PLEP statement can include general and instructional levels of performance, a distinction can be made between general and instructional strengths and weaknesses. A general strength and weakness night be excellent verbal skills and poor reading, average vocabulary but poor comprehension, or good computational skills but poor word problems skills. Whereas the general PLEP strength and weakness indicates the general direction and the magnitude of need, the instructional strength and weakness signifies what behavior or skill the measurable annual goal will address and the level of performance of the behavior or skill. For example, the general statement of strengths and weaknesses might include language arts as an area of strength and study skills and grades as areas of weakness. The specific weakness might include not completing a certain number of classroom assignments and below passing grades in social studies, science and mathematics. In addition to developing goals to address these specific weakness, the overall strength in language arts might be used to improve study skills and to address content area performance.

Present Levels of Educational Performance

Describe the child's strengths and weaknesses:

Describe how the child's disability affects involvement and progress in the general curriculum:

Describe the concerns of the parent:

In New York present levels of educational performance are designated for academic/educational achievement, social development, physical development, and management needs. Each of these areas requires a statement of Present Levels, Abilities, and Needs.

Present Levels of Performance and Individual Needs

Present Levels of Performance:

1. Academic/Educational Achievement and Learning Characteristics: Address current levels of knowledge and development in subject and skill areas, including activities of daily living, level of intellectual functioning, adaptive behavior, expected rate of progress in acquiring skills and information and learning style.

Present Levels: _____

_____

Abilities:_____

_____

Needs:_____

_____

If level of performance is defined as level of ability or skill achieved, the PLEP statement can link areas of need to corresponding goals. The purpose of the following PLEP statement is to indicate pertinent scores, observations and assessment that show present levels of performance and then what specific needs must be addressed by special instruction and related services. Although there is a correspondence between levels of performance and needs, not all needs will require a measurable annual (e.g., a child might require a related service or modification that does not result in educational improvement).

Present Levels of Performance and Individual Needs

Present Levels of Performance:_____

_____

Needs:

1._____

2._____

3._____

4._____

5._____

The purpose of the above PLEP statement is to show the linkage between levels of performance, needs, and subsequently measurable annual goals. General PLEP data might include information that a nine-year-old child is in the 4th grade and reading at the second grade level. The areas of need might involve improving reading vocabulary, reading fluency, and reading comprehension. In this situation, the PLEP statement provides the basic data, and the needs section identifies areas that must be addressed by specific measurable annual goals. Each area of need is supported by PLEP data, and each area of need has a corresponding measurable annual goal.

Strengths: Good verbal skills, follows direction, above average work when completed

Weaknesses: Difficulty relating to adults, limited interaction with other students, truant, poor grades, does not complete assigned work

PLP: Completes 0% of homework assignments

Goal: Completes 100% of homework assignments by June 15

Present Level of Educational Performance		
Strengths: Good verbal skills, follows direction, above average work when completed		
Weaknesses: Difficulty relating to adults, limited interaction with other students, truant, poor grades, does not complete assigned work		

Measurable Annual Goal		
Completes 100% of homework assignments by June 15		

Short-term Objectives	Date	Criterion
Completed homework assignments	Nov. 15	0%
"	Feb. 15	25%
"	Apr. 15	50%
"	June 15	75%

BEGINNING BENCHMARKS

There must be a beginning level of performance for each measurable annual goal. The plan for specially designed instruction is represented by measurable annual goals and short-term objectives or benchmarks, and is predicated on improving areas of performance that are affected by the child's disability.

There are certain situations when a beginning level of performance is not directly available because test administration is very controlled. For districtwide tests previous test scores or practice tests can indicate anticipated levels of performance. Statewide tests are somewhat more of a problem in that they might be given every two or three years. However, previous tests, available practice tests, sample tests or teacher-made simulations and test questions can provide some insight as to a child's performance as well as a measure for evaluating and reporting progress during the year.

The General Curriculum

The PLEP should focus on strengths and weakness arising from a child's disability to allow the child to be involved in and progress in the general curriculum. The task is not to teach the general curriculum, exactly as used with nondisabled children, to all children with disabilities; nor is the task to relate each goal to the general curriculum. The task is to define needs and corresponding levels of performance that arise from the child's disability that will allow participation in the general curriculum. In concert with the least restrictive environment philosophy of IDEA, children with disabilities are to be educated with children who are not disabled to the maximum extent appropriate.

In determining how a child can be involved and progress in the general curriculum, the child's level of performance in the curriculum must be evaluated. This is accomplished by evaluating what behavior, skill, or ability required to be involved and progress in the general curriculum is lacking. If a student cannot take notes, note-taking ability should be assessed. If a child has difficulty with expressive language, expressive language should be measured. If a child has "behavioral difficulties," exactly what behavioral difficulties the child has, and where, when, and how often they occur should be evaluated. To determine the ability to be involved in and progress in the general curriculum, curriculum performance must be evaluated. This is accomplished by curriculum-based assessment which is "the process of determining students' *instructional needs* within a curriculum by directly assessing specific curriculum skills" (Choate et al., 1995, p. 17). As stated in the 1990 regulations, goals and objectives are intended to close the gap between present levels of performance and anticipated or indicated ability. For example, if a child has a problem involving word recognition "the IEP goals and objectives would be directed toward (1) closing the gap between the child's indicated ability and current level of functioning, and (2) helping the child increase the ability to use word attack skills effectively (or to find some other approach to increase independence in reading)."[30]

There might be occasions when a need and corresponding level of performance is recognized but no educational intervention is available or possible. A student might be truant and all strategies to promote the very obvious need for school attendance might be ineffective; or a child might need to be less physically aggressive or verbally abusive to other students and/or adults, but all attempts to address this need have failed. Not every need can be addressed effectively, but the IEP should attempt honestly explicate all areas of need even if an appropriate method to address the need is less than clear.

This good-faith effort to clearly articulate a child's unique needs provides the basis for designing goals that address these needs and for measuring progress. An IEP can only be effective if there is a direct relationship between PLEP and goals. If there is a need, there should be a level of performance; and if there is a goal there should be a level of performance. If a goal does not relate to some measure of educational performance, either general or instructional, there is no meaningful way to determine whether the goal actually addresses a need or if the need is being met.

BEGINNING LEVELS OF PERFORMANCE DATA

Beginning levels of performance should be conceptualized as beginning benchmark data. If there is no data, there is no beginning benchmark. If there is no beginning benchmark, the goal is likely deficient.

Each measurable annual goal is comprised of short-term objectives or benchmarks that are used to monitor progress toward achieving the goal. In order to develop a sequence of short-tem objectives or benchmarks, there must be a beginning level of performance or beginning benchmark. That is, if the goal is to decrease a behavior to 0, the level of that behavior at the beginning of the instructional period must be known; if the goal is to increase performance to 80%, the percentage beginning level or performance must be known. If there is no beginning level of performance of a measurable annual goal, in all likelihood the ability or behavior has never been measured. A goal might be measurable, but there is a vast difference between a measurable goal and an ability or behavior that has been actually measured.

Meaningful measurable annual goals are based on measures that actually exist and are used. The major problem with most IEPs, and the major reason why IEPs do not provide reasonably calculate programs, is that specific levels of performance before, during and at the end of the school year are not determined. A goal might be measurable, but in many situations is not measured. If the goal is to improve reading, there should be a specific task, test, or activity that results in a measurement that shows how a child is performing. If a child has a need to improve phonics or word attack skills, these skills should be measured. If a child has a writing need, there should be a specific task that generates a writing sample that can be used to determine the present level of performance and progress. The "ability to demonstrate correct punctuation," "an understanding of sentence structure," or the "ability to write complete sentences with 80 percent accuracy" imply measurement or measurability but are not necessarily real measures. A measure could involve copying sentences, copying from dictation, or writing a story about a picture or sequence of pictures, or a language experience story. Or the measure

could be writing samples from reports, essays, assignments, or journals.

The importance of actually measuring performance at the beginning of the school year, during the year (short-term objectives or benchmarks), and at the end of the year (the actual goal) is critical for children having behavioral needs. If a child is classified as emotionally disturbed, the specific behaviors that gave rise to this classification must be addressed . . . and this can only be accomplished if the behavior is identified and measured. If a child has an attention deficit, the specific behaviors that suggest the attention deficit should be identified and measured. Statements like "decreasing inappropriate behavior by teacher observation" are not only vague but deceptive. Not only are specific behaviors undefined, but there is no indication that teacher observation has been used to determine the present level of inappropriate behaviors, what exactly is meant by inappropriate behavior, or how teacher observation data will be recorded. Of course, a goal to decrease inappropriate behavior as determined by teacher observation is not designed to actually address a specific need, but to *show* that a goal has been written that relates to a general area of need.

For every measurable annual goal, there should be a real measure that is used to determine the beginning level of performance before specially designed instruction is implemented to achieve the goal. For measurable annual goals involving inappropriate behavior, the measure might be a tally sheet for two or three specific behaviors to determine when, where and how frequently the behaviors occur. This is in contrast to a hypothetical measure such as "to improve classroom behavior to 80 percent based on teacher observation." Aside from the fact that 80 percent is meaningless in this context (other than giving the pretense of measurability), what will be measured and how it will be measured are not specified.

Measurable annual goals are based on measured performance. If a child has problems in reading comprehension as determined by standardized tests and the goal is "to improve reading comprehension," how comprehension is measured, before providing instruction in reading comprehension, must be determined. The result of a measurement might be that given ten questions, a child is able to answer only one correctly. On the other hand, the results might indicate that the child is able to answer all questions with 100 percent accuracy. If the child is able to answer questions with 100 percent accuracy, the goal as stated has already been achieved and the only logical recourse is either to re-examine the child's reading needs or re-conceptualize the goal.

Difficulties in specifying present levels of educational performance are often caused by vague, sometimes impractical and often poorly considered measurements of performance. If a need is adequately measured, that need can be stated in terms of a level of performance; and if a child's level of perfor-

mance is adequately stated, a measurable short-term objective can be developed that will result in measurements to determine progress toward the goal.

Each beginning or present level of performance must possess the following characteristics: First, the skill or ability must be measurable or have the capacity of being measured. Even vague, generic and imprecise goals often meet this minimal criterion. Second, a measure (e.g., test, evaluation technique) must exist to evaluate the trait, ability or skill. When the measure is "teacher observation" or a "teacher-made test," a measure often does not exist but a hope that the teacher will develop an observational protocol or a teacher-made test to evaluate the behavior. Third, the level of performance must be measured. And fourth, the measured behavior must result in a measurement (e.g., score, rating, statement of performance, etc.). The reality of a beginning level of performance does not lie in the promise of measurability, but a very real and quantifiable index of performance or behavior.

Unit of Measurement

If an ability or skill is measured, there must be a unit of measurement. The unit of measurement could be a raw score (e.g., number correct or incorrect), a frequency, a standardized score, a rating, a qualitative measurement, a statement of mastery or some other unit of measurement that represents performance. The following describes the various types of unit of measurements that can be used to interpret general and instructional levels of performance in terms of advantages and possible limitations.

Raw Scores. A raw score is generally the number of correct or incorrect responses on a test or assessment. On a 30-item reading

vocabulary test, if a student answers 15 items correctly the corresponding raw score is 15; for a test comprised of 100 primary addition facts, 80 correct answers would correspond to a raw score of 80. For many diagnostic and classroom-made tests, raw scores can provide invaluable information concerning educational performance. To report that the student has good computational skills, but can answer only one of ten end-of-chapter word problems provides important information concerning the student's strengths and weaknesses. From an instructional standpoint this information is an instructional elaboration of knowing that the student is one standard deviation below the mean on a mathematics computation test. Here, the use of a raw score is not intended to indicate the impact of the child's disability on mathematical performance, but to provide information relating to classroom performance.

Percentages. A percentage is the proportion of observed cases or events, divided by the total number of cases or events, and multiplied by 100. A student receives a score of 20 on a 25-item teacher-made spelling test and the percent correct is

$$Percent = \frac{Score}{Number} (100) = \frac{X}{N} (100)$$

so that the student's score is 20/25 (100) or 80%; a child is asked to identify 40 vocabulary words, is able to name 20, and the percent correct is 20/40 (100) or 50%; or a student does not complete homework assignments in a course where this is a significant factor so that of the 20 homework assignments, the student completes 4 or 20%. Most curriculum-based assignments are easily converted to percentages. A child answers 5 of 8 questions after reading a section in a grade level social studies book; or a child is able to identify 10 of 12 items when shown when shown a series of illustrations.

The distinction between a calculated percentage and a percentage rating is extremely important. A calculated percentage of mathematics problems completed might be 10 of 40 or 25%, but a teacher might rate the child's ability to complete mathematics problems as 10%, 50% , or 75%. The calculated percentage is empirical, while the rating percentage is an estimate which, admittedly, can be very good, or a completely arbitrary value (which is not very good). For example, a teacher assigns a grade of "75%" to an essay based on past experience and expertise in evaluating the overall quality of essays. This holistic percentage could be used as a beginning benchmark but this spe-

cific rating depends on a whole array of factors such as the teacher's frame of mind when making the evaluation, the degree of teacher expertise and experience, and the emphasis of the evaluation at the time of testing. For example, the story line or content might be emphasized for this evaluation, but spelling and writing mechanics for the next.

The advantage of a percentage is that it provides a very straightforward and easily interpretable index of performance; the disadvantage is that it does not indicate the actual or possible number of occurrences. A score of 75% on a test could be the result of correctly answering 3 of 4 items or 24 of 32 items. In the case of the former, one less correct would result in a percentage of 50, while one less for the latter would result in a percentage of 72.

Because most standardized tests have a considerable range of difficulty, a percentage can be misleading. For example, a child answer 25 of 50 questions correctly on a standardized test, yet the 50% might be equivalent to a percentile rank of 90. Of course, the purpose of the standardized test is to understand a child's performance with respect to a norm group and not to determine the number of questions that can be answered correctly.

Trials or Attempts. Trials used to indicate different attempts to consistently complete a task (e.g., a child is able to identify at least twenty-five of thirty words in three consecutive trials or in three of four trials). The concept of a series of trials adds an element of reliability or repeatability to the measurement. For instance, the task is not simply to reach the criterion but to reach the criterion on several occasions. Other terms that can be used in place of trials include attempts, occasions, occurrences, and events. The trials required to reach the criterion can occur in a relatively short period of time or over weeks or even months. For a child with a severe behavioral disorder the goal might be to exhibit less than twenty behaviors on five consecutive days. Academically, the task might be to spell at least 45 of 50 words on three separate occasions.

Measurable annual goal benchmarks could be considered as separate trials, but the total time span between benchmarks necessary to reach criterion might be excessive in terms of adjusting task or content after the criterion has been reached. For example, if the task is to identify 100 words at three consecutive benchmark points, the criterion might not be reached even if the progression toward the criterion is linear over the course of the year (e.g., the number of words identified at each benchmark might be thirty, sixty and ninety).

Indices. Indices of performance can be used to indicate the PLEP for a specific area of educational performance. A child writes a 120-word essay (paragraph, etc.), and the total number of errors (spelling, punctuation, capitalization) and the "percent" correct is determined by

$$100 - \frac{Errors}{Total\ Words}\ (100)$$

so that if the total errors for this assignment is 22, the resulting score is 100-22/120 (100) or 82 (81.67). In this case the total number of errors could actually exceed the number of errors so that the index could be greater than 100. Nonetheless, this index of writing performance might be very useful for showing the relationship between errors and the number of words written.

Instead of expressing performance as a percentage-like index, the ratio of Total Words to Errors could be used so that 120/22 signifies a ratio of Total Words to Errors of 120/22 or one error for every 5.45 words. If this measurement is used in conjunction with a measurable goal, the annual goal might be to reduce the number of ratio of errors from one every 5.45 words to one every 3.0 words.

Learning rates represent another useful form of index. For example, reading rate can be defined as (Words Per Minute)/Minutes so that if a child reads 200 words in five minutes, reading rate is 40 WPM. For writing, in addition to decreasing the number of errors, writing speed might be a point of concern. Rate of writing is seven words per minute, a goal might be to increase this rate to 10. Often the rate of performance is indicated in a goal or objective although an index of work rate is not specified (e.g., the child will write at least a 50-word paragraph in five minutes.).

Although the focal point of instruction is often to accelerate learning rate, this is not always the case. The time required for a child to read a 75-word passage might be 15 seconds for a oral reading rate of 75/15 or 5 words per second so that the reading rate per 60 seconds is 300 words. If comprehension is low, punctuation is ignored and little attempt is made to decode words, one goal might be to reduce this high rate of oral reading.

Indices can be used in a number of creative ways to measure performance. If a child is a word reader, the ratio of words to pauses might be a useful index. If a child is asked to read the following sentence, where a / is recorded by the teacher to indicate a pause, the ratio of words to pauses would be 12/6 or 2 (one pause for every two words).

Mr. Jones was/ late/ when he/ arrived/ at the/ airport/ Sunday morning.

Various indices have been developed to interpret learning performance. One measure used in conjunction with curriculum-based data is to compare a typical student's performance to that of a specific individual's performance or

$$Discrepancy\ Index = \frac{Typical\ Peer\ Performance}{Individual\ Students\ Performance}$$

so that if the typical number of spelling words known on a 50 item spelling test is 40, a significant discrepancy would be a discrepancy level of at least 2.0 or 40/20=2.0 so that a child would need a score on the test below 20 for the level of performance to be considered discrepant. If the average reading rate is 100 words per minute, and a child's reading rate is 50, the goal might be to improve performance from 2 to an end-of year goal level of 1 (or from 50 to 100). In Iowa a discrepancy criterion of 2.0 is required; that is, typical performance must be at least twice as great as individual performance before the difference is considered discrepant.[31]

Frequency. Frequency indicates the number of occurrences of an event or behavior over a period of time. The frequency of a behavior or event is a very simple index that can provide critical diagnostic information, yet one that is often overlooked. If a child exhibits a certain behavior in the classroom (e.g., cursing, refusal to participate or work, pushes other students), information should be available indicating the frequency of occurrence. Data regarding frequency of a behavior or events can be provided by regular classroom teachers, parents, and other teachers and school personnel (e.g., aides). If a child's behavior is a problem, the behavior, as well as the frequency of the behavior, should be specified. This alone would do much to improve the measurement of performance. For example, if the goal is to improve a student's self concept there must

be some reason, a behavior or a series of behaviors that indicates self concept is a problem. Assume that one reason is that the child often says "I can't" when asked to do a task or participate in an event. The task might be to reduce this class of response and to more readily participate in classroom activities.

There are a variety of ways for measuring behavior in addition to frequency. In some instances, the duration of behavior might be important. If a child is unable to attend to classroom tasks, and the goal is to increase this ability, information pertaining to the duration of behavior might be the focus of a measurable annual goal. In order to gather this type of data, the teacher or aide would need to record the amount of time that a child was able to attend to a task, the amount of time a tantrum lasted, or the amount of time needed to complete an assignment.

Frequencies are not confined to social or interpersonal skills. For a child who has a language impairment, the number of times the child demonstrates receptive understanding (e.g., follows a direction), the number of words spoken, the length of spoken sentences all might be extremely important for determining individual goals. Or when evaluating classroom work samples, the frequency of specific errors, correct responses, or completed assignments might be noted to better interpret actual classroom performance.

Indirect Measures

The measures discussed below are generally indirect assessments of level of performance; that is, the resulting unit of measurement is based on the judgement, interpretation or opinion of an evaluator as opposed to responses that are objectively scores. This is

really an oversimplification and tends to denigrate evaluations that are not objectively scores. For example, the best way to score a writing sample might be to use a rating rather than objective criteria (e.g., the number of complete sentences).

Checklist Data. There are several ways in which checklist data can be used as a beginning benchmark. First, the total number of areas checked could be used as an index of present instructional needs. If the checklist is for writing, the items might include spelling, vocabulary, syntax, ideation, capitalization, mechanics, usage, organization and handwriting. The total number of items checked can suggest the diversity of writing needs, but the checklist does not indicate the magnitude of need in each subarea. Second, if the checklist items are sequentially related, the checklist items could indicate the series of benchmarks. If the goal is to read a book, write a report and edit the report, the first objective or task is to read a book. Third, if the checklist items are specific, the checklist can provide insights for developing instructional activities (e.g., decrease word reading, teach regrouping or develop sentence organization skills). When this approach is used, each activity becomes an objective. The annual goal, based on the present level of performance, is to reduce the number of items checked. Of course, the problem with this strategy is that the checklist does not provide for a continuum of item performance. If the checklist items are general categories, this problem can be rectified by rating each item. If the checklist items are task specific (e.g., read a book, say "Bye," add 2 + 5, use a fork when eating), each item is either achieved or not achieved. In this case, the data is categorical rather than representing a linear hierarchy of tasks.

For a classroom behavior checklist, the data could be a qualitative interpretation of specific behaviors. For example, if disrupts is checked, the reason for the disruptions, where and why they occur, could be considered. For the below checklist items, if all eight categories were checked, one goal might be to select several critical areas, and develop a plan to reduce the items checked from 8 to 6.

____teases	____gossips
____exaggerates	____manipulates
____disrupts	____threatens
____fights	____interrupts

The total checklist elements checked can provide an overall index of need. Although an overall checklist index does not take into account the importance of the individual items checked. For the above, fighting and gossiping might both be checked, but this does not indicate either the magnitude or the frequency of the problem for either.

Reading tests often use checklist to denote general reading needs. The checklist categories listed below are not mutually exclusive so that a child who is a word-by-word reader might have poor phrasing, but a child with poor phrasing might not be a word-by-word reader. As is the case with all checklists, one of the primary problems is determining the elements that should comprise the list. In the below list, specific categorizes could be added for a variety of specific skills such as the ability to use blends (e.g., bl, sn, dr), digraphs (e.g., ch, th, sh), vowels combinations (e.g., ea, ay, oa), dipthongs (e..g, oi, oy, ow), etc.

____word-by-word reading
____poor word attack skills
____poor pronunciation
____can't identify root words
____can't use contractions
____difficulty with consonants
____difficulty with blends
____substitutions
____word guessing
____poor phrasing
____word guessing
____poor phonics skills
____difficulty with prefixes and suffixes
____poor syllabication

_____difficulty with vowels
_____omissions
_____additions
_____poor comprehension

Checklist data can be used to indicate specific instructional needs or as an overall index of performance. For the above checklist, one element of the PLEP might be that word guessing (the word car is read as sky) is a problem. If word guessing is a severe problem, a separate goal might be required to decrease this problem. If word guessing is just one of many items checked, overall checklist performance might provide a good description of beginning level of performance. In either case, specific objectives would need to address the needs identified by specific checklist items.

In mathematics checklists are frequently used to provide a diagnostic summary of general error types:

Check each area in which the students has difficulty:
_____counting errors
_____did not add carried number
_____wrong operation
_____did not carry
_____wrote carried number in answer

As with reading diagnostic checklists, error checklists can provide a useful summary of areas of need and specific weaknesses, but checklist data does not eliminate the need to obtain actual performance data (e.g., frequency of specific errors).

Checklists are useful when they help identify specific areas of need; they are not useful when the list includes items or skills far above or below a child's ability range. If a child is checked as having problems in all categories, this would not mean that each category requires remediation. If a child has difficulty with initial consonants, there is an extremely good probability that the child will have problems with letter combinations. Likewise, if a child has no sight vocabulary, the child will probably exhibit problems in other reading areas. The primary goal might focus on the development of sight vocabulary and not all the items on the list simply because they are checked.

For certain tasks checklists can be constructed that suggest a linear relationship between categories so that determining what a child can and cannot do indicates the beginning level of performance. As is the case with most items, the linear relationship between categories is often less than perfect (e.g., a child might not know the alphabet but is able to identify sight words).

_____knows alphabet
_____knows sight words
_____can read sentences
_____can read for meaning
_____can write sentences
_____can write a paragraph

Or combine language, reading and writing:

Check each area of need
_____Receptive vocabulary
_____Expressive vocabulary
_____Reading vocabulary
_____Reading comprehension

Checklist data are also be used in conjunction with a series of tasks (i.e., task analysis) involving anything from making a soup, writing a composition, or following a specific job sequence involving automotive repair or completing a job application form. Overall, checklists can provide very useful screening information concerning specific needs. However, for each item checked on a checklist the extent of the problem must be carefully examined. One child might have all elements of a list checked but have minimal needs, while a second child has only one element checked, but the need in this one area is exceptionally great.

Finally, if a checklist is used to determine beginning levels of instructional performance, thought must be given to how the checklist data will be used to develop an annual goal, and how progress will be monitored and reported based on PLEP checklist data.

Ratings. A rating is based on behavior, often very complex behavior, but the resulting measurement is based on a judgement of performance. Rating scales can involve a simple binary scale; that is, the child possesses the trait, ability or skill (1) or does not (0) so that work habits could be rated as

_____Able to work independently
_____Not able to work independently

Or the rating scale can be comprised of a series of points along a continuum.

_____Can Work Independently
_____Sometimes Needs Help
_____Often Needs Help.
_____Always needs help

Or the trait could be rated on a discrete continuum from 0 to 5, 1 to 5 or 1 to 7:

Work Habits:
Independent 1_/_/_/_5 Not Independent

Work Habits:
Independent 1 2 3 4 5 6 7 Not Independent

The PLEP statement could then indicate a qualitative description of the rating (e.g., sometimes needs help when working independently) or a numerical rating.

Whenever possible evaluation data should be based on actual performance rather than a rating or an indirect assessment of performance. If working independently is an area of need, the PLEP should include an assessment that measures this ability or lack thereof. For instance, simple observational data might be kept to indicate instances of working independently so that the beginning level of performance might be a frequency of 0 per day; or the frequency of instances requiring work assistance might be tallied so the the beginning level of performance is a frequency of 18 per day. In either case, the beginning level of performance provides a benchmark for evaluating subsequent short-term objectives.

When suitable curriculum-based assessments have not been developed, ratings often are the only available source for determining levels of performance. When little thought is given to actually measuring performance, a rating is often cited. If a child is substantially below average in reading comprehension, a goal is written to "comprehend grade level reading materials with 80 percent accuracy as determined by teacher observation." In other words, the teacher is required to rate the child in terms of mastery (i.e., the child has achieved an 80 percent level of accuracy as determined by the judgment of the teacher). If a measure or technique does not exist for the teacher to actually measure reading comprehension performance, the only recourse will be for the teacher to use a holistic rating to judge performance. Thus, a teacher is to answer the following:

What percent reading comprehension accuracy has _____ achieved based on your observations?

Or the percent could be obtained in the form of a rating:

Percent reading comprehension accuracy based on your observations:

10% 20% 30% 40% 50% 60% 70% 80% 90% 100%

or

| Indicate the percent of improvement based on your observations: | % |

Rather than using a rating to holistically assess performance, a more accurate approach would be to have the child read one or more passages from grade level material, ask a series of questions based on what was read, and then indicate the results in the form of a percentage. In this case, the measurement of actual performance is far more useful than a rating of performance in terms of determining need and evaluating progress.

There are constructs in which ratings can provide useful information. Although there are measures of self-concept, a teacher rating of this nebulous construct might be useful. The rating scale can be constructed so as to provide qualitative labels instead of a numerical rating such as

Poor Self-Concept
Below Average Self-Concept
Satisfactory Self-Concept
Above Average Self-Concept
Excellent Self-Concept

Or a simple numerical scale comprised of several items is easily created:

	Low		Average		High
Self-Concept	1	2	3	4	5
Peer Relationships	1	2	3	4	5
Adult Relationships	1	2	3	4	5
Motivation	1	2	3	4	5

For the above scale, if Self-Concept were rated 1, Peer Relationships 2, Adult Relationships 2, and Motivation 1, the summated rating would be 6 and the average rating would be 1.5.

Area	Low	Below Average	Average	Above Average	High
Self-Concept	✔				
Peer Relationships		✔			
Adult Relationships		✔			
Motivation	✔				

The above requires a check to indicate the selected ratings but this could be re-arranged in the form of a graphic scale as shown below:

Rate each of the following items:

Area	Low	Below Average	Average	Above Average	High
Self-Concept					
Peer Relationships					
Adult Relationships					
Motivation					

In both of these examples the qualitative labels are easily converted to a numerical rating. The low Self-Concept and Motivation ratings could be scored as a 1 and the below average Peer and Adult Relationships ratings as a 2. As is the case with the numerical rating scale, summated rating is 6 and the average rating 1.5. In this example, the annual goal might be to increase the summated rating to 12 or an average rating to 3.0.

Although rating scales can provide useful information, the limitation of these scales is often apparent when developing measurable annual goals. For a student who has a rating of "low" in the Self-Concept category, a measurable annual goal of an "above average" rating is judgmental. One teacher might consider a student's Self-Concept low, but a second teacher might view Self-Concept as average. More importantly, the rater might be influenced by several sources of error including that of the error of central tendency (a tendency to rate most traits "average"), halo effect (a tendency to give high ratings), or a severity effect (a tendency to give low ratings). Regarding this last source of error, a teacher might rate a student's Self-Concept low because of other low scores and not because of specific information that directly indicates low Self-Concept.

Ratings and rating scales can provide useful information in the determination of needs and can be very useful in developing certain goals. There is nothing inherently wrong with ratings other than they should not be used as the basis for measuring all goals. Virtually every form of measurement can be cited as the method to evaluate performance when no such measurement will ever be used (or ever exist for that matter). A goal suggests that a child will be evaluated using a teacher-made test, but if the test an assessment does not exist and one is never constructed, the statement that the "child will be evaluated by a teacher-made test" is a fiction constructed for the explicit purpose of creating a false impression of procedural compliance. A child is said to have difficulty following directions, and a check list is identified as being the method to evaluate the ability to follow directions when, in fact, there is no checklist and no real thought has been given to developing one. Or a child is said to need greater class participation and the method said to evaluate this is "class discussion" or "class participation" when no thought has been given to exactly how performance will be measured.

•

There are no restrictions concerning tasks, data, or techniques used to develop the PLEP statement. However, the key to developing an effective PLEP statement goes beyond routine testing and collecting data, and involves a focused effort to really understand "how the disability affects the child's involvement and progress in the general curriculum" and other appropriate activities. This is accomplished by determining general levels of performance, and then discerning specific instructional levels of performance to guide the development of measurable annual goals. When this is accomplished, significant needs will have been determined and the foundation for the IEP will rest in data that shows what the child is presently doing and, most importantly, what the child is anticipated to do by the end of the year.

NOTES

[1] 20 USC 1414(d)(1)(A)(i).

[2] 34 CFR 300, Appendix C, Question #36.

[3] *Ibid.*

[4] IDEA-1990, 34 CFR 300, Appendix C, Question #36.

[5] *Ibid.*, Question #36(b).

[6] *Ibid.*, Question #36(b).

[7] *Ibid.*, Question #36(c).

[8] IDEA-1990, 34 CFR 300, Appendix C, Question #39.

[9] IDEA-1990, 34 CFR 300, Appendix C, Question #36(a).

[10] 34 CFR 300, Appendix A, Question #1.

[11] Guidelines for completing the sample IEP (1998). New York State Education Department.

[12] Regulations of the Commissioner of Education, the State Education department, Albany New York (Part 200). See 200.4(c)((2)(i) for PLEP and 200.1(kk) for the four subareas.

[13] 707 KAR 1:210, Individual education programs, Section 4. (1) Present level of performance.

[14] Pennsylvania Department of Education, Bureau of Special Education, descriptions of the sections of the school age IEP Format B, Individualized Education Program (1998).

[15] Massachusetts Department of Education. (1966). Question and answer guide on the new special education individualized educational plan (IEP).

[16] Bateman, Barbara D. Writing Individualized Education Programs (IEPs) for Success, Learning Disabilities Association.

[17] Oregon Department of Education (1998). Behavioral Research and Teaching.

[18] Oregon Department of Education, Oregon Office of Special Education, Form 581-5148T (revised 7/98).

[19] IDEA-1990, 34 CFR 300, Appendix C, Question #36(a).

[20] 9th Circuit Court, No. 97-35711, 1998.

[21] Education for All Handicapped Children Act of 1975, Report N. 94-332, June 26, 1975 (to accompany HR 7217).

[22] Standards for Ohio Schools, Ohio Department of Education, 1996, Columbus, Ohio.

[23] IDEA-1990, 34 CFR 300, Appendix C, Question #36(b).

[24] *Ibid.*, Question #39.

[25] 34 CFR 300, Appendix A, Question #1.

[26] 34 CFR 300.346(e). Construction.

[27] Guidelines for Completing the Sample IEP, New York State Education Department, Albany, New York.

[28] 34 CFR 300.346(a)(1) and 34 CFR 300.347(a)(1).

[29] 34 CFR 300.346(a)(1)(i) & (ii). Also, in 346(a)(1)(iii) the IEP team must also consider the child's performance on general state or districtwide assessments.

[30] IDEA-1990, 34 CFR 300, Appendix C, Question #40.

[31] Iowa Technical Assistance Guide for Learning Disability, Iowa Department of Education, Bureau of Special Education, Des Moines, Iowa, 1997.

Chapter 6

MEASURABLE ANNUAL GOALS, SHORT-TERM OBJECTIVES OR BENCHMARKS

SPECIALLY DESIGNED INSTRUCTION means that the method of instruction, the content, or where the instruction is provided is adapted or modified to address unique needs that result from a child's disability, and to allow the child to be involved in and progress in the general curriculum so that the child can meet the educational standards of the school district that apply to all children.[1] The goal is to ensure access and to enable involvement in the general curriculum. Of course, the extent of regular curriculum involvement and progress depends on the child's needs, disability, and the severity of the disability.

The purpose of an IEP is to develop and implement an appropriate instructional plan that addresses each child's unique needs, and the essential element of this plan is defined by the measurable annual goals, short-term objectives, or benchmarks. Measurable annual goals and objectives provide the strategic framework for developing and implementing the IEP,[2] and constitutes the plan for what the child will achieve during the course of the year.

Measurable annual goals and short-term objectives not only provide a format for delineating a child's instructional plan, but serves as a vehicle for implementing the philosophy of high standards and expectations for children with disabilities. The intent of IDEA-1997 regarding general curriculum involvement is to redefine special education from a fragmented, arbitrary and teacher-defined curriculum to one in which the focus is the general curriculum and the expected level of performance is high because

> research, demonstration, and practice in special education and related disciplines have demonstrated that an effective educational system now and in the future must maintain high academic standards and clear performance goals for children with disabilities, consistent with the standards and expectations for all students in the educational system, and provide for appropriate and effective strategies and methods to ensure that students who are children with disabilities have maximum opportunities to achieve those standards and goals.[3]

Both PL 94-142 and IDEA-1990 required a statement of annual goals, including short-term instructional objectives,[4] and "appropriate objective criteria and evaluation procedures and schedules for determining, on at least an annual basis, whether the short-term instructional objectives are being achieved." The requirement for goals and objectives prior to IDEA-1997 was based on the original PL 94-142 definition of an IEP that included "a statement of annual goals, including short-term instructional objectives."[5] This definition is redefined by IDEA-1997 so that goals address needs, enable general curriculum participation, and are measurable. The IDEA-1997 requires

(ii) a statement of measurable annual goals, including benchmarks or short-term objectives, related to -
   (I) meeting the child's needs that result from the child's disability to enable the child to be involved in and progress in the general curriculum; and
   (II) meeting each of the child's other educational needs that result from the child's disability.[6]

The IEP requirement for evaluating goals and objectives also changed so that the task is to actually measure goals and not merely state a criterion and an evaluation procedure as was required by IDEA prior to 1997. For IDEA-1997, the IEP requires a statement of how the child's progress toward the measurable annual goals will be measured, the adequacy of that progress to achieve the goals, and how parents will be regularly informed, as often as parents of nondisabled children, of goal progress.[7]

The difference between the requirements for goals and objectives from 1990 to 1997 is more of an emphasis on interpretation rather than a substantive change. The IDEA-1997 requirement specifies that goals are *measurable*, while IDEA-1990 only stated the need for annual goals and short-term instructional objectives. However, the regulations for IDEA-1990 clearly intended that measurable goals and objectives should be "intermediate steps between the present levels of educational performance of a child with a disability and the annual goals that are established for the child."[8]

State Standards and Goals

With the increasing emphasis on state standards, there is an obvious relationship between IEP goals and state standards and goals. The purpose of measurable annual goals is to enable a child to be involved in the general curriculum, and state standards and goals often guide general curriculum progress. To this end effective schools "must maintain high academic standards and clear performance goals for children with disabilities, consistent with the standards and expectations for all students in the educational system."[9] Most important, schools must provide opportunities for children with disabilities to achieve these standards and goals.

State standards are extremely important, but measurable annual goals are dictated by individual need and not by a predetermined list of standards. The task is not to determine what exact state standards a child is not able to achieve but to address specific educational and disability-related needs that will enable the child to participate and progress in the general curriculum and thereby achieve, to the maximum extent appropriate, state standards.

State standards are similar to IEP measurable annual goals in that both can refer to an annual timeframe or what a child is expected to know, do, or understand over the course of a year. However, state standards often lack the specificity of IEP measurable annual goals. One of the reading/writing standards in Nebraska is that "by the end of the first grade, students will read and comprehend print, and demonstrate the understanding that reading (like conversation) communicates meaning."[10] This standard provides a very useful, albeit general, guideline for what is expected at the end of the first grade. The fact that this standard is general is a reflection of the need to consider the wide range of individual needs for all children in an elementary school setting. This standard could be measured, but a specific measure is not described, nor is a criterion specified. A general educational standard is extremely important for identifying the overall outcome of an educational experience and the general expectations relating to academic skills, knowledge, and understanding. But a general educational standard or goal does not indicate a specific skill or level of individual performance as does an IEP measurable annual goal.

If a school district requires that each IEP goal corresponds to state standards, the standards drive the development of IEP content rather than individual need. This is inappropriate for several reasons. First, state standards usually do not address specific educational needs such as sight vocabulary development, word attack skills, written ideation or organization, specific computational skills, study skills, etc. Second, state standards generally do not focus on disability-related needs such as Braille, assistive technology, and communication skills. Third, state standards for different grade levels might not correspond to a child's specific grade level needs. The standard in the first grade might be to comprehend printed material and the standard in the fourth grade might be to understand and evaluate literature, but for a child in the fourth grade who is reading at the first grade level, the specific goal might be to read content material with 75 percent accuracy. Fourth, a specific need might have no corresponding state standard or goal. If a child bites and kicks in the second grade to the point that regular classroom participation is

not possible, there is probably not a state standard that quite fits this particular need. In this situation, in order for the child to be involved in and progress in the general curriculum, the goal is to reduce these specific behaviors. Fifth, if state standards are required as the basis for each IEP goal, the goals will also require a series of short-term objectives or benchmarks that are measurable. If the state standard is to develop an appreciation of the uniqueness of others, and the child needs to reduce the occurrence of a certain classroom behavior, the short-term objectives or benchmarks must be based on a measurable behavior. This measurable behavior could be a subjective evaluation, based on the often-used teacher observation of the child's *appreciation of the uniqueness of others*, but a more relevant goal would be to reduce the behavior in question.

State standards and goals provide an excellent resource for identifying important areas that constitute the general curriculum, or at least a substantial part of the curriculum, but state standards are generally not substitutes for IEP measurable annual goals. Likewise, state standards provide an important curriculum frame of reference for selecting some IEP goals, but every IEP goal is based on individual needs that results in access to the general curriculum. State standards do not result in the achievement of IEP goals; IEP goals allow for the achievement of state standards to the maximum extent possible.

As much as possible, measurable annual goals should relate to state standards. In New Jersey, goals are related to the curriculum as much as possible so that each measurable annual goal is "related to the core curriculum content standards through the general curriculum unless otherwise required according to the student's educational needs."[11] In this situation, standards provide a general guide for developing goals but not at the expense of a child's individual needs.

Just as a state standard or goal guides regular curriculum participation, participation in the general curriculum is a general goal and not *the* goal. A child with a severe developmental disability might not be able to participate in most grade level academic tasks, but this should not prevent the child from participating, to the maximum extent appropriate, with children who are not disabled. The concept underlying regular classroom participation is not that every child can or will achieve at grade level, but that every child should be given an opportunity to develop general curriculum skills to the maximum extent appropriate. The task is to meet a child's educational needs in the context of educational participation, regardless of how little that participation might be.

Intermediate Steps

An essential feature of IEP objectives is that they are *intermediate* steps between where the child is currently functioning, or the child's present level of educational performance, and the goal. Short-term objectives represent the plan of steps that lead to goal completion. The short-term objectives or benchmarks are not independent of one another but represent a logical sequence of tasks or increasing levels of ability. Many IEPs routinely list the same vague and generic goals and objectives for each child, often unchanged from year to year, that are nothing more than activities marginally related to the goal, but activities that do not logically break down the major components of the goal.[12] The purpose of these goal-related activities is to suggest a program of specially designed instruction, but the activities are not a plan and do not establish milestones for measuring progress toward meeting the goal over the course of the year. The primary purpose of intermediate steps, milestones, and benchmarks is to "enable families, students, and educators to monitor progress during the year and, if appropriate, to revise the IEP consistent with the child's instructional needs."[13]

The need to systemically evaluate progress toward achieving goals, and reporting this progress to parents, is the rationale for short-term objectives and benchmarks. By planning a series of objectives that are designed to systematically achieve a goal, the effectiveness of the plan (i.e., series of objectives) can be evaluated. Short-term objectives are intended to enable educators the opportunity to evaluate progress and monitor progress, and to report this progress to parents as frequently as progress is reported to parents of nondisabled children.

Depending on the goal, each short term objective could be a level of ability, a task or a combination of ability level and task. Because short-term objectives represent a logical breakdown of the goal, the type of objectives developed depends entirely on the goal. If the task is to increase level of performance, such as increasing the ability to improve problem solving skills from 10 percent to 70 percent by the end of the year, each short-term objective could be a benchmark or level of performance. If the beginning level of performance is 10 percent in September, the projected level of performance might be 25 percent in November, 40 percent in February, 55 percent in April, and 70 percent in June.

Goals are defined by intermediate steps. If the goal is to write complete senetnces by the end of the year, each objective might involve increasing the child's ability from a current level (e.g., 0 percent) to 100 percent by the end of the year. Rather than using benchmarks that focus on a single task, the short-term objectives might systematically address a series of skills (e.g., identifying fractions, comparing fractions, adding simple fractions, etc.). If the goal is to receive a score on a test at the end of the year that is comprised of problems involving regrouping, decimals, fractions, and word problems, each short-term objective might focus on a specific skill required to achieve the goal.

Activity objectives. Prior to IDEA-1997, short-term instructional or IEP objectives were more than likely annual activities rather than intermediate steps designed to systematically achieve a goal or to measure progress. For example, if the goal is to "improve study skills," the following activity objectives might be listed to meet this goal:

Goal: Improve Study Skills
Activity Objectives:
1. improve ability to skim content material
2. improve ability to outline material
3. improve ability to highlighting content material
4. improve note-taking skills
5. develop an awareness of metacognitive strategies

The above objectives are related to the goal, but there is no plan to systematically measure or guide progress throughout the year. The "ability to skim content material" might be exactly what the child needs, but if this skill is not measured, the child's ability cannot be monitored, performance evaluated, and progress toward achieving the goal reported to parents. Objectives are often trivialized by generating a seemingly endless list of daily activities. However, the number of activities is not an indication of the appropriateness or effectiveness of the goal. Goal quality is a function of how it meets a

specific need, and how short-term objectives logically break down the goal into a series of steps that can be achieved during the course of a year.

Activity objectives are generally related to the goal, but this is not a breakdown of a goal into a series of logical intermediate steps that can be used to improve performance during the year. If the goal is "to improve writing," and the objectives are to improve writing mechanics, sentence structure, and spelling, each objective is definitely related to the goal. However, the objectives do not present a plan to show how these abilities would be increased during the year. A real plan of instruction might be to decrease the number of writing mechanic, sentence structure and spelling errors each quarter. A real plan is not simply listing activities, but involves progressing from point A (beginning level of performance) to point B (measurable annual goal) by identifying and projecting a series of intermediate levels of performance.

Interpreting short-term objectives to mean an objective achieved in a shorter period of time to a subactivity achieved in an annual period of time was the result of the wording of PL 94-142: the identification of "appropriate objective criteria and evaluation procedures and schedules for determining, on least an annual basis, whether instructional objectives are being achieved."[14] The intent was to develop short-term objectives that decomposed the goal into a series of steps over a period of time, but if the statutory requirement was to evaluate these instructional objectives at least annually, the need to interpret short-term objectives as intermediate steps no longer existed. For example, if the goal is "to improve reading" and the objectives are "to improve vocabulary" and "to improve reading comprehension," the objectives subdivide reading, but not into a series of intermediate steps that can be used to monitor, evaluate, and report progress to parents. In this situation, both objectives are subgoals or annual objectives, and each requires a series of short-term objectives or benchmarks that systematically show progress toward the goal at periodic intervals during the year.

If objectives are short-term, they should be evaluated on a short-term basis; if objectives are actually annual goals, they should be evaluated annually. Annual objectives can be useful, except when presented as a series of disconnected activities; but annual objectives do not monitor progress during the year, which is the very purpose of short-term objectives or benchmarks.

When short-term objectives are written as annual activities, the result can be labor intensive and result in excessive paperwork. However, when short-term objectives are used as meaningful benchmarks to anticipate projected progress, the number of objectives is generally less than five and the teacher has considerable flexibility in selecting activities that will enable children to achieve each objective. Not only will this reduce the need to list activities that are not measurable, but the short-term objectives will represent a meaningful plan (and not simply planning to comply). The result will be to reduce micro-management (see McLaughlin and Warren, 1995, p. 15), and provide a viable system for planning and monitoring progress.

If one purpose of IDEA-1997 is to focus on "resources on teaching and learning while reducing paperwork and requirements that do not assist in improving educational results,"[15] thoughtfully crafted measurable annual goals and short-term objectives that identify significant needs, are based on present levels of performance, and are actually measured will not only reduce paperwork, but will have a meaningful and measurable impact on a child's educational performance.

MEASURABLE ANNUAL GOALS

One of the most important amendments to IDEA-1997 was the change from "annual goals, including short-term instructional objectives"[16] to "measurable annual goals, including benchmarks or shortterm objectives."[17] The purpose of this change was to avoid generic and meaningless goals and objectives (e.g., improve classroom behavior) in which the actual measurement of goal progress or achievement is never a real consideration, and to indicate progress during the school year (e.g., every ten weeks or whenever school progress is reported to parents of nondisabled children).

Measurable annual goals are intended to represent a plan of high expectations, but high expectations in terms of academic and nonacademic achievement of "what a child with a disability can reasonably be expected to accomplish within a twelve month period within the child's special education program."[18] Measurable annual goals are not intended to signify levels of performance that a child has already accomplished, or levels of performance that are not challenging, but rather to show what a child can achieve with specially designed instruction during the school year.

Goal Deficiencies

Criticisms of IEP goals are many but frequently involve the following areas: (1) lack of correspondence between needs and goals, (2) lack of correspondence between goals and objectives, (3) goals that do not address general curriculum and regular classroom participation, (4) an emphasis on form rather than substance, (5) goals that are not measurable or goals that are measurable but are not measured, and (6) not evaluating and revising annual goals to meet changing learning needs.

Lack of correspondence. Assuming that a child's needs are correctly identified, if a goal is not provided for a need, or a goal is provided for a nonexistent need, the goal is deficient. If reading vocabulary is identified as an educational need, but only goals for reading comprehension and writing are listed, either the identified need is incorrect or the goals do not address actual needs. Goals that fail to address needs result in needs not being met and services provided that might well be inappropriate.

Short-term objectives must correspond to goals in terms of content and progression. In 1983 a study to evaluate special education in Skokie, Illinois, "one area of IEP development where room for improvement could be noted was in the writing of measurable short term objectives which need to be logically related to goals " (p. 61).[19] If the yearly goal is to reduce aggressive behavior toward other students, listing objectives that do not address this task (e.g., developing study skills, passing year-end tests) might be useful in their own right and worthy of being separate goals, but the objectives might have only a tangential relationship to the goal.

Just as there must be a link between need and goals, there must be correspondence between present levels of performance and goals. If a goal is to develop attention, but there is no data indicating the specific beginning level of attention, there is no way to develop a meaningful goal. Many goals are deficient because they are not data-based, and do not begin with a decisive and measured level of performance. If the goal is to improve reading comprehension to 80 percent, the beginning level of reading comprehension should be known; if the goal is to decrease a behavior to 0, the present level of behavior should be known.

General curriculum. A school district is not required to include in an IEP annuals goals that relate to areas of the general curriculum that are not affected by the child's disability. The purpose of annual goals is to offset or reduce the problems resulting from the child's disability that interfere with educational performance. The presumption is that needs that do not result from the disability or are not affected by the disability should not be addressed by specially designed instruction. A child with a disability is entitled to the same curriculum as used with non-disabled children when that part of the curriculum is unaffected by the disability.[20] Measurable annual goals, therefore, should focus on areas affected by the child's disability rather than all educational needs. If a student has an orthopedic impairment, one goal might relate to using an augmentative communication device to participate in regular curriculum social studies assessments. However, if the student's cognitive ability to deal with the regular classroom social studies content is unaffected, there would be no need to develop separate social studies goals. If goals are developed for areas unaffected by the child's disability within the context of special education, the result can be the creation of a separate and unique curriculum.

The requirement that goals address disability needs and not regular curriculum needs that are unaffected by the disability does not mean that goals should focus on skills unrelated to the regular curriculum. For example, a school district might require goals to focus on foundation skills but not specific curriculum skills (e.g., reading in the content area). Measurable annual goals must be developed that allow a child to be involved in and progress in the general curriculum and this cannot be achieved by ignoring the general curriculum.

The choice is not whether to write goals only for the general curriculum or goals that are void of regular curriculum content because of a belief that special education centers on foundation or special skills, but to write goals for needs that result from a child's disability that will enable the child to be involved in and progress in the general curriculum. The extent of this involvement might be minimal, progress slower than that of nondisabled children, but the extent of involvement or progress should not detract from the need to focus on the regular curriculum.

Form over substance. The criterion is the standard for determining success, but the criterion for goals is often misused to give a false sense of behavioral objectivity. That is, by stating a criterion a goal appears to comply with the measurability requirement. Public Law 94-142 required "appropriate objective criteria and evaluation procedures and schedules,"[21] but not actual criteria based or specific evaluation procedures. When a goal "to improve reading to 80 percent accuracy as determined by teacher observation" is included in a child's IEP, the purpose of the goal is to comply with the general format for writing goals and not to plan and measure performance. For this goal, the objective criterion (80% accuracy) and evaluation procedure (teacher observation) are stated, but in all likelihood the criterion and the evaluation will never be used.

Goal measurement. Goals are often written that cannot be measured, are not measured, or are only measured by some vague and subjective technique. On a similar basis, objectives for goals are often not designed to measure progress, but merely to indicate types of activities that appear to be related to a general area of need. If the goal is to increase regular classroom participation, the degree of regular classroom participation must be measured.

Evaluation. The greatest deficiency of most goals is that they are simply not measured. Even if measurable annual goals are specified, there must be an attempt to evaluate the progress toward the goals, report the progress to parents, and then use this information to develop or modify the educational program. The purpose of evaluation is to improve the specially designed instruction and to determine whether or not the specially designed instruction is needed. Goals are often not evaluated with the intent of modifying, eliminating, or adding more appropriate goals. The purpose of special education is to tailor an educational program to meet a child's academic and nonacademic needs, and this can only be achieved by evaluating and revising each child's measurable annual goals.

GOAL CHARACTERISTICS

Every measurable annual goal requires a timeframe to indicate when the goal will be accomplished, a measure to evaluate performance, and a criterion. Overall, the duration of annual goals is the school year or a twelve-month period if extended school year services are needed. Annual goals indicate what a child can be reasonably expected to accomplish within this timeframe. Short-term objectives are intermediate steps toward achieving the goal and are therefore usually defined in terms of months rather than an annual timeframe.

The annual timeframe provides the overall focus for developing goals. If a goal appears to be an activity that can be accomplished in a much shorter period of time, it is probably not an annual goal. For example, if the goal is *to be able to identify smaller words in compound words*, a determination should be made whether the goal requires an entire year to accomplish. Often activities are an important part of a more general goal (e.g., word attack), or might even represent a part of one or more intermediate objectives (e.g., a structural analysis objective). By focusing on what can be accomplished during the school year, a meaningful plan can be devised that is not mired down by countless day-to-day activities that are presented as annual goals.

Each goal should deal with a specific educational need, and each series of objectives should be linked to a specific goal. As with behavioral objectives, the key to an effective measurable annual goal is the identification of a specific and measurable behavior, ability, skill, or task. Improving structural analysis, phonics, or literal reading comprehension all indicate a task or behavior, but none suggests a specific procedure for actually measuring performance in these areas. If structural analysis is the focus of a goal, a teacher might create an assessment that includes compound words (e.g., snowman, workbook), prefixes and suffixes, contractions, and identifying the correct syllables in words. Based on this specific assessment, an assessment of structural analysis is constructed to actually

measure this skill.

Measurability. There is an old dictum that "if something exists, it can be measured." A measurable goal means that some element of performance is identified and quantified. If the goal is to write a paragraph by the end of the year, a task must be constructed to measure this skill before instruction (i.e., the present level of performance) and at periodic points throughout the year. The behavior for this goal, writing a paragraph, is a measurable behavior. Other variables such as sentence length, punctuation, or spelling, etc., could further clarify the conditions for achieving the goal, or exactly how the writing sample is obtained (e.g., language experience, starter sentence, from dictation).

In some instances the location of the assessment or who will conduct the assessment are important factors. If the goal is to complete more homework assignments, the regular classroom teacher might keep a log of completed assignments but the parents might also record the amount of time doing homework. If classroom behavior is a primary concern, who will actually observe and record the frequency and/or duration of the behavior should be clearly identified (e.g., the teacher, or a classroom aide).

A measurable goal means that the goal should be, can be, and is evaluated after a period of time. A vague goal does not preclude evaluation but the task of evaluation becomes more difficult. A goal to improve communication can mean most anything, and the evaluation therefore can mean most anything. However, if the goal is to improve writing mechanics (e.g., capitalization, punctuation) or to reduce the number of spelling errors from twenty-five per writing assignment to less than ten, the assessment becomes the focal point of the goal and provides a basis for evaluating and guiding future educational progress.

Criteria. When designing specially designed instruction, progress toward the criterion can be even more important than actually achieving the criterion. The criterion for success might be a score of 70 percent, less than X errors on a writing sample, or an *average* rating on a teacher rating scale. If the criterion is not achieved, the goal is not necessarily unsuccessful. If the goal is a score of 70 percent, and the student's performance at the end of each evaluation period increased from 20 percent to 30 percent to 50 percent, progress toward the goal might be an indication of success. Or consider a situation where the goal is to reduce incidents of classroom screaming from 15 to 0 per day. The plan might have been to first reduce these incidents from 15 to 10, then 10 to 5, and then 5 to 0. If the annual program reduced incidents from 15 to 7, the fact that the behavior was reduced by 50 percent might be regarded as exceptional progress. For measurable annual goals the criterion is not the standard for an effective goal; the criterion is the benchmark for gauging the extent of progress over the course of the year.

Number. The need for goals and the number of required goals is often confused. Pyecha (1980), in an early survey of IEP effectiveness, reported that "formats for about two-thirds of the IEPs tended to restrict the number of annual goals that could be listed, and almost 40 percent had a similar restriction on short-term objectives" (p. 154). The implication then and now is that form rather than need often dictates the number of goals. If space on the IEP document allows for five goals, five goals are written. If space is provided for goals in reading, mathematics, and classroom management, goals are provided in each area regardless of whether goals are needed. When goals are thoughtlessly (albeit effortlessly) generated via a computer program, the result can be pages of daily activities or annual objectives under the guise of goals. Vague goals and excessively long lists of

goals that detail day-to-day instructional activities muddle rather than promote individualized planning.

There is no ideal or set number of goals, but the number included in an IEP should be manageable, used, and evaluated. One of the criticisms of computer-generated goals is the ease with which a seemingly endless number of goals can be created but which are never considered much less evaluated. This can also occur when goals are treated as overly explicit instructional guidelines. There might well be a need for a certain goal, but creating 100 objectives is a daunting evaluation task, especially if there are ten additional areas, each with a large set of objectives.

For the most part, if five or six areas can be identified that affect, either directly or indirectly, a child's disability or educational performance, this probably represents a number of goals that can be managed effectively. As is always the case, the number of goals is dictated by need, and not a preconceived number developed to meet an arbitrary standard. One child might require one or two goals in reading, while a child with a severe disability might require dozens of special education and related service goals involving self-help, communication, social and motor skills. All other factors being equal, the number of goals will increase in direct relation to the intensity and range of a child's needs.

Need. The purpose of every goal is to address important needs that will either mitigate the effects of the disability or improve educational performance. Need implies more than just a behavior; need indicates that the behavior, task, ability, or skill is necessary to provide an appropriate education. A need might be a specific behavior, a task, an ability or a skill, and the important characteristic of a need is that it requires specially designed instruction.

The initial task when constructing IEP

measurable annual goals is to focus on what the child needs, and what can be done to meet these needs. For a child with a severe developmental disability, this might be developing receptive language and communication skills, self-help skills (e.g., dressing and eating), or gross motor skills. For a high school student, the need might be to pass a statewide proficiency examination in order to receive a high school diploma. And for a child classified as emotionally disturbed the goal might be to not scream obscenities when asked by the teacher to perform a classroom task. A teacher might feel that a child needs to read at grade level, or attend class, or spend more time in regular classes; a parent might believe that their child should receive passing grades, or homework, or develop communication skills, or receive a high school diploma. There is no limit or restriction as to what a need might be other than all academic and nonacademic needs must be identified. The development of measurable annual goals for every IEP should begin with this fundamental question: What does the child need most to enable participation in the regular curriculum and to meet the child's other educational needs?

A child could potentially need hundreds of regular curriculum and special education goals, but the IEP team must focus on goals that meet needs that result from the child's disability and enable participation and progress in the regular curriculum. Developing basic leadership skill might be an important curriculum goal, but this might not be a significant IEP goal. For a child with a writing disability, defining a goal that will "improve the ability to use a semicolon with 85 percent accuracy" is probably less important than writing a complete sentence, or organizing a series of thoughts.

Priority. Although not always possible, goals should be prioritized in the IEP document so that the most important goal is listed first, the second most important goal second, and so on. Prioritizing goals is also useful for determining the relative significance of needs. That is, the most significant need is considered first, followed by the next most significant need. For a student who is classified as emotionally disturbed, goal priority is essential. If a student requires specially designed instruction because of behavior, behavior goals should receive a high priority. If the behavior entails physical aggressiveness toward classmates and if this is the primary reason services are required, a goal dealing with this behavior should not be relegated as the last of a long list of goals. In this case, priority should be given to what caused the child to need specially designed instruction, and what can be done so that the child can participate in the general curriculum.

Achieveability. An important attribute of an effective goal is an appropriate difficulty level. If the initial difficulty is either too easy or too difficult, the goal will be quickly achieved or never achieved. If the child can already accomplish the goal, the present level of performance was probably not assessed. If the goal is exceedingly difficult, the present level of performance was either not assessed or the meaning of the evaluation data was misinterpreted in terms of projecting future progress. In either case, an overly easy or difficult goal can limit the ability of the goal to meet a specific educational need.

One of the most difficult tasks involving the development of annual goals is estimating what will be achieved within the annual timeframe. If a child's ability to accomplish a goal is underestimated, instruction will likely fall short of the "high standards and expectations" wanted for children with disabilities. On the other hand, if a child's ability is overestimated, the goal might be far too difficult to achieve. There is an important difference between a *desirable* goal and an *achievable* goal. A goal for a twelve-year-old student reading at the first grade level to increase reading ability to the sixth grade level might be desirable but not necessarily achievable. High academic expectations are exceedingly important but not to the point where the expectations are unrealistic and not achievable.

There will be many occasions when what to expect within an annual period of time is not known or is difficult to estimate. However, after one year of specially designed instruction an evaluation of goal achievement should provide an empirical basis for estimating future educational progress.

Revision. If goals are never revised, the goals are probably inappropriate. The goals completed one year should provide the basis for subsequent annual goals. A simple test for evaluating IEP goals is to determine the extent goals have been revised. If goals have not been revised, or if IEP goals have never been revised, the goals were not written to project an anticipated annual level of performance. This was the criticism in *Evans v. Rhinebeck*[22] where the goals and objectives were generic and vague . . . while repeatedly incanting phrases involving 'teacher observation' and '80% success'" (p. 97) but where no real methods were used to evaluate academic progress.

Goals often are not modified during the year, but a thoughtful annual evaluation of each goal is essential for IEP continuity; that is, the goals for one year should provide a foundation for IEP goals the following year

(if a child remains a child with a disability).

For some computerized IEPs a cloning routine is sometimes used to carry over goals from one year to the next. The inappropriateness of this becomes readily apparent when repeated over many years and goals are obviously unrelated to current levels of performance. For example, a child in the seventh grade is reading at the fourth grade level and IEP goals (which have been cloned from one year to the next) still refer to basic readiness skills such as letter identification and basic sight words that were included in the first IEP.

Considerable effort might be expended to achieve a set of goals one year, only to ignore this data the following year. A goal might be inappropriate, too easy or too difficult one year, but progress toward the goal is not used to modify the goal or create a new goal the following year. When goals are first developed for a child with a disability, projecting anticipated annual levels of performance often requires considerable guesswork. Following an initial year of special education, goals should be revised to reflect anticipated levels of performance that are based on empirical data and a thoughtful evaluation of the previous year's goals and objectives.

For every annual re-evaluation, consideration of previous goal achievement is essential. The purpose of IDEA-1997 is to promote meaningful goal review and revision; that is, annual goals are reviewed and revised to meet a child's changing needs from one year to the next.

Types of Goals

Disability-related goals. Measurable annual goals address needs that are affected by the child's disability and not for all areas of the general curriculum. If a child has a specific learning disability in reading comprehension, a goal is necessary to meet this need, but developing a set of separate and specific science goals would be inappropriate if this area is unaffected by the child's disability. On the other hand, areas affected by a disability come within the province of IEP goals. A child might have a severe reading disorder which impacts writing, and the IEP might therefore include a writing goal. Likewise, if a child has a reading disorder that affects a content area such as reading word problems in mathematics, reading in this content area might require a goal.

For children with sensory impairments, disability-related goals can have a significant impact on regular curriculum participation. For a deaf or hard-of-hearing child, goals might relate to improved speechreading skills, speech, sign language ability, or the use of residual hearing. For a child with a visual impairment, goals might involve mobility training or developing the use of Braille or assistive technology. For a child with an orthopedic impairment, developing the ability to use an augmentative communication device might be the key to regular curriculum participation.

Curriculum goals. A major focus of the IEP is to allow the child an opportunity to participate in the general education curriculum. Measurable goals are needed that allow students to be involved in and progress in the general curriculum. When designing goals, both the regular classroom and the regular classroom curriculum must be considered. For a child who is physically aggressive in the regular classroom, the goal is not just to eliminate the physical aggressiveness, but to eliminate physical aggressiveness in the regular classroom.

The role of special education to enable a child to be involved in and progress in the general curriculum is in stark contrast to the belief that special education and the regular curriculum are totally different. Nowhere in IDEA-1997 or the regulations is there a directive that goals should not deal directly

with the general curriculum. What IDEA-1997 does require,[23] and what is reiterated in the regulations, is that goals meet unique needs that result from the child's disability to enable the child to be involved in and progress in the general curriculum.

Another misinterpretation of IDEA-1997 concerning the general curriculum is that children with disabilities must be provided with exactly the same curriculum as nondisabled children. Children with disabilities must be provided with the same curriculum as nondisabled children when those portions of the curriculum are unaffected by the disability; and for those areas of the curriculum affected by a child's disability, measurable annual goals must be developed that will enable the child to be involved in and progress in the general curriculum. As a result, goals are "not required in areas of the general curriculum in which the child's disability does not affect the child's ability to be involved in and progress in the general curriculum."[24]

Special education goals. Special education goals involve adapting or modifying the content, methodology, or delivery of instruction, and can include speech-language pathology (if not a related service), travel training, vocational education, and physical education.[25] Special education goals are those goals that address the child's disability, enable the child to meet educational standards that apply to all children, or to participate in the general curriculum.

Supplementary aids and service goals. Supplementary aids and services are modifications that allow the child to participate in regular education programs. These services are essential "accommodations and adjustments necessary" for a child to participate "in particular areas of the curriculum due to the nature of the disability."[26] If a goal for a student is to receive a passing grade of at least 70 percent on a content-area test when the test is read to the student, the test accommodation of reading the test to the student might be necessary for the student to participate in that portion of the curriculum. The test accommodation itself might not require a goal, unless the student needs to develop the skill of taking content tests when given in this format. If appropriate, a goal might also be developed to de-emphasize this program modification so that the student is able to pass a content-area test without the test being read.

Supplementary aids and services may or may not require a goal, depending on whether the aid or service is intended to increase a child's skill, ability, or performance. For a child who is Other Health Impaired, frequent rest breaks might be necessary, but this would not require a corresponding goal. Likewise, an IEP might indicate that a hard-of-hearing child requires preferential seating (near the front of the room), but a goal would not be required.

Related service goals. Whether a related service requires a goal depends on whether the service is intended to result in an improved level of performance. If the related service entails transportation, a goal would not be required. If the related service entails transportation with an aid so as to reduce a certain type of behavior from occurring, then a goal might be necessary. If occupational therapy is required, there might be goals that measure progress of the therapy. If group counseling is deemed necessary, there might be a goal to measure the effectiveness of this service if the service is intended to result in improved behavior, performance, or ability. In a memorandum from the Office of Special Education Programs, the need for goals in all areas of special education (including related services and supplementary aids and services) was emphasized in that "the goals and objectives in the IEP must address all of the student's identified needs that the IEP team has

determined warrant the provision of special education, related services, and supplementary aids and services, and must enable the team to determine the effectiveness of each of these services."[27] Whether a child needs specific related service goals depends on whether the related service results in increased performance or ability. For example, if air conditioning or a transportation service is necessary for a child to attend school, but the service is not intended to improve a skill or ability, a goal is not required.

> If, however, instruction will be provided to the student to enable the student to increase the student's independence or improve the student's behavior or socialization during travel to school, then goals and objectives must be included to address the need to increase independence or improve behavior or socialization.[28]

A separate IEP section for related service goals does not mean that these goals are developed apart from the IEP team process. The IEP team does not develop special education goals while other specialist develop independent sets of goals. The IEP team is responsible for developing all goals, including all related service goals. Obviously, professionals with expertise in specific related service areas will have the primary responsibility for constructing goals to meet each child's unique needs, but the entire IEP team has the opportunity to review, modify, and approve all goals, and to add or suggest other related service goals if appropriate.

Transition service goals. Transition services are required for every student, beginning at age fourteen (or earlier if appropriate). The services or instruction are intended to assist the student in the transition from school to post-school life.[29] When transition services are provided to improve a skill or ability, measurable annual goals are required. For instance, providing a student with job information or referring a student to a state or vocational program might be important vocational services. If a student requires special instruction to learn how to apply for a job or basic job skills, these would require annual goals.

LRE goals. A major focus of IDEA-1997 is the ability of a child to be involved in and progress in the general curriculum. To this end, goals can be developed that systematically increase participation in regular classes or the regular curriculum. If a child is classified as emotionally disturbed because of unacceptable classroom behavior, a goal might be to increase the amount of participation in the regular classroom over the year. If the beginning level of classroom participation is 0, participation by November might be 2 hours a week, 4 hours a week by February, 6 hours a week by April, and 8 hours a week by June.

Nonacademic goals.[30] Nonacademic goals might involve employment skills and school-to-work activities that are developed in conjunction with the statement of transition services. In addition, goals might involve transportation, mobility skills, or the ability to participate in athletics or other extra-curricular activities. Involvement in the general curriculum is not limited to academic services but includes all areas that are affected by the child's disability. If a student expresses interest in track, a goal might be developed to teach basic track fundamentals (e.g., running, high-jump, etc.), or to develop a level of competence in each. If a child expresses an interest in a club, a goal might require developing new transportation skills or other skills relating to the activity.

Goal Development

The regulations imply a top-down approach for developing goals. That is, a general problem is identified and then subdivided or decomposed into smaller steps that will lead to goal achievement. The sequence for developing goals requires that the IEP team first develop measurable annual goals and then "measurable, intermediate steps (short-term objectives) or major milestones (benchmarks)."[31]

If the present level of performance is 30 percent in reading comprehension, the goal envisioned by the end of the year might be 70 percent comprehension. The problem is not the 30 percent reading comprehension level; the problem is achieving the 70 percent comprehension goal. Beginning with the goal or the *top* of the problem sequence, short-term objectives or benchmarks are developed that will likely result in a 70 percent comprehension level.

In contrast to a top-down approach for developing measurable annual goals, a bottom-up approach is can be used. This type of problem-solving strategy begins by determining the first level of performance, then the next level, and so on until the last level of performance is selected (the goal).

A top-down approach for determining measurable annual goals provides a structured approach for selecting realistic objectives or benchmarks and then developing a reasonable series of steps that will result in goal achievement; a bottom-up approach is useful when experience indicates that specific strategies are appropriate but there is less certainty when estimating annual performance.

SHORT-TERM OBJECTIVES

The change in IDEA from "a statement of annual goals, including short-term instructional objectives"[32] to "a statement of measurable annual goals, including benchmarks or shortterm objectives"[33] represents a major shift in how specially designed instruction is conceptualized. Short-term objectives are a series of intermediate steps for each goal and are intended to represent measurable major milestones (benchmarks) "that will enable families, students, and educators to monitor progress during the year, and, if appropriate, to revise the IEP consistent with the child's instructional needs."[34]

The emphasis on short-term objectives or benchmarks is readily apparent when comparing the IEP format before and after IDEA-1997. Following PL 94-142 guidelines many IEPs simply identified a goal, followed by a series of activities or annual objectives:

Goal: Improve reading
Objective #1: Improve word attack skills
Objective #2: Improve vocabulary
Objective #3: Improve comprehension

The short-term objective format for IDEA-1997 requires that each goal is reduced to a series of logical intermediate steps that represent a timeline toward goal achievement:

Measurable Annual Goal: Increase sight-word recognition to 75% as measured by a flash-card assessment of 100 selected sight-words by June 20.

1. Benchmark #1: Increase sight-words to 30% by November 1.
2. Benchmark #2: Increase sight-words to 45% by January 30.
3. Benchmark #3: Increase sight-words to 60% by March 20.

Behavioral Objectives

Measurable annual goals and behavioral objectives are similar with respect to behavior specificity and a stated criterion or level of performance to achieve, but annual measurable goals and IEP short-term objectives are different because of required time restraints, the relation between annual measurable goals and objectives, and the interrelation between sets of short-term objectives.

Measurable annual goals and short-term objectives often contain the three constituent parts of a behavioral objective: *behavior*, *conditions* and *criterion*. The overriding concern of both measurable annual goals and short-term objectives is that a measurable behavior is specified. However,

measurable annual goals must not only imply measurement but must clearly indicate how the behavior will be measured. The goal "to improve reading" implies a behavior (reading) and the direction of the behavior change (an increase in reading performance), but the goal does not signify how reading will actually be measured. Many short-term objectives could be improved by simply identifying real conditions that will result in real measurements.

For behavioral objectives, the conditions for a behavior further define what is measured. The behavior "to read" is measurable, but more information is required to discern exactly what will be read (unless any "reading" will suffice). The task might be "to orally read a paragraph," "to orally read a paragraph from a sixth grade social studies textbook," or "to identify sight-words."

A behavioral objective defines a level of acceptable performance or criterion. The criterion serves a twofold purpose: First, the criterion indicates what is being measured. If the criterion is to make less than ten errors, "errors" is what is being measured. If the criterion is 80 percent correct, correct responses are being measured. Second, the criterion indicates an acceptable level of performance. For a behavioral objective, reaching the criterion indicates that the objective has been achieved. For IEP short-term objectives, reaching the criterion indicates that the child is following the plan and progressing satisfactorily toward the completion of the annual goal.

A major difference between a behavioral objective and a measurable annual goal and short-term objectives is that a behavioral objective can be completely independent of other goals or objectives. Each measurable annual goal requires a subset of objectives, and the objectives within this subset must be interrelated (e.g., increasing levels of performance) to other objectives within the subset.

Another difference between behavioral objectives and measurable annual goals is that short-term objectives or benchmarks are for periods less than a year, while a behavioral objective can be for any period of time. Where a behavioral or instructional objective could include a timeline as part of the conditions for the behavior, the time period for goals is the school year or twelve months unless otherwise stated; for short-term objectives the instructional period is a designated period or term within the year.

Many IEPs include lists of objectives in which the duration for each is the school year. In other words, an IEP might have a series of behavioral objectives or annual objectives), but not a series of intermediate steps or benchmarks for each behavioral objective.

Consider a behavioral objective that is designed to improve a child's ability to recognize fifty sight words when presented on 3x5 cards to an accuracy level of 80 percent:

Behavior: To read 50 sight words
Conditions: when presented on 3x5 cards
Criterion: with 80% accuracy

The behavioral objective can be rewritten as a single statement:

To read 50 sight words when presented on 3x5 cards with 80% accuracy.

The essential element of this behavioral objective is the specification of a behavior that can be measured (the behavior and conditions) and a criterion. With several modifications, this objective could be rewritten as follows:

Behavior   To orally identify 50 sight words
Conditions   when presented on 3x5 cards
Criterion   with 80% accuracy
Date   October 30

This can be rewritten in statement form as:

To orally identify 50 sight words when presented on 3x5 cards with 80% accuracy by October 30.

For the above, the objective "to read 50 sight words" could be reduced to the basic instructional objective elements of "objective criteria and evaluation procedures and schedules."[35]

Objective	To read 50 sight words
Criterion	with 80% accuracy
Evaluation	as determined by a teacher
	made test
Date	October 30

To read 50 sight words as determined by a teacher made test with 80% accuracy by October 30.

And rewritten in statement form as:

The modified instructional objective can then be arranged in typical IEP format:

Objective	Evaluation	Criterion	Date
To read 50 sight words	Teacher made test	80%	Oct. 30

The Nebraska Department of Education (as does South Dakota) interprets benchmarks as general statements representing milestones to a goal, and short-term objectives as specific statements with conditions, behavior, criterion and time-frame.[36] These are essentially the basic elements of objective criteria, evaluation procedures, and schedules required by PL 94-142.[37] In South Dakota "short-term objectives must contain *conditions, performance,* and *criteria* if these components were not included in the annual goal," while "benchmarks are a series of 'developmental milestones' that lead to the mastery of an annual goal. Benchmarks do not require the use of conditions, performance and criteria." A benchmark does not require a statement of conditions and performance in that these elements are contained in the goal and are not repeated to eliminate redundancy. Of course, each benchmark contains a criterion because the benchmark is the criterion. In essence, a benchmark is a short-term objective, but one in which the conditions or task remain constant and are therefore not repeated in the benchmark statement.

A benchmark is often a score or frequency (e.g., number of behaviors, errors, etc.) that represents the "amount of progress."[38] Most important, a benchmark is a series of quantitative milestones that chart the expected level of progress toward a goal (e.g., 30, 45, 60, 80 percent), while a short-term objective is a breakdown of the goal itself (e.g., understand main idea, outline major points, add detail to major points, write a report from outline).

The regulations provide a fairly clear distinction between short-term objectives and benchmarks.[39] Whereas short-term objectives breakdown a skill into discrete components, benchmarks describe the amount of progress (e.g., increase the number of problems from ten to twenty to thirty). There are certainly different ways in which short-term objectives and benchmarks can be interpreted, and the two can be combined, but the essential point is that both allow the assessment of progress toward the goal "at intermediate times during the year."[40]

Planning Short-term Objectives

The purpose of short-term objectives is to provide a plan for achieving the annual goal and not to provide a guide for day-to day instructional activities. As previously described, short-term objectives, benchmarks or IEP objectives present a logical breakdown of a goal over a specified period of time. Schipper and Wilson (1978) suggested that "objectives may be more or less specific depending on the makeup of the committee but the intent of the IEP is to delineate an overall program for the child. We suggest that the child's teacher(s) may wish to treat the committee level objectives as classroom goals and in turn develop more specific objectives for the child's monthly, weekly, or daily plan" (p. 10).

Much of the confusion concerning IEP short-term objectives results from creating annual objectives or defining instructional activities rather than creating objectives that can be used to monitor and report progress toward achieving a goal. If a goal entails reading comprehension, the goal should entail what is likely to be accomplished within a twelve-month period and not a complete list of daily activities that will be used within that period. The ability to be able to use semantic mapping would be a goal if the period of time needed to develop the skill was the school year. If semantic mapping is part of a more general reading comprehension goal, this skill might be one of a series of short-term objectives or part of one objective. However, if semantic mapping is a technique to teach comprehension, and a skill that is not measured, this activity would not be listed as either an IEP goal or objective.

The interpretation of short-term objectives as intermediate steps toward goal achievement is emphasized in IDEA-1997, but this was the intent of earlier regulations. The 1990 regulations described the role of IEP objectives as "general benchmarks for determining progress toward meeting the annual goals" and "objectives should be projected to be accomplished over an extended period of time (e.g., an entire school quarter or semester)."[41] The purpose of IEP objectives was to provide a plan for achieving goals, while the objectives used in the classroom deal with more specific outcomes, accomplished on a daily or weekly, and "include details not required in an IEP, such as the specific methods, activities, and materials (e.g., use of flash cards) that will be used in accomplishing the objectives."[42]

A measurable annual goal must indicate how the task, ability or behavior is measured, the criterion, and the anticipated completion date. Short-term objectives must also indicate a measure, criterion, and anticipated completion date but the objectives represent a logical breakdown of the goal. In addition, short-term objectives represent an interrelated series of intermediate steps toward achieving the goal. A short-term objective can be a benchmark or a series of individually crafted objectives, each of which is related to one another by content, difficulty, task, setting, etc. or a combination thereof. A benchmark is one form of short-term objective in which the objectives are related by increasing levels of performance.

Short-term Objective Format

In 1995, when IDEA was introduced into the House as HR 1986, the bill redefined "the statement of annual goals, including short-term instructional objectives," to read "a statement of measurable annual objectives." The proposed change was to make each objective measurable. This was eventually modified to "measurable annual goal" but the need to develop measurable short-term IEP objectives is clear.

Consider a child who has a limited receptive vocabulary and an assessment is constructed to measure the ability to point to an object (e.g., *cup, pencil, hat, orange*) when one of the objects is named. Based on the child's performance, an annual goal is created to increase this ability from 25 percent to 80 percent accuracy. As shown by the following example, the goal is comprised of a measurable behavior and a criterion, while the annual timeframe is understood.

_____will be able to identify 20 objects in a four-item multiple choice format by pointing when given the verbal label with 80% accuracy.

Each short-term objective is written so the measurable behavior and/or criterion is modified to create a progression of learning that will result in achieving the annual goal by the end of the school year. The anticipated completion date for each objective could coincide with the reporting periods for nondisabled children, or follow a different timeline, as long as parents are informed of goal progress as frequently as parents of nondisabled children.

_____will be able to identify objects in a four-alternative 20-item multiple choice format by pointing when given the verbal label with 80% accuracy by June 20.

_____will be able to distinguish between big and small objects with 75% accuracy by October 15.

_____will be able to identify objects when shown two objects by pointing when given the verbal label 8 out of 10 times January 30.

_____will be able to identify objects in a three-alternative multiple choice format by pointing when given the verbal label with 8 out of 10 times by April 15.

Repeated measurements. In terms of monitoring and reporting progress, short-term objectives or benchmarks require repeated measurements during the year (also see p. 123). For standardized tests this is a very serious limitation in that a standardized test cannot be given on four or so occasions during the year to monitor progress. For curriculum-based assessments, which provide beginning levels of performance for annual goals, the problem is less acute. While standardized tests can be modified to a limited degree, if at all, curriculum-based assessments can be presented in a variety of ways to minimize the effects of memory, guessing, and motivation.

If each short-term objective measures a slightly different task, or the content or difficulty level is different, the assessment of one objective should have a minimal effect on the assessment of subsequent objectives. For observational assessment (e.g., frequency of behavior, completion of specific tasks), teacher-made tests and curriculum-based assessments based on different content samples (e.g., tests, writing samples), the focus is on curriculum assessment and not a normative comparison.

Standardized tests do not provide an infinite number of test versions because of cost factors, but this is much less of a problem with curriculum-based assessments. Nonetheless, the theory of reliability is based on the premise that each test represents a random sampling of items from a particular content domain. This is not possible with commercial tests but curriculum-based assessments allow greater flexibility in varying and sampling curriculum content.

Although curriculum-based assessments are easily developed for frequent use during the year, there are situations when using the same or similar assessment might unduly influence repeated test performance. For instance, if the assessment consists of math word problems or science problems, presenting the exact same problems during the year might result in inflated score performance. Using different items or making minor alternations in the order or content of items (e.g., simplifying 2/6 is changed to 3/9) can result in comparable test forms.

If the same assessment is used to measure progress at each intermediate step, randomization techniques, comparable assessment tasks or an alternate form might be used. If the task is to identify sight words presented on 3x5 cards, a simple shuffling of the cards before presentation will create a *new* test

each time the task is given. If the assessment involves twenty-five computational problems, a comparable set of items could be used to evaluate performance for each assessment period.

Instead of using a different set of items for each assessment, two forms might be used (A and B) so that form A is the first period, form B the second period, form A the third, and form B to measure final goal performance. For tasks involving writing, each writing sample could be elicited by a different stimulus sentence. For oral reading or reading comprehension, different reading selections based on readability (or increasing readability) could be used. When developing repeated curriculum-based assessments, content and difficulty comparability will often provide reasonably accurate measures of performance.

BENCHMARKS

Short-term objectives and benchmarks both indicate levels of performance "to gauge, at intermediate times during the year, how well the child is progressing toward achievement of the annual goal."[43] Short-term objectives "generally break the skills described in the annual goal down into discrete components," while benchmarks

> establish expected performance levels that allow for regular checks of progress that coincide with the reporting periods for informing parents of their child's progress toward achieving the annual goals. An IEP team may use either short term objectives or benchmarks or a combination of the two depending on the nature of the annual goals and the needs of the child.

Many IEPs provide space for either short-term objectives or benchmarks so that there is no formal distinction between the two.

The distinction between short-term objectives and benchmarks is that the former emphasizes breaking the skill described in the annual goal into "discrete components," while benchmarks are denoted by "amount of progress" and "expected performance levels."[45]

In the following example, each objective is defined by several variables, including task difficulty, the task itself and the criterion.

Objective #1: Point to concrete objects (e.g., book, can of soup) when the label is presented by the teacher with 50% accuracy by December 15

Objective #2: Point to objects in pictures when cued by the teacher with 60% accuracy March 15

Objective #3: Point to the correct drawing from among four alternatives when the stimulus word is presented by the teacher with 70% accuracy May 15

In the above example, short term objectives can easily accommodate objectives with multiple and changing variables. The hallmark of benchmarks is a constant task but where the criterion and date for each benchmark varies.

_____will be able to identify objects in a four-alternative 20-item multiple choice format by pointing when given the verbal label with 80% accuracy by June 20.

_____will be able to identify objects in a four-alternative 20-item multiple choice format by pointing when given the verbal label with 35% accuracy by November 1.

_____will be able to identify objects in a four-alternative 20-item multiple choice format by pointing when given the verbal label with 50% accuracy by January 30.

_____will be able to identify objects in a four-alternative 20-item multiple choice format by pointing when given the verbal label with 65% accuracy by March 20.

_____will be able to identify objects in a four-alternative 20-item multiple choice format by pointing when given the verbal label with 80% accuracy by June 20.

Because the stem or measure remains the same for each objective, the format can be reduced to a benchmark format:

_____will be able to identify objects in a four-item 20-item multiple choice format by pointing when given the verbal label with 80% accuracy.

Benchmark 1:
    Criterion 35%   Date: November 1
Benchmark 2:
    Criterion 50%   Date: January 30
Benchmark 3:
    Criterion 65%   Date: March 20
Benchmark 4:
    Criterion 80%   Date: June 20

And the benchmark can be neatly included in an IEP format that specifies the beginning level of performance, the criterion and date for each benchmark:

Goal: will be able to identify objects in a four-alternative 20-item multiple choice format by pointing when given the verbal label with 80% accuracy.	Criterion	Date
PLEP	20%	September 1
Benchmark 1	35%	November 1
Benchmark 2	50%	January 30
Benchmark 3	65%	March 20
Benchmark 4	80%	June 20

Or the PLEP and goal levels could be listed as the beginning and ending benchmarks for the annual goal:

PLEP	20%	September 1
Benchmark 1	35%	November 1
Benchmark 2	50%	January 30
Benchmark 3	65%	March 20
Goal	80%	June 20

If the dates for reporting progress to parents are constant and always coincide with the dates when parents of nondisabled children were sent reports, the above benchmark format could be further abbreviated as follows:

	Benchmarks				
Goal	PLEP	1	2	3	4
Identify objects in a four-alternative 20-item multiple choice format by pointing when given the verbal label with 80% accuracy.	20%	35%	50%	66%	80%

If the measurable annual goal format is also used to record results, a column for entering the measured performance for each benchmark can be added as shown below:

Goal: will be able to identify objects in a four-alternative 20-item multiple choice format by pointing when given the verbal label with 80% accuracy.	Criterion	Date	Performance
PLEP	20%	September 1	18%
Benchmark 1	35%	November 1	40%
Benchmark 2	50%	January 30	45%
Benchmark 3	65%	March 20	60%
Benchmark 4	80%	June 20	75%

Whether short-term objectives or benchmarks are used depends on child, the goal, and how progress toward the goal can best be achieved. If the goal is to pass a state competency test in mathematics, and a student has difficulty in computation, math applications, measurement and geometry, one objective might deal with computation, another with math applications, etc. In either case, short-term objectives would be appropriate because each objective would entail a different content.

Even when each objective emphasizes different content areas, benchmarks could be used to monitor progress toward goal achievement. If the goal is to pass a state competency test, mini-competency tests could be given at various points throughout the year to assess the student's progress. If an initial evaluation reveals a total score of 35 percent, each mini-competency test score would be a milestone toward goal achievement so that the projected benchmarks might be as follows:

	Benchmarks			
Goal	1	2	3	4
Receive a passing score (70%) on the State Competency Test.	45%	55%	65%	75%

The IEP format can have a separate evaluation category but this should not be used to by-pass the need for a clear explanation of the evaluation measure. In the following example a measurable behavior is stated, and space is provided for the criterion, evaluation method, and date.

This format of parsing the criterion, method of evaluation and date is in deference to the IDEA-1990 requirement that IEPs have appropriate objective *criteria* and *evaluation* procedures and *schedules* to evaluate, at least an annually, instructional objectives.[46]

Measurable Performance	Criterion	Evaluation	Date
Goal: Identify content words	80%	T	June 15
Evaluation Methods: T = teacher made tests C = checklist S = standardized tests A = activities O = observation P = class participation			

If only benchmarks are used, the IEP form can be simplified as shown below where each benchmark is indicated by the criterion (C) and level of performance (P). In

the below example, the criterion is 50 percent and the actual level of performance achieved is 60 percent:

Goal	Objective 1		Objective 2		Objective 3		Objective 4	
	C	P	C	P	C	P	C	P
Identify content words	50%	60%						

Code: C = Criterion, P = Performance

Short-term objectives and benchmarks can be combined. The first short-term objective might involve math computation, the second math computation and applications, the third, computation, applications and measurement, and the last all four areas.

In this case, the first objective might have one benchmark, the second objective two benchmarks, etc. In this example, the first short-term objective entails one benchmark, the second short-term objective two benchmarks, etc.

Short-term and Benchmark Progression

Short-term objectives and benchmarks follow a progression based on performance, task, content, environment or a combination of these factors. The time progression, as already discussed, entails the breakdown of the goals into intermediate steps of short-term objectives and/or benchmarks. The content/task progress involves increasing content difficulty, or sequencing of content and/or the task.

When benchmarks are used, the progress from one benchmark to the next is defined by an amount or level of performance. If the goal is "to write a 7-sentence paragraph from a topic sentence by June 1," the benchmarks for achieving this goal might be as follows:

Benchmark	Criterion	Date
PLEP	0	Sep 1
1	1	Nov 1
2	3	Jan 30
3	5	Mar 15
4	7	Jun 15

Table XI gives several examples of different types of benchmarks metrics that could be used to quantify levels of performance. As discussed in a later section, standard scores are by far the most difficult benchmarks to use (e.g., percentile ranks, grade equivalents) because performance cannot be measured repeatedly using the same test throughout the year, the test might not correspond to instruction/remedial content, and the test might not be sensitive to actual instructional gains.

Table XI. Examples of Benchmark Metrics

Objective	Benchmarks			
	1	2	3	4
To increase sentence writing	1	3	5	7
To improve weekly spelling	40%	50%	60%	70%
Decrease classroom outbursts	12	6	3	0
Correctly complete 50 primary facts	16 min	12 min	8 min	4 min
Time on-task	5 min	10 min	20 min	30 min
Decrease oral reading errors	40	30	20	10
Organization checklist items completed	2	4	6	8
Errors per 100 words	50%	35%	20%	5%
Grade equivalent	2.0	2.4	2.8	3.2
Reading rate (words per minute)	10	20	30	40
Proportion of writing errors	.6	.45	.3	.15
Unit Test Score (raw score)	15	20	30	50
Social Behavior Rating (1=low and 5=high)	1.3	2.0	3.0	3.5
Number of pages read	5	10	25	50

Grades. Grades are not ordinarily used as goals or benchmarks. If the regular curriculum content area is unaffected by a child's disability, there would be no reason to address this area of regular classroom performance in the child's IEP. If, however, a student in special education has never received a passing grade in a regular curriculum class or in a more restrictive setting, a goal to receive a grade of B (or whatever index is used to gauge performance) might be a quite noteworthy and would do much to promote general curriculum participation and develop curriculum-related skills. In order for the student to pass a course, each short-term objective might be to receive a C or B. If the student has never passed a regular curriculum course, the first objective might be a C- or a classroom grade of 65 (or whatever is just passing), and subsequent grades might be 70, 75 and a quarterly grade of 80 by the end of the year.

As is the case with a general standardized score, a course grade will often ignore specific instructional needs. If the goal for a child is to receive a passing grade of 65 in a course, the probability of completing the goal will be increased if specific course needs are considered. For example, a teacher gives one unit test, one major project, five graded homework assignments, and five quizzes during the course of a twelve-week unit, and the student's grades are as follows:

Student	Quizzes					Homework					Project	Test	Grade
John S.	7	6	8	6	7	0	2	2	0	0	72	70	60

For the above, homework assignments and quizzes are worth 10 points, and the unit grade is determined by adding all grades and dividing by 3. The above data indicates that one the reason for failing the course is the result of not completing homework assignments. If the student had received a 5 for each homework assignment, although 5 is below average, the result would increase the student's overall average to 65 which is passing. The short-term objectives for achieving this goal might be as follows:

Objective #1: To complete all homework assignments.
Objective #2: To receive a grade of 5 on at least three homework assignments.
Objective #3: To complete all homework assignments with an average grade of 7.
Objective #4: To receive a final project grade and test grade of of 75

Project-related objectives. If the goal is to complete a project, a series of objectives might be created that lead to the successful project completion:

Objective #1: Complete a project outline by Sept. 20.
Objective #2: Begin project by Sept. 27.
Objective #3: Complete the first draft for completing the project by Oct. 20.
Objective #4: Submit completed project Nov. 10.

The time frame for the above objectives is less than a twelve-month period, but the process of completing projects could be used throughout the year. Thus, each quarter in which there is a project, a new timeline is developed to complete the project. The annual goal is to complete all projects throughout the course of the year.

Rating scale objectives. Ratings scales can be used to evaluate behavior and a variety of academic tasks (e.g., scoring written narratives). As is the case with tests, single item ratings are less reliable than a series of items or a summated rating. If ratings are used to measure a trait (e.g., self-concept) or ability (e.g., group participation) on a scale from one (poor) to five (excellent), and the scale consists of five items, the lowest score would be 5 and the maximum score 25. If a child receives a summated score of 5 (or an average rating of 1.0), the annual goal might be to raise this rating to 15 (or an average rating of 3.0) by the following sequence of benchmarks: 7, 9, 12, 15. In spite of all the limitations of rating scales and the subjectivity of ratings, this appraoch elevates ratings from a one-time assessment to a measure for actually evaluating and monitoring progress throughout the year.

Checklist objectives. As discussed in Chapter 4, a checklist can be used to indicate types of behavior or skills. If a behavior checklist indicates that a child exhibits 15 of the 20 behaviors listed, the goal might be to reduce this number from 16 to 0 by the end of the year using the following sequence of benchmarks: 16, 12, 8, 4, 0. The overall plan indicates the projected level of performance, and the teacher's responsibility is to develop interventions and strategies that will achieve these anticipated benchmarks.

Standard-score Benchmarks

Standard scores frequently provide the basis for goals and objectives, but often without due consideration to the nature of the scores or what is required to achieve progress. If the beginning level of performance is a grade equivalent of 1.5 and the goal is a grade equivalent of 3.5 by the end of the year, objectives must be created that are designed to achieve this goal by carefully considering the sequence of test content measured by the test.

For a child in the fifth grade who has a grade equivalent in reading comprehension of 1.5, a goal is created to increase this beginning level of performance to a grade equivalent of 3.5. Instead of using grade equivalents, percentile ranks or standard scores could be used as the beginning level of performance. In this example, the standardized test used to measure reading comprehension consists of passages of increasing length and difficulty, followed by a series of questions. In order to improve grade equivalent performance (or to increase the performance using any other test score), the following objectives are defined:

PLP: Reading Comprehension 1.5

Objective #1: 50% accuracy in reading comprehension using second grade material.
Objective #2: 75% accuracy in reading comprehension using second grade material.
Objective #3: 50% accuracy in reading comprehension using third grade material.
Objective #4: 70% accuracy in reading comprehension using third grade material.

Goal: Reading Comprehension 3.5

Instead of grade level reading material, the content could be three-sentence paragraphs, five-sentence paragraphs, etc., or a teacher-made test comprised of two paragraphs, each followed by five questions.

What is important when using standard scores to measure annual gains is the need to consider the type and sequence of content required to achieve a specific level of standard score performance. This must be accomplished without teaching the test, and by using measures other than the standardized test to assess short-term objective or benchmark performance. If increased score performance is the goal, test content and difficulty cannot be ignored in the design and implementation of instructional activities. Test scores will not magically improve by teaching content unrelated to the test.

SHORT-TERM OBJECTIVE CHARACTERISTICS

Annual goals and short-term objectives are similar in many ways in that both are defined in terms of measurability, criterion and time frame, but the emphasis for each is somewhat different.

Measurability. An annual IEP goal must be measurable, while a short-term objective is a measurable intermediate step or milestone used to monitor progress toward achieving the goal.[47] Short-term objectives are not just measurable, they are *the* measure for evaluating progress.

The change from IDEA-1990 to IDEA-1997 regarding objectives is more a clarification than a redefinition of IEP goal and objectives. The clarification is that short-term objectives or benchmarks are not unrelated instructional activities but, as described in the 1990 regulations, intermediate steps between the present levels of educational performance and annual goals.

Criteria. For measurable annual goals, the criterion is a level of performance or anticipated levels of performance at the end of the year. For short-term objectives, the measure of success can be a series of criteria or a single criterion for different short-term objectives. If the goal is to increase writing sentences from 0 to 8 sentences, the criteria for the short-term objectives might be 2, 4, 6, and 8 sentences where the last benchmark signifies the goal criterion (8 sentences). If the goal is to receive passing grades on quarterly tests in mathematics, the criterion for each short-term objective (i.e., a quarterly test in mathematics) might be 70 percent.

If there is difficulty envisioning a level of annual progress for an annual goal, the goal criterion could be arrived at by first determining the anticipated progress for the first short-term objective, then the second, etc. so that the last objective criterion is the annual goal criterion.

Goal-based objectives. Annual goals can be independent, interdependent, or relate to a common area of need. Short-term term IEP objectives are predicated on a logical breakdown of the annual goal, and are designed to subdivide the annual goal into meaningful segments that can be evaluated during the course of the year. Short-term objectives must be written with the expressed purpose of achieving an annual goal and not as activities that are independent of the goal.

Interrelated objectives. There is an interrelationship and/or an interdependence between short-term objectives. The short-term objectives or benchmarks for a goal are sequentially related based on a sequence of performance, environments, content, tasks, time or a combination of these factors. Because the focus of special education is the regular curriculum, objectives can also relate to a series of environments that increase regular classroom participation and/or decrease the need for specially designed instruction. If the goal is to enable the child to remain in the regular classroom 50 percent of the time by the end of the school year, the first objective might be to decrease a behavior, a second objective to decrease the behavior in the regular classroom, and the third objective is to decrease the behavior in the regular classroom with minimal special education (e.g., consultant teacher services).

Because short-term objectives or benchmarks for a goal are interrelated, the IEP documentation should not separate goals and objectives. By allowing one page for each goal and corresponding objectives, as well as the beginning level of performance, additional goals and objectives are easily added, removed or modified as necessary based on the evaluation of performance.

Number. Unlike activity objectives which can result in an excessive number of annual activities, the number of short-term objectives will correspond to the number of required reporting periods for nondisabled children. Although there should be at least two short-term objectives or benchmarks, IDEA-1997 regulations suggests that "generally, benchmarks establish expected performance levels that coincide with the reporting periods for informing parents."[48] If a school has four reporting periods, four benchmarks (or objectives) would coincide with these periods. If a school has eight reporting periods, eight benchmarks would coincide with the number of reporting periods. The number of objectives can be less than the number of reporting periods, but progress toward the goal must still be reported as frequently as progress is reported to parents of nondisabled children. If regular education report cards are given in November, January, March, and June, these would be obvious rimes to report progress toward goals. For the student who has two objectives, actual measurements for the two objectives could be used to report progress in addition to two informal evaluations or ratings of performance. If the number of short-term objectives corresponds to the number of yearly reports sent to parents of nondisabled children, the dates that these reports are sent can be used as the anticipated completion dates for the short-term objectives. If the first report is sent to parents of nondisabled children on November 15, this could be the anticipated completion date for the first short-term objective.

Pyramid objectives. Pyramid objectives include and expand the content and/or task difficulty from one objective to the next. A reading task might begin with a word bank of 20 words, and 20 new words are added following the successful completion of an objective. For the fourth objective the task entails 80 words, 60 of which have been part of previous objectives. For a mathematical computation task, the first objective might involve 9 facts, the second objective 36, the third objective 64, and all 100 facts are presented for the last objective. As shown by the following example, this type of format can be paired with varying criteria as shown below:

Objective #1: Knows facts with addends from 0-2 with 100% accuracy by December 15

Objective #2: Knows facts with addends from 0-5 with 95% accuracy February 15

Objective #3: Knows facts with addends from 0-7 with 90% accuracy March 31

Objective #4: Knows facts with addends from 0-9 with 85% accuracy by June 15.

If the goal is to reduce the number of writing errors per one hundred words when writing an essay, each short-term objective could be represented by an error benchmark:

Objective #1: Reduce total writing errors from 40 to 30

Objective #2: Reduce total writing errors from 40 to 30

Objective #2: Reduce total writing errors from 30 to 20

Objective #3: Reduce total writing errors from 20 to 10

Or a pyramid objectives could be created in which the instructional task is enhanced systematically for each objective:

Objective #1: Reduce errors in spelling from 15 to 10
Objective #2: Reduce errors in spelling from 12 to 9, in capitalization from 10 to 6
Objective #3: Reduce errors in spelling from 9 to 5, in capitalization from 6 to 3, and in punctuation from 5 to 1

Benchmark Criteria

Benchmark criteria provide the framework for individualizing instruction. The criterion for a goal period depends on the content, the content difficulty, the beginning level of performance, and the anticipated level of performance. If the task is to increase (or decrease) a behavior, a linear sequence of benchmarks might be appropriate (e.g., 20, 40, 60, 80 percent). If the task is to demonstrate ability with different content (e.g., a different group of words each week), the criteria might remain the same for each benchmark period (e.g., 75, 75, 75, 75 percent).

For each objective, the selection of an appropriate criterion depends on the beginning level of performance. The cavalier use of the *80 percent criterion*, is meaningless without a beginning level of performance frame of reference. If the goal is to identify 100 sight words with 80 percent accuracy, the difficulty and rate of progress depends on the child's beginning level of performance and previous learning history. The different

ways in which a sequence of objectives can be arranged is virtually infinite when different levels of content and task difficulty are combined with different criteria. Table XII provides several examples of how content difficulty can be matched with different criteria. For student A the first objective entails low content or task difficulty and only a 30 percent criterion, but the difficulty and criterion increases for each subsequent objective. For student B the criterion remains the same for each objective (70 percent), but the content difficulty increases. The appropriate combination of content and criterion depends on the child and the purpose of the goal. There might be occasions when the final criterion is not 70 percent or 90 percent, but 50 percent or even 30 percent (Students C and D in Table XII). Or the content difficulty and criteria might be high (E), or there might be an inverse relationship between content and criteria (Student F):

Table XII. Examples of Short-term Objective Difficulty/Criteria

Student	Objective #1		Objective #2		Objective #3	
	Difficulty	Criterion	Difficulty	Criterion	Difficulty	Criterion
A	Low	30%	Moderate	50%	High	70%
B	Low	70%	Moderate	70%	High	70%
C	High	30%	High	30%	High	30%
D	Low	10%	Low	30%	Low	50%
E	High	90%	High	90%	High	90%
D	Low	90%	Moderate	80%	High	70%

Task Objectives

Not every skill, behavior or task must be defined by a quantitative index such as a raw score, frequency or percentage. For certain tasks, the criterion is the completion of a single task or mastery as shown in the below examples:

Objective #1: Press switch when assisted by teacher
Objective #2: Press switch when given verbal cue by teacher
Objective #3: Press switch when cued by computer
Objective #4: Press switch when "diffe ent shape" is scanned

or

Objective #1: Read a one-page article
Objective #2: Read a short story
Objective #3: Read novel

For a nonacademic goal, the analysis of the task might result in the following objectives:

Objective #1: Stand with teacher help
Objective #2: Stand without teacher help
Objective #3: Walk 25 feet with teacher help
Objective #4: Walk 25 feet without teacher help

The sequence of tasks can simply follow a logical sequence of steps which may or may not involve increasing task difficulty:

Objective #1: Select topic
Objective #2: Discuss topic
Objective #3: Write story
Objective #4: Edit story

For transition service goals, the objectives often involve a series of complex skills such as the skills necessary for a student to be able to apply for a job.

Objective #1: Review different jobs
Objective #2: Visit job sites
Objective #3: Prepare job application
Objective #4: Apply for job

Analyzing the specific task needs of a child has an important role in the history of developing specially designed instruction relating to communication, self-help, socialization and basic motor skill development. For a child with a severe disability the annual goal might involve going from point X to Y on a bus, ordering a hamburger at McDonald's, catching a ball, reading functional words, drinking from a cup, making a sandwich, playing with others, or walking across the room unassisted. The only requirement for this approach is that the overall task is accomplished over an annual period, and that each short-term objective represents a task that results in progress toward achieving the final goal.

Rewriting Annual Objectives

When objectives are written as annual goals and not as intermediate steps, the objectives must be rewritten as short-term objectives or defined by benchmarks. For example, if the goal is to achieve each of the following by June 15, each objective would need to be defined by intermediate criteria and completion dates.

Goal: Improve reading readiness
Objective #1: Discriminate among three
  objective (e.g., ● ● ■)
Objective #2: Identify 10 sight words
Objective #3: Write letters from dictation
Objective #4: Recite the alphabet
Objective #5: Identify random letters

Acluster of annual objectives could relate to fine motor activities (e.g., cutting with a scissors, classifying objects), motor ability (e.g., balance, walking, running, throwing), self-help skills (e.g., eating, dressing, cleanliness), or a variety of academic or work-related tasks. Annual objectives most often represent a listing of goal-related activities that might be appropriate or might be used during the year, but not skills and abilities that are actually measured at intermediate intervals.

There are several approaches that can be used to change annual objectives to measurable annual goals or short-term objectives. First, each objective could be changed to a goal and short-term objectives or benchmarks developed for each new goal. An analysis of the various tasks might indicate that each task does not justify a separate goal, each with a series of short-term objectives. Second, the task can be couched in terms of short-term objectives by affixing dates to the objectives. In the above example, the completion date for the first objective might be December 15, February 15 for the second, etc. If the tasks are related hierarchically, this can effectively change the annual objectives to short-term objectives. However, if the tasks are not related hierarchically or are cannot be taught in a specific order throughout the year, the sequence of activities might not result in a logical breakdown of the goal.

A third method for dealing with annual objectives or activities is to redefine the objectives or activities into a series of planned short-term objectives. For example, consider the following activities which are presented in no particular order or sequence.

Objective #1: Pronounces words containing diphthongs
Objective #2: Pronounces two letter blends
Objective #3: Differentiating initial consonants
Objective #4: Differentiating final consonants
Objective #5: Names other words beginning with specified consonants
Objective #6: Pronounces words containing silent letters

The above cluster of activities could be reconceptialized as a series of three short-term objectives, the last of which represents the final or goal level of performance:

Objective #1
  Differentiating initial consonants with 50% accuracy
  Differentiating final consonants with 40% accuracy
Objective #2
  Differentiating initial consonants with 65% accuracy
  Differentiating final consonants with 60% accuracy
  Names words beginning with consonants with 50% accuracy
  Pronounces two letter blends with 40% accuracy
Objective #3
  Differentiating initial consonants with 80% accuracy
  Differentiating final consonants with 80% accuracy
  Names words beginning with consonants with 80% accuracy
  Pronounces two letter blends with 80% accuracy

Pronounces words containing silent letters with 70% accuracy

Pronounces words containing diphthongs with 70% accuracy

Individualized Goal Assessment

A fourth approach for redefining annual objectives into measurable annual goals and short-term objectives is to create an Individualized Goal Assessment (IGA). If the cluster of annual activities includes stacking blocks, sorting objects, folding paper, tracing objects, cutting with scissors, etc., an IGA can be created in which the overall performance of the related activities is evaluated for each benchmark period.

Task	No Progress	Some Progress	Progress	Good Progress	Completed
Stacking Blocks					
Sorting Objects					
Folding Paper					
Tracing Objects					
Cutting					

If No Progress is assigned a value of 0, and Some Progress a value of 1, etc., each item has a maximum value of 4 and the overall assessment has a maximum value of 20. If a child receives a summated score or rating of 1 (or an average score of .2), the annual goal might be a score of 10 or an average rating of 2.0. Benchmarks would then be developed to anticipate this level of progress by the end of the year. For each objective, the teacher decides what to emphasize during each intermittent time period or whether all the activities will be the focus of instruction.

Rather than using an overall IGA rating scale, performance for each item could be evaluated in terms of actual performance. If the present level of performance for stacking blocks is 1, the anticipated levels of performance might be stacking 2, 3, 4 and then 5 blocks. Each objective signifies an increased level of performance that is used to indicate progress rather than a rating scale.

Stacking Blocks	1	2	3	4	5

An IGA can combine different types of criteria. In the following example the IGA is comprised of six areas relating to written expression. The first three items show the anticipated progression of performance (beginning with the present level of performance) for spelling, punctuation, syntax. The last three items are ratings of vocabulary, handwriting and ideation where 1 is low and 5 is excellent. The child's performance is rated each benchmark period. If the child receives ratings of 20%, 12, 12, 3, 2 and 2, these would correspond to ratings of 1, 1, 2, 2, 1 and 1 or a summated rating of 8 and an average rating of 1.33. The first benchmark might be an average rating of 1.0 and the goal an average rating of 4.0.

Task	PLEP (0)	1	2	3	Goal (4)
Spelling	25%	20%	15%	10%	5%
Punctuation	15	12	9	6	3
Syntax	20	16	12	8	4
Vocabulary	1	2	3	4	5
Handwriting	1	2	3	4	5
Ideation	1	2	3	4	5

Whether or not to treat a cluster of goals/objectives as one goal or as separate goals depends on the importance of the goal in meeting a child's specific needs. The above might be reconfigured so that spelling is a separate goal and the IGA is comprised of the remaining categories. Or spelling, punctuation and syntax might be separate goals or even combined into a single IGA.

Short-term Objective Progress

The purpose of short-term objectives and benchmarks is to provide a mechanism for evaluating IEP progress, reporting IEP progress to parents, and to make decisions concerning the effectiveness of goals and objectives.[49] However, an agency, teacher, or service provider is not "held accountable if a child does not achieve the growth projected in the annual goals and benchmarks or objectives."[50] The IEP is not a guarantee that progress planned by IEP goals and objectives will be achieved. Nonetheless, schools and teachers are required to make a *good faith effort*[51] to achieve the goals and objectives or benchmarks. Furthermore, parents always have the right to request IEP revisions if the goals and objectives are thought to be inappropriate or ineffective.

Progress toward annual goals must be reported to parents as frequently as progress is reported to parents of nondisabled children, but the report must also include "the extent to which that progress is sufficient to enable the child to achieve the goals by the end of the year." A child might not achieve a goal, but the parents should be informed during the year concerning the child's ongoing progress toward goal achievement. Only when parents are given a realistic evaluation of ongoing progress toward goal achievement can parents and educators develop educational strategies or, if necessary, revise or change goals and/or objectives.

Changing objectives. Short-term objectives or benchmarks provide the plan for instruction, and are not intended to detail specific daily instructional activities. When objectives focus on instructional minutiae, overall planning is ignored and instructional activities are given precedence over planning; that is, the purpose of instruction is to follow a plan to achieve certain objectives and not to conduct instructional activities apart from the overall plan. As indicated in the Senate report for PL 105-17, teachers are invested with considerable flexibility to develop and implement instructional activities to meet goals and objectives. However, if a substantive change is "contemplated in the child's measurable annual goals, benchmarks, or short term objectives, or in any of the services or program modifications, or other components described in the child's IEP"[52] the IEP team must reconvene in a timely manner to address the change.

There are a occasions when a short-term objective or benchmark will require reconsideration. If a short-term objective requires a substantive change, this change must be made by the IEP team. One of the reasons why considerable care is taken when first constructing goals and objectives is that not doing so will often result in inappropriate or ineffective goals or objectives that will need change. When a goal or objective is clearly inappropriate, the goal or objective should be changed. As is the case with goals, objectives must be given an opportunity to work. The goal might be to write a five sentence paragraph with fewer than five misspellings, or to identify twenty-five sight words, but progress toward achieving this objective might be nonexistent during the initial three weeks of instruction. However, after three or four weeks, progress accelerates. Obviously, to change an objective during this initial period would preclude the opportunity to progress.

Ideally, each short-term objective is achieved on schedule and when the last objective is achieved, the goal has been accomplished. Short-term objectives indicate anticipated progress and are not intended to be exact determinations of performance. Often a child will not meet the anticipated level of progress, or progress will be in excess of what was anticipated. This does not mean that the remaining objectives are inappropriate, or that the IEP team must create new goals and objectives.

There are infinite number of progress curves that could reflect a child's progress toward a goal. One child might exhibit fairly linear performance gains, a second child might achieve the criterion for a goal immediately, and a third child might show small but significant gains throughout the year. A child might show inconsistent or no gain throughout the year because the goal is too difficult or the instructional activities ineffective. Another child might show no gain for five months then exhibit a dramatic increase in performance. If anything, a curve showing steady linear progress toward a goal is probably an atypical depiction of most performance curves.

The purpose of the yearly plan is to identify significant needs, anticipate growth in areas that will meet these needs and to monitor progress so that instructional activities can be modified to create a new and higher set of expectations (or goals). If a short-term objective must be modified, there is strong likelihood that the goal requires modification. If after a period of two months a student has learned only 5 sight words when the objective is 50, the goal of learning 200 sight words by end of the year might be unrealistic. There is less urgency in changing the overall goal than changing an objective that is clearly not attainable. If there is even a remote possibility that a goal might be reached, the instructional activities should be reconsidered to achieve the short-term objectives or benchmarks. The annual evaluation of IEP goals then considers any lack of expected progress toward the annual goals and the child's anticipated needs.[53] If at all possible, and if goals and objectives have been thoughtfully written to begin with, the annual review is the ideal time to create new measurable annual goals, delete goals and

objectives that are no longer suitable, and modify and increase the performance expectations based on prior goal and short-term objective performance.

•

The purpose of special education is to provide specially designed instruction, and measurable annual goals and short-term objectives or benchmarks provide the framework for specially designed instruction. The IEP is the comprehensive plan to address a child's needs, and measurable annual goals

and short-term objectives or benchmarks provide the instructional plan to improve abilities, skills or behaviors. To determine whether an IEP is a real plan to address real needs, one need look no further than the goals and objectives and how they are evaluated during the course of the year.

NOTES

[1] 34 CFR 300.26(b)(3). Special education.

[2] 34 CFR 300, Appendix A, Question #1.

[3] 20 USC 1451(a)(6)(A).

[4] 20 USC 1401(a)(20)(A) & (E).

[5] PL 94-142, 20 USC 1401(a)(19)(B).

[6] 20 USC 1414(d)(1)(A)(ii).

[7] 20 USC 1414(d)(1)(A)(viii).

[8] IDEA-1990, 34 CFR 300, Appendix C, Question #39.

[9] 20 USC 1451(a)(6)(A).

[10] Nebraska Standards, Reading/Writing, Grades K-12, Nebraska Board of Education, 1998, Standard 1.1.4.

[11] New Jersey IEP form, New Jersey Department of Education, 1999.

[12] IDEA-1990, 34 CFR 300, Appendix C, Question #39.

[13] 34 CFR 300, Appendix I. Involvement and Progress in the General Curriculum.

[14] PL 94-142, 20 USC 1401(a)(19)(E).

[15] 20 USC 1400(C)(5)(F) & (G).

[16] IDEA-1990, 20 USC 1401(a)(20)(B).

[17] 20 USC 1414(d)(1)(A)(ii).

[18] IDEA-1990, 34 CFR 300, Appendix C, Question #38.

[19] Evaluating Special Education (1983). ED 227 176. Department of Education, Washington D.C.

[20] 34 CFR 300.347 interprets the general curriculum as "the same curriculum as for non-disabled children."

[21] PL 94-142, 20 USC 1401(a)(19)(E).

[22] Evans v. Rhinebeck, 930 F. Supp. 83 (S.D.N.Y, 1996).

[23] 20 USC 1414(d)(1)(A)(ii).

[24] 34 CFR 300, Appendix A, Question #4.

[25] 34 CFR 300.26.

[26] Senate Report 105-17, p. 20.

[27] Thomas Hehir, Director, Office of Special Education Programs, October 4, 1994.

[28] *Ibid.*

[29] 34 CFR 300, Appendix A, Question #11.

[30] 34 CFR 300.306. Nonacademic services.

[31] 34 CFR 300, Appendix A, Question #1.

[32] 20 USC 1401(a)(20)(B).

[33] 20 USC 1414(d)(1)(A)(ii).

[34] 34 CFR 300, Appendix A, Question #1.

[35] IDEA-1990, 20 USC 1401(a)(20)(F).

[36] Nebraska Department of Education, Nebraska IEP Technical Assistance Guide, September, 1998.

[37] PL 94-142, 20 USC 1401(19)(E).

[38] 34 CFR 300, Appendix A, Question #1.

[39] *Ibid.*

[40] *Ibid.*

[41] IDEA-1990, 34 CFR 300, Appendix C,

Question #39.

[42] *Ibid.*

[43] 34 CFR 300, Appendix A, I. Involvement and Progress of Each Child With a Disability in the General Curriculum.

[44] *Ibid.*

[45] *Ibid.*

[46] 20 USC 1401(a)(20)(F).

[47] 34 CFR 300, Appendix A, Question #1.

[48] *Ibid.*

[49] 20 USC 1414(d)(1)(A)(viii).

[50] 34 CFR 300.350(b).

[51] 34 CFR 300.350(a)(2).

[52] Senate Report 105-17, p. 20.

[53] *Ibid.*, p. 24.

Chapter 7

IEP SERVICES

An IEP outlines a plan of individual- ized instruction and supports that can be monitored throughout the year, and documents services necessary to provide them. The IEP service requirement must include

> a statement of the special education and related services and supplementary aids and services to be provided to the child, or on behalf of the child, and a statement of the program modifications or supports for school personnel that will be provided for the child.[1]

For each service described above the IEP must also include "the projected date for the beginning of the services and modifications . . . and the anticipated frequency, location, and duration of those services and modifications."[2]

In addition to special education, related and supplementary aids and services, IDEA-1997 also requires a statement of modifications to state and districtwide assessments, alternate assessment services if necessary,[3] and transition services. Every child who receives services under IDEA must have a defined program of special education; all other services provided are based on individual need. To receive special education, a child must have unique educational needs that require specially defined instruction.

A large portion of IEP content is devoted to the provision of services. In addition to basic special education, related and supplementary aids and services, individual assessment modifications, and transitional services,[4] a child is also entitled to extended school year services, and other services that will allow the child to benefit from an educational environment, or promote inclusion in a regular educational environment. Other services cited in IDEA and the regulations include adult services, counseling services, educational services, extracurricular services, mental health services, nonacademic services, physical education, private school services, psychological services, rehabilitation services, social work services, supportive services, and vocational instruction. Specific services that are addressed by special education include academic and nonacademic instruction, related services, supplementary aids and services, and transition services. The timeframe for services is usually the school year unless extended school year services are required beyond the normal 180-day school year in order to provide a child with FAPE.

In addition to the variety of services described above, several other services directly or indirectly can play an important role in meeting a child needs. Section 504 services can provide special education, related services, or supplementary aids and services to a child who is not disabled under IDEA or eligible for IDEA services. Assistive technology services include any item, equipment, or system that is used to maintain or improve the functional capabilities of a child. Mediation services[5] entail a free, voluntary, and confidential mediation process, conducted by an impartial mediator in a timely manner, and resulting in a *written mediation agreement.* Coordinated services are described as developing a system to improve service delivery, accountability, service coordination, and improving interagency financial and personnel strategies and development. In certain situations, direct services involving special education and related services can be provided directly by the State Education Department. For at-risk infants and toddlers early intervention services are available for children "under 3 years of age who would be at risk of experi-

encing a substantial developmental delay if early intervention services were not provided to the individual."

Service overlap. The various services available to a child with a disability are not mutually exclusive. If a child is disabled under IDEA, specially designed instruction is required but this could be provided in the regular classroom via an itinerant teacher as a supplementary aid or service.[6] A related service (e.g., speech pathology) can entail special education, if the service involves specially designed instruction provide to meet the unique needs of a child. Section 504 services often entail specific modifications (e.g., additional test time) or classroom aids (e.g., humidifier) but Section 504 can be used to provide the full range of services if a child has a disability that is under Section 504 but not IDEA.

IEP Service Documentation

How and where services are specified in the IEP depends on the child's needs and the nature of the service. The IEP does not list every day-to-day activity, and nothing in IDEA-1997 "may be construed to require the IEP team to include information under one component of a child's IEP that is already contained in another component."[7] Certain services are age specific such as transition services which must be included in the IEP by age fourteen (or earlier if deemed appropriate by the IEP team), while the provision of other services is permissive (e.g., on-site private school services).

Where the service appears on an IEP also depends on whether the service is instructional or support-related. An instructional

service is provided to achieve a measurable annual goal to meet a disability, academic, or nonacademic need. Transition services might require either measurable annual goals, support services or both. If a student requires specific job skills, a measurable annual goal might be developed to assist the student in acquiring the necessary skill. On the other hand, a support service might be necessary to access different work settings or to increase vocational awareness. If a transition goal is developed for a student, the goal might be listed with the special education goals or included in a separate transition service section or as part of transition service plan.

SPECIAL EDUCATION SERVICES

The services associated with special education focus on *instruction*, and result in educational growth, enhanced learning or improved educational performance. Because of a child's disability, academic and/or nonacademic needs, instruction must be modified or changed. The purpose of measurable annual goals is to provide a annual plan for modified or changed instruction, as well as short-term objectives or benchmarks to plan and monitor progress during the year.

The IDEA-1990 regulations noted the importance of the definition of special education "since a child does not have a disability under this part unless he or she needs special education."[8] In other words, for a child to receive services under IDEA, the disability must affect educational performance, thereby requiring specially designed instruction and measurable annual goals to guide the course of instruction. If a child does not need special education, but has a disability and needs a related service or supplementary aid or service, the service would be provided under Section 504 but not IDEA.

Specially Designed Instruction

Special education is concerned with providing an appropriate educational program, and this is accomplished by specially designed instruction which is "instruction, at no cost to the parents, to meet the unique needs of a child with a disability, including (1) instruction conducted in the classroom, in the home, in hospitals and institutions, and in other settings; and (2) instruction in physical education."[9]

Special education is the focal point of IDEA services, and specially designed instruction is the essence of special education. For every child receiving services under IDEA, the child must need instructional content, methodology or delivery adapted or modified. The purpose of specially designed instruction is to adapt "to the needs of an eligible child under this part, the content, methodology, or delivery of instruction," to address needs that result from the child's disability, and to ensure access to the general curriculum.[10]

Special education and related services must address all special education and related services needs and must not be based on a child's disability. For example, the special education service for all children with specific learning disabilities could not be a resource room in which an individual child's need for resource room services were not considered. If a service is a necessary part of a reasonably calculated plan to provide educational benefit, the service should be provided. For each special education and related service, the frequency, location and duration of services must be specified in the IEP "so that the level of the agency's commitment of resources will be clear to parents and other IEP team members."[11] The overriding concern is to address all of the child's unique needs but cost for services can be a factor if the cost is so great that the education of other children is impacted.[12]

Special education services are provided by qualified personnel who have met "recognized certification, licensing, registration, or other comparable requirements that apply to the area in which the individuals are providing special education and related services."[13] An aid, paraprofessional or a regular classroom teacher not recognized by the state to provide special education could not provide specially designed instruction.

Services for Nondisabled Children

The emphasis on participation in the general curriculum often requires a special education service that directly or indirectly benefits children who do not have disabilities. Under IDEA-1997 funds can be used "for services provided in a regular class or other educationrelated setting to a child with a disability in accordance with the individualized education program of the child, even if one or more nondisabled children benefit from such services."[14]

In order to best provide for a child with a disability in the regular classroom, a special education teacher can work with children who are nondisabled if the activities are necessary to promote the regular classroom participation of the child. A special education teacher might provide instructional activities in the regular classroom on a one-to-one basis, with small groups of children with disabilities, with small groups of children with and without disabilities, and general classroom activities in which a child with a disability is a part. There might be occasions when working with only children who are nondisabled by the special education teacher promotes the regular classroom participation of a child who is disabled.

To emphasize the importance of the location of services, IDEA-1997 amended the IEP provision requiring the projected date for initiation and the duration of services to "the projected *date* for the beginning of the services and modifications . . . and the anticipated *frequency, location,* and *duration* of those services and modifications."[15] The *frequency* and *location* of services were added because where services are located can influence the type of services provided. For special education, a service might be required in a resource room one hour each day rather than a general assignment to a self-contained room. In the case of a related service, the appropriate location for the service "may be the regular classroom, so that the child does not have to choose between a needed service and the regular educational program."[16] For both special education and related services, the regular classroom might be the appropriate location for all or a part of services. The following IEP table shows how location, frequency and duration are often documented in the IEP:

Service*	Beginning Date	Location**	Duration	Frequency

*Type: Special = Special Education, Related = Related Service, Supplementary = Supplementary Aids and Services, Transition = Transition Services, Extended = Extended School Year Service
**Location: RC=Regular Classroom, SS=Support Service, CT=Consultant Teacher, RR=Resource Room, SP=Special Classroom, SC= Self-Contained Classroom

The description of services can be enhanced by requiring additional information such as ending service dates and the name of the service provider. Although indicating the service provider is not required, this does provide an important contact for parents and eliminates possible ambiguity concerning who will provide specific services.

Service	Beginning Date	Ending Date	Times Per Week	Duration Each Session	Location	Service Provider

For children receiving a variety of services, there is considerable collaboration and planning between teachers and service providers so that services do not interfere with one another, and services are coordinated with regular classroom activities. There might be a need to remove a child from the regular classroom for speech therapy, but not during reading or language arts, and not if the child has a specific learning disability in reading. Many problems involving conflict of services can be avoided by having all service providers attend the IEP meeting, or at least communicating with the IEP case manager, the primary service provider and/or each teacher of the child concerning location, duration and frequency of services. If an aide is responsible for specific services, the aide should attend the IEP meeting to clearly understand his or her role and responsibilities. The following illustrates an IEP format that combines the various services with basic information for the initiation, location, duration and frequency of the services.

Service	Type	Beginning	Location	Duration	Frequency
Special Education					
Related Services					
Supplementary Aids and Services					
Transition Services					
Extended School Year Services					
Other Services and Modifications					

The location, duration and frequency of services can also be integrated with measurable annual goals and short-term objectives and benchmarks as shown below. This format could also be used to provide a standard format for services requiring goals by related services providers. The resulting IEP would include a collection of goals, each requiring a single page and written in the same format:

Service:		
Goal:	Benchmark 1	
	Benchmark 2	
	Benchmark 3	
	Benchmark 4	
Beginning Date:		
Location:		
Duration:		
Frequency:		

Private School Services

Services might require other locations, including on-site private school services, homebound instruction, and special school or residential facility settings. The location of services is especially important for children with disabilities attending private schools. As a result of *Russman v. Board of Education of Watervliet*, the wording of the statutory[17] and regulatory guideline that on-site services "provided to children with disabilities may be provided on-site at a child's private school, including a religious school, to the extent consistent with law" is regarded as permissive (e.g., *may* be provided) and not mandatory. Because of scheduling conflicts, the availability of service providers and the coordination of public school services with those of the private school, services provided in the public school might be different in terms of the amount or frequency than the services provided at the private school location.[19] Nonetheless, what, how and when services are provided to children with disabilities attending private schools should be determined "in a timely and meaningful way" by representatives of private school and public school district.[20]

Extended School Year Services

If there is evidence that the gains made by a child during the school year regress significantly during the summer, extended school year services (ESY or ESYS) can be provided beyond the normal district school year. Extended school year services are defined as special education and related services provided to a child with a disability, beyond the normal school year (180 days), in accordance with the child's IEP, at no cost.[21] In *Armstrong v. Kline*, the parents of a student who was severely and profoundly impaired, challenged the rule limiting free public education to 180 school days because this "deprived handicapped children and members of their class of opportunity of attaining level of self-sufficiency which they would otherwise achieve given their handicap, and thus the 180-day rule deprived children and the class they represented of appropriate education" (p. 584).[22]

Extended school year services are not provided because a child has a particular disability category, because the service is available, as a summer recreational program or activity, or as a convenience to parents; extended school year services are provided explicitly to ensure that a child receives a free and appropriate public education. Also, the availability of summer school for nondisabled children does not require summer programs for all children with disabilities. The need for extended school year services is always made on an individual basis, based on the probability of regression, and indicated in the child's IEP in order to meet the FAPE mandate.

How the need for extended school services is determined varies from state to state, but many states follow *Armstrong* concerning regression of skills or abilities during the summer. If the regression rate during the summer of skills and abilities acquired during the year exceeds the recoupment rate, or the length of time to re-acquire these skills during the normal school year, extended year services might be necessary to develop an appropriate program to deal with the discrepancy. Most children, disabled and nondisabled, will experience some degree of regression during the summer, but for some children with disabilities, especially children with severe disabilities, the disparity between regression and recoupment can be significant. In *Armstrong* the plaintiffs argued that during the summer break the "children regress to such an extent that the time required to regain lost skills and development once programming resumes is so great that it renders impossible progress and the learning required for reaching their otherwise obtainable goals in the area of self-sufficiency" (p. 592).

There is no formula for determining regression or recoupment, or for comparing the two. The IEP team must consider previous regression and recoupment by comparing short-term objective performance at the end of one year and the beginning of the next school year. The deciding factor is whether there is a likelihood to fail or lose skills during the summer based on parent input and other data, and whether the child is embarking on a critical learning stage that requires immediate attention. For a child who has just begun to develop expressive language using single words, the discontinuation of language activities during the summer might have a negative impact on language acquisition.

Many of the court cases supporting the need for extended school services are based on students with severe disabilities. In *Alamo Heights Independent School District v. State Board of Education*, a child born with cerebral dysplasia (an abnormal development of the brain) needed extended school year services because he "would suffer at least substantial regression without continuous, structured programming during summer months" (p. 1154).[23] The child in this case had been making progress in areas such as feeding, dressing, and verbalization, but showed a significant loss of skill following the summer break.

For children with severe disabilities, a strong argument can be made that extended school year services are necessary to limit the effects of regression and thereby provide an appropriate program that develops self-sufficiency. A decision not to provide extended school year services might seem to be primarily cost-related, but there are several important reasons why such services might not be appropriate. For some children with disabilities, the summer months provide a respite from school, and an opportunity to generalize school-learned skills to authentic situations; for other children, extended school year services are simply not needed.

When the determination for extended school year services is made depends on state guidelines in addition to several practical considerations. If summer services are deemed necessary, these services can be included in the initial IEP. If the initial IEP is for ten months, the determination for extended school services might be made prior to the end of the school year. If extended services are not provided in the initial IEP, an evaluation of regression and recoupment the following year will provide baseline data for determining the appropriateness of these services for the following summer.

The quality and location of services during the summer will not necessarily be the same as those provided during the school year. Services located at School A during the school year might be relocated to School B during the summer if School A is not in session during this time. The least restrictive environment is often most affected by extended school year services. Because summer educational services do not always follow the regular year schedule, certain settings might not be available or might not be available in the same location, with the same class, or at the customary time.

Nonacademic Services

There is considerable emphasis on participation in the general curriculum in IDEA-1997, and participation in nonacademic services can play an important role in enabling a child to reach a level of self-sufficiency. Nonacademic activities can include clubs, intramural sports and activities, athletics, school specials, school projects, fund raising, meals, recess, study halls, special programs, recreational activities, physical education, or special physical education. The regulations state that "nonacademic and extracurricular services and activities may include counseling services, athletics, transportation, health services, recreational activities, special interest groups or clubs" referrals to outside agencies, and employment services.[24]

If necessary, specific nonacademic services can be included in the child's IEP if there is reason to believe a service or activity in which all children are entitled will not be provided.[25] The importance of nonacademic participation is also addressed in the Rehabilitation Act of 1973 regulations so that "in providing or arranging for the provision of nonacademic and extracurricular services and activities, including meals, recess periods, and the services and activities" the school district must ensure that children with disabilities participate with children who are not disabled to the maximum extent appropriate.[26]

Direct Services

As a type of special education service, a direct service can mean either specially designed instruction provided to a child with a disability in the regular classroom by a special education teacher (e.g., direct consultant teacher services)[27] or services provided directly to a child with a disability by a state or regional program. If a school district is unable to provide a service or when a regional program can best meet a child's needs, the State educational agency can provide services directly.[28] If the state agency provides direct services by means of a regional service-delivery system or program, the services must be consistent with the least restrictive requirement provision by educating children with disabilities, to the maximum extent appropriate, with children who are nondisabled.[29]

LEAST RESTRICTIVE ENVIRONMENT

The concept of Least Restrictive Environment (LRE) applies to all special education, related services, supplementary aids and services, and program supports and modifications. Every service provided to a child under IDEA must ensure that

> to the maximum extent appropriate, children with disabilities, including children in public or private institutions or other care facilities, are educated with children who are not disabled, and special classes, separate schooling, or other removal of children with disabilities from the regular educational environment occurs only when the nature or severity of the disability of a child is such that education in regular classes with the use of supplementary aids and services cannot be achieved satisfactorily.[30]

The primary focus of IDEA-1997 is the general education curriculum and participation in the least restrictive environment which is the regular classroom. Special education, related services, supplementary aids and services, and program modifications or supports for school personnel are provided so that the child can "be involved and progress in the general curriculum . . . and to participate in extracurricular and other nonacademic activities."[31] The emphasis

> is intended to produce attention to the accommodations and adjustments necessary for disabled children to access the general education curriculum and the special services which may be necessary for appropriate participation in particular areas of the curriculum due to the nature of the disability.[32]

The IEP requirements concerning participation and progress in the regular curriculum are not the same as the regulations concerning the least restrictive environment. There is no provision for a statement in the IEP to justify a restrictive environment although the extent of nonparticipation must be documented as described in the next section.[33] The LRE is the rationale underlying every service provided under IDEA, including special education, related services and program modifications. For every receiving child receiving IDEA services the placement must be based on the child's IEP,[34] and that if the IEP does not indicate a restrictive placement, "the child is educated in the school that he or she would attend if nondisabled."[35] In addition, consideration must be given to any potential harmful effects of a placement, and that a child is not removed only because the general curriculum must be modified.[36]

For special education, all services should be provided in the least restrictive environment, each support service should be as least restrictive as possible, and all restrictions concerning regular curriculum participation should be minimized. If a service can be provided in the regular classroom, it should be provided in the regular classroom. If a child does not need extended testing time, and this accommodation is cited in the IEP solely because of the child's disability (e.g., all children with disabilities receive extra time) and not actual need, this would be an overly restrictive accommodation. Likewise, if a child is excused from a foreign language requirement because of a specific learning disability designation, this would be a restriction to the child's regular curriculum access.

Continuum of Services

The obligation to provide the least restrictive environment is accomplished by providing a continuum of services. The Senate Report for IDEA-1997 has reaffirmed this need and

> supports the longstanding policy of a continuum of alternative placements designed to meet the unique needs of each child with a disability. Placement options available include instruction in regular classes, special classes, special schools, home instruction, and instruction in hospitals and institutions. For disabled children placed in regular classes, supplementary aids and services and resource room services or itinerant instruction must also be offered as needed.[37]

Although there is a policy of a continuum of services, there is no policy that a restrictive service placement precludes non-restrictive services by virtue of the placement. If a child is placed in a self-contained classroom, this does not prevent or otherwise limit participation, to the maximum extent appropriate, in regular classroom activities. Also, if the funding mechanism used by a state is made "on the basis of the type of setting in which a child is served, the funding mechanism does not result in placements that violate the" LRE requirements.[38]

Figure IV illustrates the continuum of alternative placements in IDEA-1997 regulations which must be included.[39] Although the regulations[40] identify specific types of placements (e.g., regular classroom, special classes, special schools, etc.), the continuum of placements is not a series of discrete placements, and a child's placement can involve different combinations of regular classroom, special classroom, and instruction in other settings.

Figure IV. Continuum of Alternative Placements

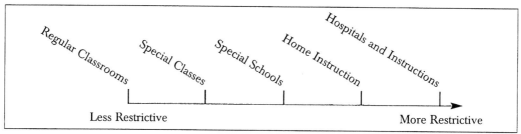

For every child with a disability, the question is not either a regular classroom or a restrictive placement but providing a continuum of services in relation to each child's needs. An appropriate education requires an education in the least restrictive environment; the continuum of service is used to provide this environment. One child might receive all services in the regular classroom; another child might receive most services in regular classes; and a third child might receive supplementary aids and services for language arts, resource room services to develop organizational and study skills, and speech pathology services outside of the regular classroom. By this interpretation, a full inclusion program that does not provide a continuum of services is just as inappropriate as an overly restrictive setting. Indeed, complete inclusion without a continuum of services runs afoul of both the FAPE and LRE provisions of IDEA.

As is the case with the provision of services, the location of services plays an important role in the availability of the least restrictive environment. If a child requires one hour of specially designed instruction a day, the location could be the regular classroom, a resource room, or a support classroom. In other words, special education and related services need not be equated with a special class, and a placement in a special classroom should not preclude the availability of other less restrictive environments.

The least restrictive environment. The least restrictive environment for providing special education is the regular classroom. Although special education is sometimes synonymous with a separate special education class, IDEA-1997 does "contain a presumption that children with disabilities are to be educated in regular classes,"[41] and that the LRE requirement creates "a strong preference in favor of mainstreaming."[42] For every child, regular classroom participation must be considered in conjunction with supplementary aids and services, or the "whole range of supplemental aids and services, including resource rooms and itinerant teachers."[43] The first test for determining the least restrictive environment is whether participation in the regular classroom has been considered with supplementary aids and services. This includes determining the benefits of services[44] and considering the needs of nondisabled children so the placement does not have a deleterious affect on the education of nondisabled children in the classroom.

The most restrictive environment is one in which there is the least opportunity to participate or progress in the general curriculum (e.g., residential school). Least and most restrictive environments do not imply a level of appropriateness; that is, a less restrictive environment is not more appropriate than a very restrictive environment. The appropriate educational setting is guided by individual needs, and the environment is selected to best meet these needs in the least invasive and restrictive manner possible.

A rationale in the IEP document for the LRE placement is not required, but only that the following factors are reviewed and considered prior to placement:

1. To the maximum extent appropriate children with disabilities are educated with children who are nondisabled.

2. Special classes, separate schooling or other removal from the regular educational environment occurs only if the nature or severity of the disability is such that education in regular classes with the use of supplementary aids and services cannot be achieved satisfactorily.[45]

3. Provisions are made for supplementary services (such as resource room or itinerant instruction) to be provided in conjunction with regular class placement.[46]

4. A continuum of alternative placements is available to meet the needs of children with disabilities for special education and related services.[47]

5. The placement decision is made by a group of persons, including the parents, and other persons knowledgeable about the child, evaluation data, and placement options.[48]

6. The placement is as close as possible to the child's home.[49]

7. Unless the IEP requires some other arrangement, the child is educated in the school that he or she would attend if nondisabled.[50]

8. Consideration is given to any potential harmful effect or the quality of services in the selection of the LRE.[51]

9. A child is not removed from education in age-appropriate classrooms solely because of needed modifications in the general curriculum.[52]

10. To the maximum extent appropriate, each child with a disability participates with nondisabled children in non-academic and extracurricular services and activities, including meals, and recess periods.[53]

Several states have developed checklists of LRE factors to consider prior to placement. The Arkansas IEP uses a ten-item checklist for Criteria for Determining Least Restrictive Environment as shown by following items:

1. [ ] To the maximum extent appropriate, children with disabilities, including children in public private institutions or other care facilities, are educated with children who do not have disabilities

2. [ ] Special classes, separate schooling or other removal of children with disabilities from the regular educational environment occurs only if the nature or severity of the disability is such that education in regular classes/appropriate preschool environment with the use of supplementary aids and services cannot be achieved satisfactorily

3. [ ] A continuum of alternative placements is available to the extent necessary to implement the IEP for each student with a disability, including instruction in regular classes, special classes, special schools, home instruction, and instruction in hospitals and institutions

4. [ ] Provisions have also been made for supplementary services (such as resource room or itinerant instruction) to be provided in conjunction with regular class placement/appropriate preschool environment

The justification for an LRE placement is based on the consideration of all pertinent factors by the IEP team and parent input, but the justification should not be generalized to all opportunities for less restrictive participation. If the justification for a self-contained classroom is that the child needs intensive academic accommodations and instruction because of a developmental disability, or when education in the regular classroom cannot be achieved satisfactorily, the justification should not preclude participation in all regular classroom activities, even if the participation is minimal. The justification for a restrictive placement, such as the need for *individualized instruction* or *the ability to complete goals and objectives* in a restrictive setting, should not ignore the presumption that a child is entitled to regular classroom participation.

The statement of special education services, related and supplementary services must also indicate how the child will be involved and progress in the general curriculum. Many IEPs follow the IDEA-1990 guideline that suggested "one way of meeting this requirement is to indicate the percent of time the child will be spending in the regular education program with non-disabled students. Another way is to list the specific regular education classes the child will be attending."[54] A separate regular education/ service matrix can be used to denote the extent of regular classroom participation for elementary, middle school, junior high, and high school students; or a matrix could be individualized based on the child's exact class schedule. As suggested in the 1990 regulations, regular classroom participation could be indicated by percentages or by check marks to indicate which regular education courses will be attended.

For the LRE-IEP format shown below, regular classroom participation could be indicated by a check, time value (e.g., ten minutes, thirty minutes) or a percentage. The advantage of a time value or percentage is that it does provide an opportunity to indicate some level of regular classroom participation. This might be thirty minutes a week for certain lessons or activities.

Class/Period	Regular Classroom	Consultant Teacher	Resource Room	Special Classroom
Language arts				
Social studies				
Mathematics				
Science				
Art				
Physical education				
Music				
Health				
Foreign language				
Study				

The continuum of services can include other categories such as transition or support programs for students who have been declassified. Special education classes can also be defined in terms of student-teacher-paraprofessional ratios. For example, a 15:1 class indicates a maximum of 15 students for every teacher, a 12:1 ratio represents 12 students for one teacher, and a 6:1:1 ratio signifies six students, one teacher, and one paraprofessional. As was discussed above, a child can be placed in a restrictive setting (12:1) classroom for most of the day, but participation in the regular classroom might be possible with or without support for a specified portion of the day. If a child is placed in a special school because of serious developmental or behavioral needs, special provisions might be made to include the child in a local school district to the maximum extent appropriate. If participation in the regular curriculum is not possible, a child in a special classroom might receive some services in the resource room (which is less restrictive).

Subject/Class	Regular Classroom	Support Services	Consultant Teacher	Related Service	Resource Room	15:1 Class	12:1 Class	6:1:1 Class
Language arts								
Social studies								
Mathematics								
Science								
Art								
Physical education								
Music								
Health								
Foreign language								
Study								

Rather than listing each placement, the IEP format can integrate regular classroom participation with the location, duration and frequency of services as shown below. For a child at the elementary level, classes generally follow a group schedule. For older students, where schedules are made on an individual basis, the least restrictive regular classroom schedule can be determined first, and then special education and related services specified as necessary.

Subject/Class	Regular Classroom	Service	Location	Duration	Frequency
Language arts					
Social studies					
Mathematics					
Science					

Art				
Physical education				
Music				
Health				
Foreign language				
Study				

The time when a service is provided is an important consideration in to avoid conflicts between different services or regular classroom activities and services. This can be addressed by considering where regular classroom participation and other services are provided according to defined school periods or classroom periods.

Period	Regular Classroom	Service	Location	Duration	Frequency
1. 8:00 – 8:44					
2. 8:45 – 9:14					
3. 9:15 – 9:59					
4. 10:00 – 10:44					
5. 10:45 – 11:29					
6. 11:30 – 12:14					
7. 12:15 – 12:59					
8. 1:00 – 1:44					
9. 1:45 – 2:29					
10. 2:30 – 3:14					
10. 3:15 – 3:59					

Rather than listing the schedule by designated time periods, a child's schedule could be listed by specific subject areas for each day of the week to show when and where special education services are provided:

C = consultant services
RR = resource room
P = pull-out (related service)
S = self-contained classroom

Subject/Class	Monday	Tuesday	Wednesday	Thursday	Friday
Language arts	RR	C	C	C	RR
Social studies					
Mathematics	RR	RR	RR	RR	RR

Science					
Lunch					
Art					
Physical education					
Health or Music					
Foreign language					
Study	C		RR		

If a child's anticipated regular classroom schedule is listed, participation in regular education, as well as needed special education and related services, can be described over a one week period. One important advantage of this type of schedule is that special education is not provided apart from the regular curriculum. If resource room services are indicated for eight periods a week, when this time is scheduled is an important factor. If the primary disability is in mathematics and reading, these periods could provide the needed time for resource room services. Of course, removing the child from the regular classroom can affect participation in the regular curriculum, especially if the resource room teacher does not follow the regular curriculum. For example, removing the child from regular classroom reading for resource room instruction in reading might detract rather than enhance involvement and progress in the regular reading curriculum; that is, the child might need regular classroom reading and resource room reading.

One solution to regular/special education scheduling that is not recommended is to sacrifice content area courses or nonacademic participation to provide time for pull-out services. In the case of physical education, these services must be made available to every child with a disability.[55] For children who receive pull-out services, a determination must be made as how and when a child can participate in the regular curriculum while being provided with the necessary services in the more restrictive setting.

Additional factors that must be considered when placing a child in the least restrictive environment include the need to base the placement on the child's IEP.[56] In other words, the IEP must include goals and services that cannot be provided in a less restrictive environment, and a child cannot be "removed from education in age-appropriate regular classrooms solely because of needed modifications in the general curriculum."[57] The substance of the IEP (e.g., PLEP, measurable annual goals, services, etc.) must provide a compelling argument why a less restrictive setting is necessary, and the need for regular classroom modifications is not a valid argument.

Regular Curriculum Participation.

Schipper and Wilson (1978) observed that one element that was omitted from many IEP forms was "mention of the percent of time the child will spend in regular classroom" (p. 13).[58] Very often this data is readily available and an index of regular participation can be used to compare participation from one year to the next, and also in conjunction with measurable annual goals that are designed to improve regular curriculum participation. An easily calculated index of the extent of regular classroom participation is the percent of total regular school/classroom academic and non-academic periods in which a child participates. In the exhibit below the school week is defined by eleven daily periods for a total number of fifty-five weekly periods. Instead of using time periods, the daily periods could be defined by subject areas (e.g., language arts, math, lunch, etc.). As shown below, special education services are defined by C (consultant teacher services in the regular classroom), R (resource room services), P (pull-out services), and S (self-contained classroom services). Pull-out services could include related services (e.g., speech), or resource room services.

Period	Mon.	Tues.	Wed.	Thurs.	Fri.
1. 8:00 – 8:44	C		C		C
2. 8:45 – 9:14	R	R	R	R	R
3. 9:15 – 9:59					
4. 10:00 – 10:44	R	R	R	R	R
5. 10:45 – 11:29					
6. 11:30 – 12:14	P		P		P
7. 12:15 – 12:59					
8. 1:00 – 1:44	R	R	R	R	R
9. 1:45 – 2:29					
10. 2:30 – 3:14					
10. 3:15 – 3:59					

The percent of total special education services is determined by Total Special Education Periods/Total Periods (100), and the total regular school participation is Periods in Regular Classroom/Total Periods (100). Instead of using time periods, actual time in minutes or percentages could be used to designate regular and special education participation. If a child is in a self-contained classroom, and no time is spent in the regular classroom or with nondisabled children, all periods would need to be marked either S (self-contained) or P (pull-out). If a child does not participate with nondisabled children during lunch or recess, this would need to be indicated.

For the above data the percent of total special education services is 21/55 (100) or 38 percent, the percent of special education services outside of the regular classroom is 18/55 (100) or 33 percent, the percent of special education services in the regular classroom is 3/55 (100) or 5 percent, and the percent of regular curriculum participation is 37/55 (100) or 67 percent. For children who are in self-contained classrooms, the amount of time spent in a less restrictive environment other than the regular classroom (e.g., resource room) will provide useful information for increasing participation in less restrictive environments.

In addition to providing a basis for developing overall program goals, indices of regular curriculum participation can also be used to develop individual annual goals (e.g., increasing the amount of regular classroom participation), or increasing the amount of regular classroom participation from one year to the next. If a major goal of IDEA-1997 is to increase participation in the general curriculum, there should be data available to evaluate the success of this goal.

Defining participation. The Office of Special Education Programs (OSEP) uses the following criteria to differentiate placement alternatives: (1) Regular class placement: 80% or more of the school day in the regular class; (2) Resource room placement: 40 to 79 percent of the school day in the regular class; and (3) Separate placement: 39 percent or less in the regular class. Using these criteria, from 1990–91 to 1994–95 the percentage of students from six to twenty-one receiving services in the regular class has increased from 32.8 percent to 44.5 percent.[59] In the above example where the total participation in the regular classroom is 67 percent, the amount of regular classroom participation falls into the resource room category.

Indicating the amount of regular classroom participation on the IEP requires a consideration of actual time spent in the regular classroom and in other placements. South Dakota requires a determination similar to the percentages used by OSEP described above,[60] but also a list of time spent in different settings (e.g., regular classroom, recess, art, between classes) with "typical peers."

Continuum of Alternative Placements

❑ 0100 General Classroom with Modifications 80-100%
❑ 0110 Resource Room 40-79%
❑ 0120 Self-Contained Classroom 0-39%
❑ 0130 Day Program > 50% out of home school
❑ 0140 24 Hour Program
❑ 0150 Home/Hospital

STATEMENT OF NONPARTICIPATION

A statement of nonparticipation added to the list of IEP requirements must include "an explanation of the extent, if any, to which the child will not participate with nondisabled children in the regular class and in"[61] in special education, related services, supplementary aids and services, program supports and modifications, involvement in the general curriculum, and participation in extracurricular and other nonacademic activities.

If a child is receiving all services in regular classroom settings, there is obviously no need for a statement of nonparticipation. However, a claim that a program is inclusionary, when in fact a child is pulled from the regular classroom for special education or related services, does not abrogate the need to provide a statement of nonparticipation. Likewise, if a child's IEP specifies all services in the regular classroom, removing the child from the regular classroom requires either changing the type of services indicated in the IEP or stating the reason for nonparticipation in the IEP.

The nonparticipation statement is intended to serve as a verification of the presumption that a child will be educated in the regular classroom, and as a method for evaluating the decision to remove a child from regular classroom participation. If there is a reason for nonparticipation, a more restrictive environment will be needed to meet the child's educational needs. If a child ordinarily has science at a certain time, but the IEP indicates that the child's goals cannot be achieved in regular classroom science or the level of science difficulty is too high, the reason for nonparticipation in the least restrictive setting must be addressed; that is, if regular classroom science is not appropriate, appropriate science goals should be written. If a child cannot participate in the regular classroom because of disruptive behavior, the reason for nonparticipation should highlight the behaviors that must be addressed via specially designed instruction in the restrictive setting. Every child is entitled to be involved in and progress in the general curriculum to the maximum extent appropriate, and nonparticipation does not mean that certain parts of the general curriculum are simply ignored. The Senate report for IDEA-1997 states "when the decision is made to educate the child separately, an explanation of that decision will need, at a minimum, to be stated as part of the child's IEP."[62]

As with all attempts to mandate the least restrictive environment, a statement explaining nonparticipation can easily be reduced to a perfunctory remark that the child "will not benefit from the regular classroom." For content areas, if a student has a reading disability, but has the cognitive skills to achieve in different content areas, the child's reading disorder should not prevent nonparticipation in content areas. A reason for nonparticipation cannot be the child's categorization; that is, stating that a child cannot participate because he or she is mentally retarded, learning disabled, etc. is inappropriate.

The statement of nonparticipation requires consideration of the many ways in which a child can be included in the regular curriculum. The statement should clearly indicate why a child cannot participate in art, a technology class, a home and careers course, a language arts class, extracurricular activities, etc. If the statement indicates that a child cannot participate in *all* class and school activities, there is a strong likelihood that the diverse ways in which regular class and school activities are accessed have not been thoroughly considered.

By simply considering the extent of nonparticipation in the regular classroom the IEP team might detect areas or times when participation is possible, even to a very minor extent. Just as important, the statement of nonparticipation provides a criterion for participation; that is, when the reason for nonparticipation is no longer valid because of specially designed instruction, the IEP team can reconsider increased involvement in the regular curriculum.

An open-ended statement of nonparticipation could require an explanation as to why a child cannot participate in each academic and nonacademic activity.

Regular Classroom Nonparticipation
(Explain the extent the child will not participate in the regular class)

The IEP statement of nonparticipation can be subdivided in several ways by academic/nonacademic areas, academic courses, or areas of instruction. The following requires a statement of nonparticipation for each period in a child's schedule:

Reason for Nonparticipation **(State the reason for nonparticipation and exceptions within each class period)**
Language Arts
Social Studies
Mathematics
Art
Lunch
Physical Education
Science
Technology
Other

Rather than indicating a reason for nonparticipation for each period, a checklist provides an easy-to-use solution for the statement of nonparticipation requirement. As is the case when providing a justification for a specific LRE placement, a checklist provides little room for considering the extent of nonparticipation. Not being able to achieve IEP goals in the regular classroom might be an explanation for a certain level of nonparticipation, but this assumes that the regular classroom goals and the IEP goals are completely different.

> **Reason for Nonparticipation**
>
> ❏ The child is not able to achieve IEP goals in the regular classroom.
>
> ❏ Instruction in the regular classroom would be disruptive to other students.
>
> ❏ The child is not able to participate in regular classroom instruction because of level of difficulty.

An overall checklist for all classes was not the intent of the nonparticipation statement. What is required is "an explanation" for nonparticipation so that possible participation is given serious consideration. The statement of nonparticipation not only describes why a child cannot participate in regular classroom activities, but the extent of nonparticipation. A child might not be able to participate when using a basal reader, but the child might be able to participate in story telling or language experience activities. In the below example, the relative extent of nonparticipation for different categories could be included in the statement:

Reason for Nonparticipation	Percent of Nonparticipation
The child is not able to achieve IEP goals in the regular classroom.	
Instruction in the regular classroom would be disruptive to other students.	
The child is not able to participate in regular classroom instruction because of level of difficulty.	

The statement of nonparticipation requires that an explanation be given why a child cannot participate in regular classroom activities, but the real question in terms of a continuum of services is why the child cannot participate in a lesser restrictive placement. Arkansas provides an interesting approach concerning nonparticipation by requiring in the IEP a "lesser restrictive placement option which the program developers considered and the reasons(s) why that option was rejected." If a child is placed in a self-contained classroom, the reason for rejecting a resource room setting should be stated; if a child is placed in a resource room, an explanation should be given for rejecting a regular classroom placement with supplementary aids and services.

When providing services, regular classroom participation, the reason for nonparticipation, and the location, duration and frequency of services should all be considered. The following IEP format combines these three elements in a single statement. If the percentage of regular classroom participation is less than 100, a nonparticipation statement is added; and if nonparticipation is indicated, the location, duration and frequency of services is specified:

Beginning date(s) of services:						
Subject/Class	Regular Class (%)	Nonparticipation	Service	Loc.	Dur.	Freq.
Language arts						
Social studies						
Mathematics						
Science						
Art						
Physical ed.						
Music						
Health						
Foreign lang.						
Study						

If at all possible, an attempt should be made to have services received outside of the regular classroom correspond to what the child would receive if participating in the regular classroom. If the first period of the day is devoted to reading in the regular classroom, this same period should provide reading in the more restrictive setting; a child with a severe reading disability might be unable to participate in regular classroom reading activities initially, but increase to some degree, even if for only one day of the week or ten minutes a day. If reading in the restrictive setting is in the afternoon, regular classroom participation might require rescheduling.

RELATED SERVICES

Related services are defined to mean "transportation and such developmental, corrective, and other supportive services as are required to assist a child with a disability to benefit from special education."[63] A related service often means a specific service provided directly to the child such as occupational or speech therapy, but the term includes a wide range of services such as counseling by a social worker or guidance counselor, parent counseling, vocational rehabilitation and transportation services such as adapting a bus for children with physical disabilities. Related services are defined in IDEA-1997 as

> transportation, and such developmental, corrective, and other supportive services (including speechlanguage pathology and audiology services, psychological services, physical and occupational therapy, recreation, including therapeutic recreation, social work services, counseling services, including rehabilitation counseling, orientation and mobility services, and medical services, except that such medical services shall be for diagnostic and evaluation purposes only) as may be required to assist a child with a disability to benefit from special education; and includes the early identification and assessment of disabling conditions in children.[64]

Speech pathology was expanded to "speech-language pathology" in IDEA-1997 to indicate the growing emphasis on the importance of identifying and remediating language disabilities; psychological services includes psychological assessment, evaluating assessments, behavioral evaluations and developing behavioral intervention strategies; orientation and mobility services was added to the list of related services to indicate that children with disabilities other than visual impairments might profit by such services.

Related service personnel can include regular classroom teachers, special education teachers, aids, paraprofessionals or persons from varying professional backgrounds and with a variety of operational titles, depending upon individual state requirements. Counseling services might be provided by social workers, psychologists, or guidance counselors." In addition, certain related services require administrative activities for planning and evaluation. For aids and paraprofessionals, the only restriction is that the paraprofessionals and assistants must be appropriately trained.[66]

As is the case with special education services, the amount of each related service must be specified with respect to frequency, location and duration. As can be seen from the list of possible related services shown in Table XIII, there must be careful coordination between regular classroom participation, special education and related services, especially if a child needs extensive services in several areas.

Table XIII. Examples of Related Services

Related Services

Adapted buses	Habilitation of hearing	Parent counseling and training
Art therapy	Habilitation of speech or language	Physical therapy
Artistic and cultural programs	Hearing aid selection	Psychological services
Assessment of disabilities	Hearing evaluation	Psychological testing
Assistive technology services	Hearing loss prevention	Recreation
Audiology services	Independent living services	Rehabilitation counseling
Auditory training	Individual hearing amplification	School health services
Career development	Individual counseling	Social work services
Corrective services	Language habilitation	Specialized equipment
Counseling services	Leisure education	Speechlanguage pathology
Counseling regarding hearing loss	Lifts and ramps	Speech conservation
Dance therapy	Medical services for evaluation	Technical assistance
Early identification	Mobility training	Therapeutic recreation
Early intervention	Music therapy	Transportation services
Employment preparation	Nutrition services	Travel training
Evaluating amplification	Occupational therapy	Vocational rehabilitation
Group counseling	Orientation and mobility services	services
Guidance counselors	Paraprofessionals	

Instructional and Noninstructional Services

As with specially designed instruction goals, related service goals require a statement to indicate the beginning date for services, and frequency, location, and duration of services as shown by the below IEP component:

Related Service	Date	Time	Frequency	Location	Duration	Provider
Adaptive P.E.						
Counseling						
Occupational Therapy						
Physical Therapy						
Speech and Language						
Transportation						
Vocational Training						
Other						

The IEP team is responsible for all instructional and noninstructional services, including related services, so that the instructional component of related services (e.g., goals and objectives) is not developed apart from the IEP. For example, the IEP team might provide a list of possible related services, but provide no connection between the related services and measurable annual goals. If a related service has an instructional component, measurable annual goals and short-term objectives or benchmarks must be included in the IEP.

SUPPLEMENTARY AIDS AND SERVICES

Supplementary aids and services focus on regular classroom participation. The goal of a supplementary aid or service is to allow a child to participate in the regular classroom. As a result, supplementary aids and services are not unique activities that are used in the regular classroom, but include all special education, related services, and modifications that promote and allow regular classroom participation. Supplementary aids and services include "aids, services, and other supports that are provided in regular education classes or other educationrelated settings to enable children with disabilities to be educated with nondisabled children to the maximum extent appropriate."[67] This means that the "removal of children with disabilities from the regular educational environment occurs only when the nature or severity of the disability of a child is such that education in regular classes with the use of supplementary aids and services cannot be achieved satisfactorily."

Supplementary aids and services have been "referred to as the 'mainstreaming' or placement in the 'least restrictive environment'" in which "Congress created a statutory preference for educating handicapped children with nonhandicapped children."[68] In *Greer v. Rome* supplementary aids and services are not merely modifications but include what the court referred to as "the whole range of supplemental aids and services, including resource rooms and itinerant instruction."

The preference for mainstreaming has been raised to an IEP mandate by the inclusion of a statement of the special education and related services and supplementary aids and services to be provided to the child, and a statement of the program modifications or supports for school personnel.[69] As indicated in *Greer v. Rome*, "the full range of supple-

mentary aids and services that may be provided in conjunction with regular education"[70] must be considered during the development of the IEP. Thus, the supplementary aids and services requirement is not a list of activities or modifications but the consideration by the IEP team of the full range of services, modifications, and supports that might be used to include a child in the regular classroom. As a result, supplementary aids and services could entail special education (e.g., a resource room teacher), a related service or program supports or modifications in the regular classroom.

The essence of supplementary aids and services is to enable children with disabilities to be educated with nondisabled children to the maximum extent appropriate by providing aids, services, and other supports in regular education classes or in other educationrelated settings. In *Oberti v. Board*[71] inclusion was defined as a full-time placement in a regular class with supplementary aids and services, but that another placement on the continuum might result in a mixed placement "in which a child might be a member of a regular class but obtain certain supplementary services in a separate resource room, or where he or she might be a member of a self-contained special education class."[72] In this context, "supplementary" means supplementary to the general education curriculum which might result in modifying the curriculum or providing supports and services that will allow the child to progress in the general curriculum, albeit in a more restrictive setting. Regardless of where supplementary aids and services are provided, the focus of such services is always the general curriculum and the regular education classroom.

Because the IEP need not be redundant, a

special education service (e.g., itinerant teacher) might be listed under special education, and additional aids and services listed under supplementary aids and services. In other words, the first task is to determine what special education services are necessary, then what related services are necessary in order to profit from special education, and then to consider what additional supplementary aids and services, modifications and supports are necessary for the child to be educated with nondisabled children to the maximum extent appropriate.

The importance of the "consideration" of supplementary aids and services is not limited to a vague IEP option that indicates that "the full range of supplementary aids and services were considered," but rather specific supplementary aids and services must be considered (e.g., assistive technology, an aide, direct special education services, curriculum modification) to allow regular classroom participation. If a particular aid or service is cost-prohibitive so as to "significantly impact upon the education of other children in the district,"[73] the aid or service might not be appropriate but the district must show that this is the case. Finally, although the district need not "actually implement supplemental aids and services before choosing an alternative to mainstreaming,"[74] the district must "give serious consideration to including handicapped children in the regular classroom."[75]

Table XIV lists a variety of services and aids that can be provided in the regular classroom by teachers, specialists, parents, paraprofessionals, teacher aids, tutors, volunteers and other individuals. As is the case with related services, supplementary aids require goals if the result of the service is instructional progress.

Table XIV. Examples of Supplementary Aids and Services

Supplementary Aids and Services

Aids	Services
Acoustics	Assistant
Amplification devices	Assistive technology specialist
Assistive technology devices	Behavior specialist
Braille lessons and materials	Braille specialist
Breaks during lessons/tasks	Consultant teacher
Calculator	Direct services
Cassette recorder	Individualized instruction
Class location	Indirect services
Class size	Interpreter
Computers/aids	Itinerant teacher
Dehumidifier	Mobility specialist
Extended time to complete tasks	Note taker
Headphones	Occupational therapist
Lighting	Paraprofessional
Magnification devices	Physical therapist
Reading stand	Peer tutor
Reduced time for tasks	Reader
Scheduling	Recorded notes/lessons

Seating arrangements	Remedial reading teacher
Software	Resource room teacher
Sound buffer	Speech therapist
Special chairs	Teacher aid
Special tables	Teaching assistant
Vaporizer	Tutor
Visor cap	Volunteer

ASSESSMENT MODIFICATIONS

The presumption that children with disabilities are to be educated in regular classes[76] also applies to state and districtwide assessments which can have a significant affect on educational access and opportunities. Prior to IDEA-1997, many IEPs included test modifications to address possible discrimination so that a child with a disability is not "excluded from participation in, denied benefits of, or be subjected to discrimination."[77] If a child requires a test in Braille in order to participate in a testing program, and to receive benefits from such testing, not providing the test in Braille would be discriminatory. The basic issue is fairness and testing a child's ability rather than disability so that

> tests are selected and administered so as best to ensure that when a test is administered to a child with impaired sensory, manual, or speaking skills, the test results accurately reflect the child's aptitude or achievement level or whatever other factors the test purports to measure, rather than reflecting the child's impaired sensory, manual, or speaking skills (unless those skills are the factors that the test purports to measure).[78]

Because of the importance of state and districtwide tests, IDEA-1997 requires a statement that addresses test accommodations and modifications that will enable participation in such assessments, or, if this is not possible, why state and districtwide assessments are not appropriate and how the student will be assessed.[79]

The need for test accommodations also must be balanced with issues of test validity and fairness. A test is valid when it measures what it purports to measure. The regulations require that standardized tests "have been validated for the specific purpose for which they are used," and "are administered by trained and knowledgeable personnel in accordance with any instructions provided by the producer of the tests."[80] If a standardized test is not conducted under standard conditions, the conditions must be explained.[81]

Virtually every change relating to the administration or modification of a test will have some impact on the test's validity. However, if the adaptations and modifications do not significantly alter test difficulty or inadvertently create a different test, most changes will not give the child an undue advantage but will allow the child to participate in the standardized test program. Table XV lists a variety of test accommodations, strategies and techniques that can be used to enable participation in schoolwide testing programs.

Table XV. Examples of Test Accommodations

Possible Test Accommodations

Accessibility (test site)	Exemptions (test or subtest)	Recorded tests
Acoustics (test site)	Facilitated communication	Reduced text per page
Adaptive furniture	Foreign language	Reduced time
Adaptive response	Guessing strategies	Respond in any manner
Additional test examples	Highlight text	Response strategies
Alternative assessment	Increased spacing	Scripted tests
Amplification aids	Individualized testing	Short instructions
Arithmetic tables allowed	Item layout	Signing instructions
Assistive technology	Item pacing	Signing items
Auditory amplification	Item placement	Simplified format
Augmentative communication	Large print bubble sheet	Simplified instructions
Between-test breaks	Large print test	Single switch technology
Braille	LEP format	Small group testing
Braille materials	LEP instructions	Special location
Bubble format	Magnification aids	Special marker/pen
Calculators	Manipulatives	Special seating
Cassette	Markers for answering	Special tables
Color coding	Masks for reading items	Spell check
Communication device	Modified grading	Student-determined time
Comparable time	Multi-day testing	Test breaks
Computational aids	Multiple choice modifications	Test environment
Computers	Nonverbal responses	Test location
Credit prorated	Note taker	Time cues
Critical-range testing	Oral responses	Time management
Developing rapport	Practice tests	Time of day (specified)
Developing test strategies	Preferential seating	Time strategy
Diagnostic interpretation	Presenting instructions	Transcriber
Eliminating biased items	Problem-solving aids	Translator
Eliminating subtests	Questions omitted	Using a scribe
End-of-test strategies	Reading aids	Using an abacus
Enhanced instructions	Reading content questions	Visual aids
Examiner aid	Reading instructions	Waive time
Examiner feedback	Reading stands	Within-test breaks
Examiner rapport	Record answers in test booklet	Writing aids
Examiner training	Recorded responses	Writing on test

There are several ways for listing test accommodations in a child's IEP (see Burns, 1998). Many IEPs include a checklist of possible accommodations. The problem with this approach is that consideration is often not give for the need for the accommodation or how the accommodation will be implemented. For example, if increased test time is indicated, there might be no apparent reason or supporting data for this accommodation, when the accommodation is used, or what exactly increased test time means (e.g., unlimited time, thirty minutes, etc.).

____Large print
____Braille
____Read test items

_____Sign test items
_____Simplify directions
_____Extra sample items
_____Preferential seating
_____Calculator
_____Increased test time
_____Alternate test location
_____Extended test breaks
_____Multiday testing
_____Assistive communication
_____Using a scribe
_____Test exemption

Least restrictive test accommodations. There are a number of factors that must be considered when determining the appropriate type of test accommodations. First, there must be a need for the accommodation. Test accommodations are provided to meet a specific need and not because a list of accommodations is provided on an IEP. Second, test accommodations should address specific needs. A child with attention deficit disorder might require multiple test periods or a wide-range test that requires less total test time. On the other hand, a child using Braille or a test that is read to a student might require from two to three times more test time. Third, test accommodations should

be as least restrictive as possible. A least restrictive accommodation might be to allow a student to sit near the test proctor, while the most restrictive is a test exemption. Fourth, and most important, the test accommodation should not invalidate what the test measures. If writing is being measured, and a scribe is indicated as a test accommodation, the scribe's task is to record and not add text, correct grammar or spelling, or interpret or otherwise change ideas. If spelling is being tested, a spell check or list or words to spell should not be available. A calculator is allowed for many tests, but not when what is being measured is basic computational skills.

The test accommodation of reading test questions raises test validity concerns. If questions are read to a student, the reader must be give clear instructions concerning how questions are read so as not to give inadvertent clues for answering questions. If questions are read, this accommodation should be restricted to only content area tests and not used with reading tests as that would completely invalidate the test, ignore the very purpose of the test and how it is administered, and is likely discriminatory.

TRANSITION SERVICES

The transition services required in an IEP concern the outcomes associated with special education and are designed to promote the transition from school to work. In IDEA-1997, transition services are defined as a set of coordinated activities for a student with a disability that

1. Are designed within an outcomeoriented process, that promotes movement from school to postschool activities, including postsecondary education, vocational

training, integrated employment (including supported employment), continuing and adult education, adult services, independent living, or community participation;

2. Are based on the individual student's needs, taking into account the student's preferences and interests; and

3. Include instruction, related services, community experiences, the development of

employment and other postschool adult living objectives, and, if appropriate, acquisition of daily living skills and functional vocational evaluation.[82]

The original purpose of transition services was to include a statement in the IEP no later than the age of sixteen (or before if appropriate) describing the coordinated set of activities, using an outcome-oriented process, that facilitates the transition from school to postschool activities.[83] Because of the importance of transition services as a necessary element to promote self-sufficiency, IDEA-1997 added a second provision beginning at age fourteen. The rationale for this provision is to

> focus attention on how the child's educational program can be planned to help the child make a successful transition to his or her goals for life after secondary school. This provision is designed to augment, and not replace, the separate transition services requirement, under which children with disabilities beginning no later than age sixteen receive transition services including instruction, community experiences, the development of employment and other post-school objectives and, when appropriate, independent living skills and functional vocational evaluation.[84]

The IDEA-1997 IEP requirements for transition services are as follows:

1. beginning at age 14, and updated annually, a statement of the transition service needs of the child under the applicable components of the child's IEP that focuses on the child's courses of study (such as participation in advanced placement courses or a vocational education program);

2. beginning at age 16 (or younger, if determined appropriate by the IEP Team), a statement of needed transition services for the child, including, when appropriate, a statement of the interagency responsibilities or any needed linkages.[85]

The transition services at age fourteen include courses and activities within the school that will promote independent living and the transition from school to work. The IEP team must begin to consider the postschool needs of the student and how these can be addressed. Appropriate activities might include vocational interest assessments, vocational counseling, or course work that will ready the student for postschool activities. For children with intensive needs, skills that will prepare for participation in more advance programs (e.g., job coach) and to maximize self-sufficiency in adult life can be addressed. Transition services can entail special education if the task is to develop a skill or ability as a result of specially designed instruction. These goal-related transition services might develop interview skills, improve specific job skills, or increase independent living skills (e.g., money management, driving, etc.).

Specific courses within the school curriculum should be identified that will contribute to the transition from school to work such as home economics, life skills, vocational courses, family planning, driver education, typing, etc. The types of school-based activities courses that might be offered in a school district to facilitate the transition from school to work (either with or without supplementary aids and services) include the following: applied science, civics, computers, consumer math, criminal justice, drawing, early childhood education, effective writing, ESL skills, food services, health education, industrial arts, keyboarding, life skills, office skills, physical education, restaurant operation and work study.

If necessary, new courses might be developed to address vocational needs and interests. Most important, beginning at age fourteen or earlier, the interests and preferences of the child should be given very serious consideration, especially in the development of the IEP. At age fourteen the task is to meet these needs within the school curriculum and develop linkages within the school to meet individual needs; at age sixteen (or earlier) the emphasis is on postschool needs and developing necessary linkages between various agencies to meet these needs. For many children with disabilities, the availability of clubs, organizations, and postschool activities provide ideal opportunities to acquire and generalize skills in a reasonably controlled environment. An important reason for beginning transition services before age sixteen is that many students with disabilities need more than two years of transition services, especially for students with intensive needs and students who are at risk of dropping out of school.

A close connection between age fourteen and sixteen transition services is important when considering the transition from school to work, and from the role of student to an independent and productive adult. The primarily in-school transition services beginning at age fourteen provide the foundation for the types of linkages and school-to-work activities provided at age sixteen.

IEP Team Student Participation

A key factor in the development of an effective transition service program is the participation of the student in the IEP development process and as an integral IEP member. Prior to the need for a statement of transition services, decisions are generally made on behalf of the child in the development of the IEP. Because the success of transition services is inextricably linked to the student's interests and preferences, the regulations for student participation in the IEP process is greatly expanded when transition services are considered. When transition services are considered by the IEP team, a student with a disability of any age is invited to the IEP meeting. If the student does not attend the IEP meeting, student preferences and interests must be considered.[86]

Transition Service Linkages

The statement of transition services requires the determination of needed linkages. A student might require not only a variety of transition services in order to move successfully from a school to a postschool environment, but the responsibilities and relationships between different agencies to achieve this goal must be planned and coordinated. For example, the IEP team, rehabilitation services, and a private agency might develop a coordinated plan to prepare a student for a work environment. Or a student might require counseling from a community college counselor, or a workshop developed by several agencies to acquaint the student with community college programs, expectations, requirements and general information. In addition to this type of postschool transition service involving linkages with other agencies, the student might require a college-type course provided by the local educational agency to prepare the student for this next level of study. Table XVI lists examples of different agencies and activities in which post-school linakges might be developed:

Table XVI. Postschool Transition Service Activities

Transitional Service Considerations

Acquisition of daily living skills	Family member services	Pre-employment training
ACT training	Family planning	Psychological services
Adult education	Family resource service centers	Recreational enhancement
Adult foster care	Financial assistance	Referral services
Adult goal identification	Food stamps	Regional occupational center programs
Adult services	Functional vocational evaluation	
Application services	GED preparation	Regional specialist program services
Applied technology education	Group home living	
Apprentice programs	Health insurance	Rehabilitation services
Assistive technology training	Household management skills	Rehabilitation technology
Career counseling	Identification of responsible agencies	Related service needs
Career planning		Residential care living
Church groups	Independent activities	SAT exam training
Church participation	Independent living	Seeking postsecondary assistance
Civic participation	In-home support services	
Club participation	Integrated employment	Semi-independent living
College placement	Integrated work services	Shelter care group home
College placement exam training	Intermediate care facility	Sheltered workshop programs
Communication skills training	Job application skills	Special education needs
Community based adult education programs	Job club services	Specialized equipment transportation
	Job coach services	
Community experiences	Job Opportunities and Basic Skills program (JOBS)	Specialized shelter care group home
Community job placement		
Community participation	Job placement assistance	Speech and language therapy
Compensatory education	Job retention skills	Supplemental Security Income
Competitive employment	Job search skills	
Computer assisted technology	Job skill training	Supported employment
Continuing and adult education	JTPA (Job Training Partnership Act)	Supported work models
Counseling services		Supportive services
Department of Rehabilitation Services	Junior college placement	Training material
	Medical and dental needs	Vehicle modification
Determining adult outcomes	Money management	Vocational aptitude assessment
Development of daily living skills	Occupational licenses	
Development of employment objectives	On-site job training	Vocational goal development
	Personal management skills	Vocational needs assessment
Development of interview skills	Plan for Achieving Self Support (PASS)	Vocational technical centers
Development of job search skills		Vocational training
Draft registration	Postschool objectives	Volunteer placement
Employment search	Postsecondary counseling	Work activity programs
Employment objectives	Postsecondary disability services	Work experience placements
Employment training	Postsecondary education	Work/Transportation training

The 1990 regulations required that the transition statement include instruction, community experiences, and the development of employment and other postschool adult living objectives.[87] Although this was deleted from IDEA-1997 regulations, some IEPs still require a justification for not providing transition services as shown below:

Transition Service	Yes	No	If No, Justification
Postsecondary Education			
Vocational Training			
Employment			
Adult Services			
Adult Education			
Independent Living			
Community Participation			

Individual Transition Plan

A separate Individual Transition Plan (ITP) or Individual Vocational Plan is not required, but doing so highlights this extremely important IEP component. As is the case for all special education services, the individual transition plan includes measurable annual goals and short-term objectives or benchmarks, if necessary, and the beginning date, frequency, location, and duration of transition/vocational services. The individual transition plan might also require the identification of transition or vocational activities, classes or coursework when necessary, and linkages with outside agencies.

School Transition Planning

In terms of the IEP document itself, many children with disabilities below the age of 14 will not have a transition service component, while other students require a very elaborate plan and coordinated set of activities. Nonetheless, a general emphasis on transition services throughout a child's schooling will greatly facilitate school-to-work transition services at the secondary level.

Although IDEA-1997 highlights the need for school-to-work transition services, this is really only one element of more general transition needs. The need for promoting a "smooth and effective" transition from one level to the next was addressed directly in IDEA-1997 with respect to the transition from early-intervention programs (under Part C of IDEA-1997).[88] By a child's third birthday, an IEP or an IFSP is developed and implemented and "the local educational agency will participate in transition planning conferences arranged by the designated lead agency."[89]

A child receiving special education at the elementary level might need specific program help to effectively deal with the transition from elementary to middle school (or from middle school to high school). The transition for children in regular education from one school program to the next is not always easy, and the task is sometimes even more difficult for children receiving special education services. For a child receiving elementary school services, this might include sample classes to familiarize the child with middle school classes and expectations, or specific programs that will prepare the child for this next level of education. The key to promoting an effective transition from one level to the next is be aware that each educational level is not an isolated entity and that by coordinating a steady transition throughout a child's education, the likelihood of success (i.e., the maximization of individual potential) is greatly enhanced.

OTHER SERVICES

Remedial Services

A child with a disability is entitled to all benefits of the regular curriculum, including access to remedial services in areas that are unrelated to the disability. If a child is identified as emotionally disturbed but has only minor problems in reading that would benefit from remedial reading, the child is entitled to remedial reading as is every child. However, if the child has a specific learning disability in basic reading, remedial reading could not replace special education as the appropriate service; that is, if the child has a disability involving reading, special education and not a remedial service is required. If a service is available to all students, as are most remedial services, then these services are not be considered in the realm of specially designed instruction. The distinction between remedial services and special education services also concerns the service provider. Special education is provided by a special education teacher so as to provide specially designed instruction as detailed in the IEP. A remedial activity is not necessarily provided by a special education teacher, and students in most remedial programs are generally not subject to IEP accountability. However, New York State does allow school districts to use certified reading teachers to provide specially designed instruction for children with specific disabilities in reading.[90] In this situation, services provided by the certified reading specialists are separated for funding purposes into those pertaining to Title I (remedial reading) and those involving special education and funded under IDEA. If services are provided by a reading specialist, the specialist should be part of the IEP team that formulates measurable annual reading goals and corresponding short-term objectives or benchmarks.

Section 504 Services

Part or all of IDEA-1997 services and modifications, including the development of an IEP, can be offered under Section 504 of the Rehabilitation Act of 1973. Children are eligibile for IDEA-1997 services if they are determined to have one of the 13 disabilities defined in the regulations, and they need special education.[91] However, a child can receive a related service or specific modification if they meet the more general definition of a disability under Section 504 as discussed in Chapter 1 (p. 16).

Declassification services. Declassification is a process that can occur at any time during a child's eligibility for special education and related services. Declassification can occur either because the child no longer has a disability, or no longer needs special education. As a result, and as per Section 504, services can be required for a child who either has a record of an impairment or is regarded as having an impairment. Declassification services include activities, supports and modifications that will promote the continuation of a child in the general curriculum without special education. In addition to Section 504 services, a school district might involve remedial personnel and provide school-based activities that will support the child's ability to be involved in and progress in the general curriculum following declassification.

NOTES

[1] 20 USC 1414(d)(1)(A)(iii).

[2] 20 USC 1414(d)(1)(A)(vi).

[3] 20 USC 1414(d)(1)(A)(v).

[4] 20 USC 1414(d)(1)(A)(vii).

[5] See *Federal Register*, Vol. 64, No. 48, March 12, 1999, Rules and Regulations, Major Changes in the Regulations, p. 12411.

[6] As is required by 34 CFR 300.551(b)(2).

[7] Senate Report 105-17, p. 23.

[8] IDEA-1990, 34 CFR 300.17, Note 1.

[9] 34 CFR 300.26(a).

[10] 34 CFR 300.26(b).

[11] 34 CFR 300, Appendix A, Question #35.

[12] Greer v. Rome, 950 F.2d 688 (11th Cir. 1991), p. 697.

[13] 34 CFR 300.23.

[14] 20 USC 1413(a)(4)(A).

[15] 20 USC 1414(d)(1)(A)(vi).

[16] Senate Report 105-17, p. 21.

[17] 20 USC 1412(a)(10)(A).

[18] 34 CFR 300.456.

[19] 34 CFR 300.455(a)(2) & (3).

[20] 34 CFR 300.454(b).

[21] 34 CFR 300.309.

[22] 476 F. Supp. 583 (1979).

[23] 790 F.2d 1153 (5th Cir. 1986).

[24] 34 CFR 300.306(b).

[25] 34 CFR 300.307(b).

[26] 34 CFR 104.34 Educational setting.

[27] New York State provides consultant teacher services which include both direct and indirect services (Part 200–Students with Disabilities Section 200.1(l). Indirect services include support and consultation that allow the regular classroom teacher to meet, at least partially, the instructional needs of a child with a disability in the regular classroom.

[28] 20 USC 1413(h)(1).

[29] 34 CFR 300.550(b)(1).

[30] 20 USC 1412(a)(5)(A).

[31] 20 USC 1414(d)(1)(A)(iii)(II).

[32] Senate Report 105-17, p. 20.

[33] 34 CFR 300.347(a)(4).

[34] 34 CFR 300.552(b)(2).

[35] 34 CFR 300.552(c).

[36] 34 CFR 300.552(d) & (e).

[37] Senate Report 105-17, p. 11.

[38] 20 USC 1412(a)(5)(B)(i).

[39] 34 CFR 300.551.

[40] 34 CFR 300.551(b)(1).

[41] Senate Report 105-17, p. 21.

[42] Daniel v. State, 874 F.2d 1036 (5th Cir. 1989).

[43] Greer v. Rone, 950 F.2d 688 (11th Cir. 1991).

[44] Hudson v. Rowley, 458 U.S. 176.

[45] 34 CFR 300.550(b).

[46] 34 CFR 300.551(b)(2).

[47] 34 CFR 300.551(a).

[48] 34 CFR 300.552(a)(1).

[49] 34 CFR 300.552(b)(3).

[50] 34 CFR 300.552(c).

[51] 34 CFR 300.552(d).

[52] 34 CFR 300.552(e).

[53] 34 CFR 300.553.

[54] IDEA-1990, 34 CFR 300, Appendix C, Question #52.

[55] 34 CFR 300.307.

[56] 34 CFR 300.352 Placements.

[57] 34 CFR 300.352(e).

[58] Schipper, W., and Wilson, W. (1978). *Implementation of individualized education programming: some observations and recommendations.* National Association of State Directors of Special Education, Washington, D.C.

[59] See the Nineteenth Annual Report to Congress on the Interpretation of the Individuals with Disabilities Education Act. U.S. Department of Education, page III-2 (footnote 1) and page III-3.

[60] State of South Dakota, Department of Education and Cultural Affairs, Office of Special Education. (1998). Individual Education Plan (IEP). Pierre, S.D., Page 8A.

[61] 20 USC 1414(d)(1)(A)(iv).

[62] Senate Report 105-17, p. 21.

[63] 34 CFR 300.4(a).

[64] 20 USC 1401(22).

[65] IDEA-1990, the note following 34 CFR 300.16.

[66] 34 CFR 300.136(f).

[67] 20 USC 1401(29).

[68] Greer v. Rome, 950 F.2d 688 (11th Cir. 1991).

[69] 20 USC 1414(d)(1)(A)(iii).

[70] 950 F. 2d 688 (11th Cir. 1991), p. 696.

[71] 789 F. Supp. 1322 (D.N.J.) 1992), p. 1326, Footnote #6.

[72] *Ibid.*

[73] 950 F.2d 688 (11th Cir. 1991), p. 696.

[74] Poolaw v. Bishop, 67 F.3d 830 (9th Cir. 1995), p. 835.

[75] *Ibid.*, p. 835.

[76] Senate Report 105-17, p. 21.

[77] 29 USC 797.

[78] 34 CFR 300.532(e).

[79] 20 USC 1414(d)(1)(A)(v).

[80] 34 CFR 300(c)(1).

[81] 34 CFR 300.532(d).

[82] 20 USC 1401(30) or Section 602(30).

[83] IDEA-1990 (PL 101-476) and 34 CFR 300.18(a).

[84] Senate Report 105-17, p. 22.

[85] 20 USC 1414(d)(1)(A)(vii).

[86] 34 CFR 300.344(b)(1) & (2).

[87] IDEA-1990, 34 CFR 300.18(b)(2)(i) to (iii).

[88] 20 USC 1412(a)(9).

[89] 20 USC 300.637(a)(8). To ensure a smooth transition for toddlers to preschool.

[90] New York State Education Department, Regulations of the Commissioner of Education, Section 200.6, 1997.

[91] 34 CFR 300.7.

Chapter 8

IEP EVALUATION

IEP PERFORMANCE AND PROCESS EVALUATION

THE IEP EVALUATION CONCERNS THE REVIEW, collection and interpretation of disability and educational data, the overall evaluation of IEP results, the determination of IEP team satisfaction with the process, the degree of IEP compliance, the quality of IEPs, and the extent IEPs promote participation in and progress in the general curriculum. The need to evaluate IEPs is consistent with the intention to "improve Federal program effectiveness and public accountability by promoting a new focus on results, service quality, and customer satisfaction."[1] For IEPs, the basic accountability issues concern compliance, reasonably calculated program development, overall program quality, and the evaluation of progress toward goals.

The IEP evaluation is comprised of *performance* and *process* evaluation. The IEP performance evaluation involves the assessment of ongoing and annual program effectiveness. The IEP process evaluation entails compliance with the regulations, satisfaction with the IEP process, overall IEP effectiveness, and the overall quality of IEPs. The IEP performance and process evaluation both require formative and summative assessments. The formative evaluation involves a continual shaping or *forming* of the IEP process to constantly improve the delivery of services. The formative evaluation entails the collection of ongoing information and data while the IEP is being implemented, and then using this information to make adjustments to individual programs and the delivery of services. Formative evaluation data and information include measured short-term objective performance, feedback from parents, teachers, and service providers during the school year. As shown in Table XVII, the formative IEP evaluation involves feedback relating to ongoing performance, procedural compliance during the year, and ensuring that the IEP plan is implemented and followed. The summative evaluation includes the annual evaluation of IEPs, the evaluation of overall IEP effectiveness and the general satisfaction with the IEP process as determined by an overall program review. The IEP annual evaluation concerns the need for individual IEP revision; the general program review centers about overall district-wide or school-wide IEP quality and effectiveness.

Table XVII. IEP Evaluation

Evaluation	Formative	Summative
IEP Performance	Progress Reports Ongoing Feedback	IEP Annual Evaluation
IEP Process	Compliance Evaluation Implementation Evaluation	General Program Review

Timelines

The IEP performance evaluation is comprised of on-going feedback, periodic reports to parents and an annual review of each IEP. There is not a specific timeline for progress reports and the annual evaluation other than the need to report progress toward achieving goals as often as progress is reported to parents of nondisabled children, and that the IEP is reviewed periodically (but not less than annually).[2] The general timeline shown in Figure V illustrates the various elements of an IEP evaluation.

The IEP process evaluation is comprised of a compliance evaluation, an implementation evaluation and general IEP program review. The compliance evaluation is conducted in conjunction with the development of the IEP to ensure that the IEP process and the IEP itself following statutory, regulatory and State guidelines. The implementation evaluation is conducted to ensure that goals are actually addressed, short-term objectives or benchmarks actually measured, and services actually provided. Although a compliance and implementation evaluation are not required by regulation, both can do much to improve the quality of IEPs and the IEP process.

Figure V. IEP Evaluation Timeline

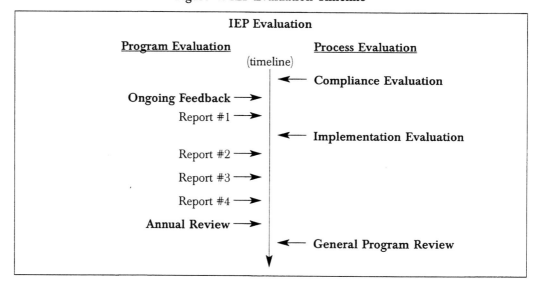

PERFORMANCE EVALUATION

The IEP performance evaluation concerns the measurement and reporting of progress toward annual goals, feedback during the school year from parents, progress reports concerning services, adjustments and needed revisions to IEPs required during the year, and a periodic review (at least annually) to determine whether measurable annual goals are being met.[3]

Feedback

Ongoing feedback requires a channel of communication between parents, regular education teachers, and special education service providers. For parents, the written consent for special education services provides an initial opportunity to consider proposed goals, program supports and modifications, and input concerning implementation and coordination with home-based activities and interventions. Although the parent is part of the IEP team, parents must have an opportunity to review the IEP document, voice concerns, and provide input concerning the IEP before services are provided.

The report to parents concerning progress toward goals is essential for obtaining parent feedback. These reports allow parents, teachers, and service providers to give feedback concerning goals, objectives, services, and needed program supports and modifications. In addition, periodic progress reports provide teachers and other service providers with information and data to make ongoing program adjustments and modifications to better meet each child's needs. Above all, progress reports provide teachers and parents with an understandable and straightforward evaluation of progress toward achieving the measurable annual goals as indicated by the achievement of short-term objectives or benchmarks.

Progress Reports

The assessment of short-term objectives or benchmarks is a key source of data in the evaluation of IEP performance. Each short-term objective or benchmark constitutes an evaluation of goal progress. Measurable annual goals address individual needs and provide the direction for special education and related services; short-term objectives or benchmarks provide the basis for reporting progress to parents, determining the adequacy of progress toward the annual goals, and whether "progress is sufficient to enable the child to achieve the goals by the end of the year."[4] Although IDEA-1997 requires that parents of disabled children be informed as frequently as parents of non-disabled children are informed of their child's progress, regular classroom teachers and other service providers should also be informed of progress toward achieving annual goals.

As important as formative evaluation is to the development of a viable IEP, goals and objectives should not be changed every several weeks because a child is performing below or above expectations. Often an understanding of needed IEP changes requires a reasonable period of time to discern trends, new or additional areas of need, and the overall effectiveness of services. If goals and services are constantly changed, initial planning might be suspect or that a reasonably calculated plan was not developed.

Annual IEP Reviews

At least annually, the IEP team must consider goal achievement, lack of progress, re-evaluations, current needs, parent input, and any other matters of concern.[5] Although these periodic reviews can occur as frequently as necessary, most reviews will take the form of an annual review. The annual review provides an opportunity to evaluate the measurable annual goals, short-term objectives and benchmarks, as well as related services, modifications, program supports, and the extent of regular classroom participation for each child's IEPs.

Short-term objective performance provides an opportunity during the year to consider a child's progress and, based on this information, whether the child is likely to achieve the annual goal. Periodic reports are necessary for monitoring progress, but the ultimate test is whether goals have been achieved. The purpose of the IEP review is to evaluate whether goals have been achieved, revise the IEP by deleting unnecessary goals, modifying existing goals, or modifying short-term objectives or bench-marks for goals, or developing new goals to meet anticipated needs based on re-evaluations and/or parent input.[6]

If IEP annual progress is not considered, there is little likelihood that IEPs will be modified or revised. The failure to adequately revise IEPs is most obvious when IEP goals and objectives are carried over from one year to the next without change. The extent each goal has been achieved or whether the goal should be revised, must be considered annually. If the goal has not been achieved, either a more appropriate goal is required, or the short-term objectives or benchmarks must be reconsidered. If goals and objectives are carried over from one year to the next, often word-for-word, the IEP is most likely not a real plan for addressing educational needs. An IEP should reflect a gradient of improvement in terms of ability, performance, or skill. If there is no change in an IEP from one year to the next, there will probably be no change in the child's ability, performance, or skill.

PROCESS EVALUATION

The IEP process evaluation consists of a determination of whether IEPs are written in compliance with the regulations, the extent IEPs provide reasonably calculated plans, and the assessment of overall IEP quality. The evaluation of the IEP process includes the evaluation of IEP completeness, the implementation of IEPs, satisfaction with the IEP process, the evaluation of quality indicators and other relevant program information such as the extent of regular curriculum participation, and the number of children classified and declassified.

Compliance Evaluation

Compliance evaluation, the first prong of the *Hudson v. Rowley* test concerning IEP appropriateness, concerns compliance with the procedures set forth in IDEA.[7] Compliance with IDEA-1997 involves adhering to regulations that directly and indirectly define the IEP process and IEP content. Compliance is achieved by meeting the letter of the law and a good-faith effort to adhere to the regulations before, during, and after IEP development and implementation. The language of the law and regulations sometimes leaves no question as to whether compliance is mandated or strongly encouraged. For example, "a meeting to develop an IEP for the child *must* be conducted within 30-days of a determination that the child needs special education and related services."[8] For other regulations a good-faith effort is required as to when to comply such as when a school district "shall take steps to ensure that one or both of the parents"[9] attend IEP meetings.

Noncompliance, intentional or not, can undermine the integrity of an IEP. If a child does not have a disability, does not need special education, or has needs that are the result of lack of prior instruction, an IEP that is developed is inherently flawed. If the IEP does not contain all the required elements, the IEP is clearly not in compliance. The regulations require measurable annual goals that enable a child to be involved in and progress in the general curriculum, but the likelihood of this occurring is made more difficult if the regular classroom teacher or parents are not active IEP team participants. If the IEP team does not review and evaluate IEP progress, and make appropriate revisions, the IEP is not in compliance.

One method for conducting a compliance evaluation is to use a checklist to note each required IEP element or procedure. New York State has developed several checklists relating to initial evaluations and reevaluations, IEP requirements for implementation, and procedural safeguards.[10] The checklist for implementation places emphasis on changes in IDEA-1997 requirements and provides an overall guide for school districts to ensure compliance with the law and regulations. The following sample items from the New York checklist illustrates this type of format for IEP implementation:

✔ Amend the IEP document to ensure all the required components are included.

✔ Establish administrative policies and practices to ensure training on these requirements is provided to all parents and members of the Committee on Special Education, Subcommittee on Special Education, and Committee on preschool Special Education.

✔ Ensure that the Committee reviews a student's prior instruction, and lack thereof, in reading and math and limited English Proficiency in relation to the student's eligibility for special education and related services.

California has a rather lengthy 72-item Individualized Education Program (IEP) Checklist that uses a simple checklist format as shown by the following items:

1. ❏ A statement of the child's present levels of performance including how the disability affects the child's involvement and progress in the general curriculum.

27. ❏ Transition language in the IEP supports the movement of students from special to general education classrooms, from middle to high school, and from infant to preschool to kindergarten to first grade programs.

43. ❏ Interpreters for the IEP meeting are obtained for parents who are deaf or whose primary language is other than English.

Compliance checklists often identify exact regulations that must be met, or should have been met, rather than focusing on IEP quality. The survey used in the Skokie, Illinois study focused not only on the existence of specific IEP content but also IEP quality.[11] The questions used in this evaluation are quite timely and illustrate an awareness for needed IEP quality and not merely IEP compliance. Specifically, this survey highlighted two areas of goals for PL 94-142 that are emphasized in IDEA-1997: Short-term objectives must be related to the goal and short-term objectives must be logically sequenced. Noteworthy in this survey is the reference to what constitutes quality short-term objectives by evaluating whether the objectives are related to the goal, logically sequenced and measurable. And most important, whether an evaluation was actually done.

	Yes	No	Questionable
6. Does the IEP have short-term (instructional) objectives (STOs)?	___	___	___
Are the STOs:			
a) Related to the goal?	___	___	___
b) Logically and cumulatively sequenced?	___	___	___
c) Measurable?	___	___	___
7. Does the IEP include evaluation measures for each STO?			
a) Are the evaluation measures repeatable?	___	___	___
b) Was the evaluation done?	___	___	___

Even when the intent is to comply with the regulations, not knowing the regulations, or the underlying intent of a regulation, can jeopardize compliance. This is likely to occur when the majority of IEP team members do not have a background in assessment or special education. One approach for dealing with this problem is to use a simplified checklist during the IEP meeting, or at least have a checklist available to each IEP member for reference purposes. The checklist in Table XVIII includes items required in IEPs as detailed in IDEA (see 20 USC 1414(d)):

Table XVIII. IEP Checklist

IEP Checklist

Instructions: Has each of the following been considered and, if necessary, included in the child's IEP?

❏   1. General levels of educational performance
❏   2. How the disability affects general curriculum involvement
❏   3. How the disability affects nonacademic performance
❏   4. Measurable annual goals
❏   5. Measurable goals for each identified need

❑ 6. Measurable annual goals meet disability-related needs
❑ 7. Short-term objectives (STOs) or benchmarks
❑ 8. STOs or benchmarks represent intermediate steps
❑ 9. Each STO or benchmark has a measure
❑ 10. Each STO has completion date, and criterion
❑ 11. Special education services
❑ 12. Related services
❑ 13. Supplementary aids and services
❑ 14. Program modifications or supports
❑ 15. Regular curriculum involvement
❑ 16. Nonparticipation statement
❑ 17. Test accommodations
❑ 18. Alternate assessments (if necessary)
❑ 19. The beginning date of services
❑ 20. Location, duration, and frequency of services
❑ 21. How goal progress will be measured
❑ 22. How progress will be reported to parents
❑ 23. Age 14 school transition plan
❑ 24. Age 16 school-to-work transition plan
❑ 25. Transfer of rights statement (if appropriate)

Rating scales for IEPs provide a method for allowing each IEP member to indicate their satisfaction with the IEP process for each IEP (Table XIX). Indeed, the IEP membership should decide what is included in the IEP survey. The primary purpose of the survey is provide each team member with an opportunity to give feedback and a method for discerning major areas of disagreement (or agreement).

Table XIX. IEP Evaluation

IEP Evaluation

To what degree:	Low	Acceptable			High
1. Does the IEP address academic needs?	1	2	3	4	5
2. Does the IEP address nonacademic needs?	1	2	3	4	5
3. Are the goals appropriate?	1	2	3	4	5
5. Do the goals relate to needs?	1	2	3	4	5
6. Do the objectives breakdown the goals?	1	2	3	4	5
7. Are services provided to achieve the goals?	1	2	3	4	5
8. Are the IEP services in the IEP appropriate?	1	2	3	4	5
9. Does the IEP provide the least restrictive environment?	1	2	3	4	5
10. Does the IEP contain necessary program supports and modifications?	1	2	3	4	5
11. Is the measurement of goal progress clearly defined?	1	2	3	4	5
12. Is progress reported to parent on a regular basis?	1	2	3	4	5

Because the purpose of the of the evaluation is for the IEP team to consider the overall quality of IEPs, a simplified rating scale with fewer items and scale values might be more than adequate (Table XX).

Table XX. Simplified IEP Evaluation

IEP Evaluation

To what degree:

1. Does the IEP meet educational needs?	No	Somewhat	Yes
2. Are the goals appropriate?	No	Somewhat	Yes
3. Are services provided to achieve the goals?	No	Somewhat	Yes
4. Are the IEP services in the IEP appropriate?	No	Somewhat	Yes
5. Does the IEP provide the least restrictive environment?	No	Somewhat	Yes
6. Is progress reported to parent on a regular basis?	No	Somewhat	Yes
7. Does the IEP seem to be in compliance?	No	Somewhat	Yes

The Nebraska Department of Education has a satisfaction survey that is very parent/consumer oriented and includes the following types of questions: Has the IEP team meeting been helpful in planning the child's educational program? Can the goals set for the child be accomplished during the current school year? Did you have all of your questions concerning the child answered at the IEP meeting? Which participant talked the most? Which participant talked the least? How much influence do you think you had in defining the child's curriculum?[12]

Implementation Evaluation

The implementation evaluation is described by Stevens, Lawrenz, and Sharp (1997), as a check of the reality of the planned activities: "Before you can evaluate the outcomes of a project, you must make sure the project is really operating, and if it is operating according to its plan or description" (p. 6).[13] The purpose of the implementation evaluation, or quality check, is to identify problems or potential problems at a time in the year when changes can be made.

Shortly after the first progress report is sent to parents, a small sample of IEPs should be reviewed by the IEP team or a small ad hoc evaluation team to determine whether short-term objectives are actually being measured, if services are provided as described in the IEPs, and whether modifications and program supports have been made. The IEP document is a reality, but what is actually accomplished by the IEP may or may not be real, depending on whether the IEP item is a real plan to address needs or a document to show compliance.

Compliance is important in the implementation evaluation in that progress must be reported to parents, the IEP must be reviewed and revised, and due process procedures must be followed. However, the focus of the implementation evaluation is to ensure that services, modifications and supports are *actually* being implemented, and that performance toward annual goals is actually measured.

One of the objectives in the evaluation of special education and the IEP process in the Skokie survey was "to measure the quality of IEPs by using a team of readers to study a random sampling of IEP documents to rate each according to a desired standard."[14] A controlled evaluation of the IEP process at set intervals would be ideal, but this is not generally practical when considering such factors as time, effort and available resources. Nonetheless, an implementation evaluation does not require an exhaustive investigation but is designed to rectify problems in the IEP process as soon as possible.

The implementation evaluation need not consider every IEP, but a small sample of IEPs might be sufficient. An implementation evaluation team could be conducted by a small group (two or three persons) knowledgeable about the IEP process, and the resulting evaluation should not require a lengthy report. Considering that most school districts do nothing in the way of an implementation evaluation, even evaluating one IEP by one evaluator would be better than nothing at all.

For an implementation evaluation, the sampling of IEPs and corresponding progress reports should be evaluated by someone other than the special education teacher or service provider. A school administrator (e.g., director of special education) might randomly select a small sample of IEPs following the first reporting period, visit the service provider, inspect the actual assessments used to measure progress, and provide a brief summary that can be used by the IEP team to improve the IEP process.

An implementation evaluation should be conducted by the school district after the first reporting period. At this point in time, how (or if) short-term objectives or benchmarks are actually measured can be determined, how progress is reported to parents assessed, and the degree of progress toward achieving annual goals evaluated. As shown in Table XXI, the implementation evaluation need not be an excessively long survey, but should provide an opportunity for parents and service providers to provide feedback concerning whether services are being provided, and the quality of the IEP services.

Table XXI. IEP Implementation Evaluation

Implementation Evaluation

Category	Yes	No	If No, Explain
1. Are all of the services specified in the IEP being provided?			
2. Are all of the modifications specified in the IEP being provided?			
3. Are the measurable annual goals appropriate?			
4. Are the short-term objectives or benchmarks appropriate?			
5. Was short-term objective or benchmark progress measured?			
6. Are there actual assessments that show levels of progress?			
7. Were results reported to parents?			
8. Did the parents provide feedback or respond to the report?			
9. Are there any immediate concerns about IEP services?			
10. Are there any concerns about goals, objectives or benchmarks?			

The evaluation of IEP implementation can also consider the appropriateness of goals and objectives, and individual needs. A need might have gone undetected during the initial development of the IEP, or a specific need becomes apparent during the school year. The implementation evaluation is not just the evaluation of IDEA requirements but the evaluation of the *plan* designed to address individual needs and participation in the regular curriculum.

One area that is often overlooked when reviewing services and program supports is the need and effectiveness of test modifications and classroom supports. If extra time is listed as an IEP test modification or tests are read to the student, a determination should be made whether this modification is being used and whether it is effective.

General Program Review

Following the school year a summative evaluation should be conducted to evaluate the overall annual progress of each individual IEP,[15] and an evaluation of IEP effectiveness as determined by selected quality indicators (viz., goals achieved, parent/teacher satisfaction). On an individual basis, a decision must be made concerning the overall effectiveness of each child's IEP and needed IEP revisions. In addition, the IEP team should consider the overall effectiveness of each IEP in terms of progress toward goals, trends, and possible IEP process changes that will improve the delivery of services.

Although overall program effectiveness should be considered, this does not mean that program success is determined by the percent of goals achieved. A single index for evaluating IEP program effectiveness would likely encourage the development of easily achieved goals and individualized programs that are not educationally challenging. The IEP evaluation process assumes a multidimensional character in which many variables and inputs are considered.

Outside Evaluators

Many of the problems associated with IEPs could be effectively dealt with if the school district and IEP team were provided with an unbiased evaluation of IEPs based on a sampling of IEPs after the first reporting period as part of the implementation evaluation. This evaluation could be undertaken by school personnel or the IEP team, but this can involve a conflict of interest.

An outside consultant can be very useful in providing a relatively unbiased perspective concerning IEP compliance, planning, and implementation. Whether a school district hires an outside consultant or develops and evaluation exchange with another school district or school, outside expertise can provide excellent insights for evaluating basic compliance and IEP implementation issues.

If an outside consultant is not available, an evaluation agreement could be developed between different schools so that each school evaluates a small sample of IEPs from another school. When the goal is to improve the quality of IEPs and IEP process, fair criticism is generally appreciated; when the goal is to generate a document that seems to comply with the regulations, criticism is less welcomed. Even a cursory examination of disparate IEP forms used by different school districts suggests that collaboration between school districts and agencies regarding the design and evaluation of IEPs would do much to improve the quality and format of IEPs.

IEP METRICS

IEP metrics refer to quantifiable indices that can be used to evaluate the quality and effectiveness of IEPs at individual and programmatic levels. The major difficulty in developing metrics is the diversity of ways in which measurable annual goals and short-term objectives or benchmarks are measured and the myriad indicators that can be used to measure program quality. For a specific IEP, one goal might be based on a teacher rating, another on a percentage, and a third on a raw test score. In addition, goals and objectives can be qualitative or quantitative, range in terms of complexity, and deal with very diverse disabilities, educational and non-academic tasks, skills, and abilities.

If the overall effectiveness of IEPs and the IEP process is evaluated, a method should be available to reduce annual goal and short-term objective data to a quantifiable format. This section offers several approaches for interpreting and quantifying progress toward goal data. These are only suggestions in that the type of data collected, the frequency of data collection, and the resources to collect and interpret data will vary from one school district to the next. How data is quantified and interpreted also depends on how goals and objectives are measured. If most goals and objectives are based on objective assessments, a simple percentage might be the best index to evaluate overall program effectiveness. If goal and objective progress is measured by subjective teacher ratings, or if goals and objectives are defined in qualitative rather than quantitative terms, a different data reduction format might be necessary. Most importantly, there is simply no single procedure for evaluating overall program effectiveness. What is important is that program quality and overall program effectiveness are considered in spite of the fact that the evaluation methodology is less than perfect.

IEP Benchmarks

The quantification of an IEP, and evaluating IEP annual goals and benchmarks, is a difficult task at best. There is no standard for evaluating IEP annual goals and objectives. For one child, one goal might be appropriate, while for a second child ten or twenty goals might be necessary. Likewise, for a child with ten goals, achieving one goal, or even one objective for one goal, might be reason for celebration. With the understanding that IEPs are predicated on individual needs are not easily quantifiable, several IEP indices are available to evaluate IEPs. The purposes of these indices is not to create an IEP calculus but to generate indices that are heuristically useful and assist in understanding IEP quality and effectiveness.

Program statistics. Basic IEP team decision data concerning classification decisions, types of placements, the number of children declassified, Section 504 services, and the services provided should be reviewed annually.

Number of goals. The number of goals per IEP can be useful for highlighting the intensity of an individual's needs and for overall program evaluation. Although some school districts require a minimum of two or three goals, there must be at least one special education goal. There is no limit as to the maximum number of goals that can be included in an IEP but the number should be manageable and address all of a child's needs that result from the disability.

Number of objectives. If short-term objectives or benchmarks are intermediate steps for measuring progress, the number will often correspond to the number of reporting periods and therefore should not fluctuate greatly as is the case when objectives are really year-long activities. If the number of short-term objectives equals the number of reporting periods used by the school district, this value might be constant. If the number of short-term objectives varies greatly, the objectives might be annual activities or subgoals rather than short-term objectives.

Need-goal linkage. There should be a strong linkage between needs, goals and objectives. The importance of this linkage is essential for providing services that address each child's needs. One method for considering need-goal linkage is to first match each IEP goal with a corresponding need, and then determine whether there are needs without corresponding goals. Selecting goals is a relatively easy task, but determining the underlying need is more difficult. Ideally, the individual evaluation report, the IEP, or

PLEP statement will contain a section that deals with areas of need but this is not always the case. Test scores or teacher observation might indicate a need for specialized instruction in reading comprehension, but there will not necessarily be a statement that highlights reading comprehension as an area of need that requires an IEP goal. Likewise, classroom behavior might be an area of need but exactly what would be an appropriate goal might require a careful reading of all available observational reports.

Just as there can be goals without clearly identified needs, there can be clearly identified needs without goals. Because needs are not always explicitly indicated, finding needs without goals is a more difficult task. Nonetheless, an attempt should be made to consider data from the evaluation report and the PLEP statement to determine whether additional goals are required.

The following example shows two separate lists of needs as determined by evaluation reports and data, and areas of need for which IEP goals have been developed. Ideally, areas of need and goals will correspond but this is not always the case. In this example, one IEP goal centers about reading vocabulary, but the area of need involves reading comprehension; organization skills and attention are listed as goals and also as areas of need, while attendance is as area of need but not listed as a goal.

Areas of Need	Actual IEP Goals
Reading Comprehension	Reading Vocabulary
Organization Skills	Organization Skills
Word Problems	Mathematics Computation
Attention	Spelling
Attendance	Attention

For the above lists of needs and goals, there are two goals in which there is a stated

need (organization skills and attention), three goals in which there is not a specific need (reading vocabulary, mathematics computation, and spelling), and three areas of need that do not have corresponding goals (reading comprehension, word problems, and attendance). There are a number of reasons why a goal might not have a corresponding need such as progress, the inclusion of outdated goals from previous IEPs, goals that are not measurable, or goals written more for compliance than to meet individual need. For example, in the second grade a goal might have been written to address the need for group participation, but this need no longer exists in grade three; or a goal might have been written to develop

basic sight-word vocabulary in an earlier grade but this goal has been achieved.

There will always be a degree of ambiguity when determining whether a goal has a need or vice versa, but the very task of attempting to show the relationship between needs and goals provides insight into the integrity of the IEP. In this example, the analysis of IEP needs and goals suggests that three goals should be added to the IEP and three goals reconsidered or deleted. As was already said, deleting goals must be done with caution so that a child's legitimate needs are not ignored.

Goals with Need	Goals Not Needed	Goals Needed
Organization Skills Attention	Reading Vocabulary Mathematics Computation Spelling	Reading Comprehension Word Problems Attendance

The above can be summarized as follows.

Goals	IEP Goals	Goals Needed
Goals with Need	2	3
Goals Not Needed	3	
Total Goals	5	

Simply considering goal-need linkage is often sufficient to obtain an understanding of necessary goal revisions. If an index of goal-need linkage is desired, one method is to

consider all the goals listed, plus areas of need that should have goals, as the total IEP goals, and then to calculate an index of need-goal linkage by

$$Goal\ Linkage\ Index = \frac{Goals\ with\ Need}{Total\ Goods + Goals\ Needed}\ (100)$$

or $2/(5+3)(100) = 25\%$. Although a need might not be listed or indicated in the IEP, this might be more apparent in the evaluation report. For the above data, information might reveal that there is, indeed, a need for reading vocabulary, mathematics computa-

tion and spelling goals. If this is the case, the index would be $5/(5+3)(100)$ or 63%. For the above formula, the index is 100% when Goals with Need is equal to the Total Goals and no additional goals are needed. Again, the task of linking goals and need is far more important than a resulting index (which will be, admittedly, quite arbitrary) of goal/need linkage.

Areas of need for which there are no goals is more critical. If a child has a problem in a specific area, there should be a corresponding goal unless there is a rationale for not including a goal. For the above data, attendance might be affected by health problems and no goal can be developed to effectively address this need. However, the likelihood that a goal will not be achieved because of extraneous factors should not prevent the goal from being included in the IEP.

Rating reliability. Reliability concerns the consistency, accuracy and repeatability of a measurement. In the case of the reliability of goals and services, the question is whether different interpretations of the same data result in different goals or services. If there is little accuracy in defining goals and services, the end result is a high degree of disagreement, inaccuracy, and overall unreliability.

The IEP team must not become not become bogged down in a morass of data and statistics when considering IEP reliability. There is, however, one situation when the accuracy of goals and services determination can be useful. At one of the initial IEP team meetings, team members might independently evaluate several IEPs to consider matters of consistency and accuracy. The goal is not to reach perfect reliability but to develop a common frame of reference for developing IEPs and reaching consensus.

Another approach to reliability is to evaluate the general agreement among IEP team members. Consider a simple five-item IEP evaluation scale as shown in Table XXII.

Table XXII. Five-item IEP Evaluation

Areas to Evaluate	Poor		Average		Excellent
Identifying Needs	1	2	3	4	5
Developing Goals	1	2	3	4	5
Providing Services	1	2	3	4	5
Regular Curriculum Participation	1	2	3	4	5
IEP Team Participation	1	2	3	4	5

If the IEP team consists of six members, and each member evaluates the IEP using the above scale, the resulting data will give a sense of the reliability of the ratings as well as the satisfaction for each of the rating scale items:

Team Member	IEP Rating Scale Item				
	Needs	Goals	Services	Regular	Team
1	5	4	4	4	4
2	3	3	3	3	3
3	5	4	4	3	3
4	4	3	3	4	2
5	3	3	3	3	2
5	4	3	3	4	3
Item Mean	4.0	3.3	3.3	3.5	2.8

The above data provide an opportunity to consider IEP items of interest, how these items are perceived by team members, and the overall agreement among team members. Even more important than the data, or analyzing the data, is the opportunity to consider IEP team agreement. Although this type of rating scale would need to be modified to reflect the needs of each school district and IEP team, this type of simple rating scale can be administered quickly and can be useful for gathering input from all team members, especially parents.

Although an index of reliability could be calculated to evaluate the consistency of ratings, this presents several statistical problems such as having relatively few raters or little variance among raters. If all raters evaluated an IEP as excellent (5),[16] the variance would be 0 and the reliability also 0. In this situation, simple percentages for each rating category would provide the best description of IEP reliability (e.g., 100% rated the IEP as Excellent).

Regular classroom participation. Every IEP should clearly indicate the amount of regular classroom participation in terms of a percentage. To this end, every IEP should have a matrix of services and an overall index of participation that details the amount of regular curriculum participation, special education in the regular classroom, and all special education and related services provided outside of the regular classroom.

Regular curriculum indicators. In addition to the amount of time children with disabilities participate in regular classes, the number and performance of children with disabilities in state and districtwide assessments should be considered. Likewise, a summary of students receiving regular high school diplomas and IEP diplomas should be noted. Graduation is important in that a student who receives a regular high school diploma is no longer eligible for services

under IDEA, but eligibility is retained if the student receives an IEP diploma or certificate other than a regular high school diploma.[17]

Beginning levels of performance. The importance of measurable annual goals cannot be overemphasized in the IEP development process. The problem is not simply to have measurable annual goals, but goals that are actually measured. A simple index that will reveal the likelihood of a goal actually being measured is the number of goals that have beginning levels of performance or beginning benchmarks. If the goal is to increase expressive vocabulary to 50 words, the current level of performance should be known; if the goal is to receive a score of at least 80 on a test of written expression, the beginning level of performance or score should be stated. Even if the always vague and much maligned *teacher observation* is the assessment technique, the present level of performance as actually determined by *teacher observation* should be indicated.

When the beginning level of performance for an annual goal is indicated, there is little doubt how the objective is measured because the skill or ability has already been measured. Even if the beginning level of performance is represented by a vague index or subjective rating, this is far better than no measurement or only a promise of measurement at some distant time.

Parent participation. Parent attendance at IEP meetings should be noted and the overall percent of parent attendance determined every year. There are very few indices where the need to achieve 100 percent is more obvious. If parent attendance is low, this must be addressed by the school administration and the IEP team.

Student IEP participation. As a matter of course, the number of students who attend IEP meetings should be noted, although the importance of this statistic becomes much more prominent for middle school, junior high, and especially high school students (or

when transition services are included in the IEP).

GOAL/BENCHMARK DATA

Progress toward goals, as measured by short-term objectives, can be tracked by using the IEP document or a data recording chart or sheet. The exact data tracked depends on the type of goals and objectives used, the number of goals and objectives, the type and variety of criteria, what data is deemed important, what data is used to review overall program progress, and what and how progress is reported to parents. Using the IEP to record data can be cumbersome, is not easily accessible for interpretation, and often results in data not being recorded. A data summary sheet clearly shows a child's overall measured performance, and represents an invaluable source of data for teachers, parents, and the IEP team.

The following methods for recording performance data are intended to show how important variables that affect progress can be considered and recorded. In view of the unique IEPs used by school districts, whatever data system that is selected should be evaluated to indicate what data is useful, what data is repetitious or not available, and

what unique problems occur when recording or interpreting data.

Table XXIII illustrates the basic data that is required to evaluate progress toward goals as determined by the achievement of short-term objectives or benchmarks. As shown, each goal is followed by an abbreviated description, the present level of educational performance for that goal, and the criterion or anticipated level of performance for each intermediate step.

The data sheet is not intended to replicate the IEP, but to provide a means to record, evaluate, and review performance progress toward goals. A very brief description for each IEP goal is provided, followed by four objectives for each goal that are listed horizontally. Each objective has a criterion (C), a measured performance (P) index, and an evaluation (E) of performance. The PLEP column illustrates different types of data that can be used such as percentages, raw scores, ratings, and time metric. For many IEPs the number of goals will probably be less than ten and the data will not be as disparate as shown in Table XXIII below:

Table XXIII. IEP Data Recording Sheet

Goal	Description	PLEP	Measurement of Performance											
			1			2			3			4		
			C	P	E	C	P	E	C	P	E	C	P	E
1	Sight words	27	40	30	2	80			120			160		
2	Reading errors	50	<40			<30			<20			<10		
3	Reading comp.	36%	50			60			70			80		
4	Disruptions	>25	<20			<15			<10			<2		
5	Passage detail	0	2			4			6			8		

6	Sight words	R30%	R40			R55			R70			R85		
7	Sentences	0	1			3			6			12		
8	Reg. Class	0 hours	1			4			8			12		
9	Social studies	52%	65			75			85			85		
10	Science	F	C			C+			B			B		

For the first goal, the task is to increase basic sight words from an initial level of performance level of 27 to 160 over the course of four periods. The criterion (C) for each benchmark provides a standard for evaluating performance.

Goal	Description	PLEP	Measurement of Performance											
			1			2			3			4		
			C	P	E	C	P	E	C	P	E	C	P	E
1	Sight words	27	40	30	2	80			120			160		

At the conclusion of the first reporting period, the child is evaluated and performance is recorded in the P (Performance) column. Using an evaluation scale from 0 to 4, where 0=no progress, 1=some progress, 2=progress, 3=good progress and 4=completed, a 2 is recorded in the E (Evaluation) column.

	1	
C	P	E
40	30	2

As shown by the examples of levels of performance in Table XXIII, the data recorded can be quite varied. The first goal is based on raw scores, the second goal entails reducing reading errors, the third goal involves increase reading comprehension and goal #6 is based on rating scale and as indicated by an R. The last goal shown above indicates regular classroom performance as measured by course grades.

Recording measurements. When short-term objectives measure different abilities, there are several ways in which data can be measured and recorded. Consider the example shown below where the goal is to pass a state competency test composed of four areas: computation, measurement, applications and geometry. One method for measuring and recording data is to emphasize one area each period. Another approach is to pyramid skill development so that computation is measured each period, measurement is assessed for periods 2, 3 and 4, applications for periods 3 and 4, and geometry is measured in period 4. A third possibility is to measure each area each recording period.

Goal	STO	Description	PLEP	Criterion	Measurement			
					1	2	3	4
Ex. 1	1	Computation	8	20	24			
	2	Measurement	4	20		15		
	3	Applications	7	20			21	
	4	Geometry	5	20				19
Ex. 2	1	Computation	8	20	10	14	18	24
	2	Measurement	4	20		8	15	21
	3	Applications	7	20			14	22
	4	Geometry	5	20				19
Ex. 2	1	Computation	8	20	10	14	22	23
	2	Measurement	4	20	6	10	19	18
	3	Applications	7	20	10	24	23	22
	4	Geometry	5	20	7	12	22	18

REPORTING PROGRESS

The Senate report for IDEA-1997 suggested five rating categories for evaluating objectives[18] that can be recorded by either a numerical or alphabetical scale:

0	NP	No Progress
1	SP	Some Progress
2	GP	Good Progress
3	AC	Almost Complete
4	C	Completed

The above is not an unreasonable scale but it does suggest a certain unevenness between the rating intervals (see Figure VI). One possible improvement might be to add *Progress* and *Good Progress* categories:

Figure VI. Senate Report Evaluation Scale

Evaluation Scale

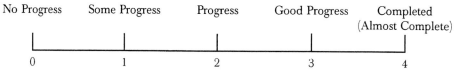

The Senate report suggested that checkboxes or an equivalent option be used to review and judge performance. The example given in this report was to rank a goal or benchmark using a multipoint scale so that if the goal is "'Ted will demonstrate effective literal comprehension,' the ranking system would then state the following, as indicated by a checkbox: No progress; some progress; good progress; almost complete; completed."[19]

The following is an example of the type of

rating scale suggested in the Senate report. For the goal "Ted will demonstrate effective literal comprehension," benchmarks must exists to evaluate progress toward the goal. For example, the ability to comprehend literal information from reading sections is measured before instruction and at the end of each reporting period. If this is done, each objective is evaluated using the criterion established for the objective, performance is compared to the criterion for each objective, and a rating is assigned (viz., no progress, some progress, etc.). If the measure is *teacher observation*, and no real measurement of literal reading comprehension is made using teacher observation, a rating of Some or Good Progress is meaningless. Even if the child's goal performance is rated as completed at the end of the year, this does not indicate what the child has accomplished.

IEP Progress Report						
Goal	Objective	No Progress	Some Progress	Good Progress	Almost Complete	Completed
1	1	✔				
1	2			✔		
1	3			✔		
1	4					✔

The example given in the Senate report is a measurable objective, but the behavior, criterion, and task are vague. The purpose of a measurable objective is to clearly indicate what will be measured, and not merely that some behavior will be measured or demonstrated. Rather than "Ted will demonstrate effective literal comprehension," a measurable annual goal might be "Ted will answer 70% of comprehension questions," or "Ted will orally answer 70% of literal comprehension questions from a third grade basal reader."

Table XXIV presents several different rating scale formats that could be used in lieu of the basic 0-4 scale. Scale A is actually a seven-point scale in which regression or performance less than the beginning level of performance is signified by -1. The rating format used is arbitrary. Instead of using -1, 0, 1, 2 and 3, a simple linear rule of 0, 1, 2, 3, or 4 could be used. For interpretative purposes -1 seems to better convey the idea of regression, but for computational ease the latter is probable more convenient. Of course, every scale could be extended upward or downward to include these extreme possibilities. Scale B is a simple binary mastery scale (No Progress or Completed), and scales C, D and E vary with respect to the number of possible scale values.

Table XXIV. IEP Progress Report Scales

Interpretation	Scale				
	A	B	C	D	E
Regression	-1				
No Progress	0	0	0	0	0
Some Progress	1			1	1
Progress	2		1		2
Good Progress	3			2	3
Completed	4	1	2	3	4
Exceed Goal	5				

REPORTING PROGRESS

Reports to Parents

There are a number of ways in which IEP short-term objective or benchmark data can be reported to parents. The most convenient method for reporting results is to use the IEP goal/objective sheet included in the child's IEP as shown below:

Goal: student will be able to read 200 content words from a fourth grade mathematics book with 80% accuracy.	Criterion	Date	Performance
PLEP	20%	September 1	
Objective 1	35%	November 1	42%
Objective 2	50%	February 15	48%
Objective 3	65%	April 15	61%
Objective 4	80%	June 15	

A numeric scale for reporting progress is appropriate, but a series of numeric entries might be less than meaningful to a parent. Reports to parents should provide an unambiguous assessment of each child's short-term objective or benchmark performance. Instead of a numerical scale, objectives could be evaluated by None, Progress, and Completed or Achieved, or by whatever scale is used to evaluate progress. Although reports can include an abundance of data, the task is not to inundate parents with all possible data, but to indicate progress toward goals.

Goal vs. Objective Progress

While developing the report card to report progress to parents, a decision must be made whether the report indicates progress toward goals, or whether the report represents short-term objective or benchmark performance which, in turn, indicates progress toward goals. In both cases, progress toward achieving goals is defined as sufficient progress to enable the child to achieve the goals by the end of the year. For example, if the benchmarks are <20, <15, <10 and <5, a frequency of <19 indicates that the first objective has been met. However, if 19 is recorded for each subsequent benchmark, the report to parents could indicate *Progress* or *Some Progress* because the level of performance has improved from the initial level, but the level of progress might be minimal and not suggest that the goal of <5 will be achieved by the end of the year. Although individual short-term objective or benchmark performance is important, the purpose of reporting progress to parents is to indicate the likelihood that the goal will be achieved

based on the periodic evaluations during the year. If the initial level of performance is a score of 20 percent and the goal is 80 percent, and a child receives a score of 21 percent for each benchmark evaluation, reporting *Some Progress* would be accurate but hardly a fair indication of the likelihood that the goal of 80 percent will be achieved.

When the report indicates overall goal progress (i.e., each reporting period rating signifies the likelihood that the annual goal will be achieved), a rating of *Progress* is given if the benchmark is achieved and a rating of *Completed* is given if the goal is achieved. Instead of using a multipoint scale, a simple binary scale could be used such as *Progress (P)* or *No Progress (NP)*, or *Sufficient (S)* or *Insufficient (I)* progress. As shown below, each goal could be briefly described (or presented in its entirety) and the report shows, based on the most current benchmark data, whether "progress is sufficient to enable the child to achieve the goals by the end of the year."[20]

Progress Report				
Goal	Description	PLEP	Performance	Goal
1	Sight words	27	Progress	40
2	Reading errors	50	No progress	<40
3	Reading comp.	36%	Progress	50
4	Disruptions	>25	Progress	<20
5	Passage detail	0	Progress	2
6	Cooperation	R30%	No Progress	R40
7	Sentences	0	Progress	1
8	Reg. class	0 hours	Progress	1
9	Social studies	52%	Progress	65
10	Science	F	Progress	C

This format represents the basic requirement for reporting progress to parents: the extent of progress toward goals and whether progress is sufficient to achieve the goals. A report could be generated for each reporting period, or the report could be expanded to include a multipoint scale of goal progress for each reporting period. In the below example, the amount of data presented is further simplified by excluding specific beginning performance and goal data. In this example, the 8th goal, regular classroom participation, is *Completed*. Because these data indicate overall goal progress, *Completed* signifies that the goal has been achieved and not simply the first benchmark.

Goal	Description	Progress toward Goals			
		1	2	3	4
1	Sight words	Progress			
2	Reading errors	No progress			
3	Reading comp.	Progress			
4	Disruptions	Progress			
5	Passage detail	Progress			
6	Cooperation	No Progress			
7	Sentences	Progress			
8	Reg. class	Completed			
9	Social studies	Almost			
10	Science	Some			

The advantage of reporting overall goal progress is that progress is has a very clear frame of reference (i.e., progress means progress toward goal achievement) and the amount of data presented is simplified. The disadvantage is that specific short-term objective or benchmark data is not provided that would unequivocally show the extent of progress made.

Instead of directly reporting progress toward goals, individual short-term objectives can be evaluated that indirectly indicate progress toward goals. That is, if each short-term objective or benchmark is completed, and the short-term objectives or benchmarks are sequentially related, progress toward goals is indicated. As shown below, each progress rating refers to a specific short-term objective or benchmark. The task is to achieve each objective which, in turn, results in logical and sequential progress toward achieving the annual goal. In this example, *Completed* means that the short-term objective has been achieved and not that the goal itself has been achieved.

Progress Report					
Goal	Description	Objective			
		1	2	3	4
1	Reading vocabulary	Completed	Progress		
2	Reading comprehension	Progress	Completed		
3	Study skills	Progress	Progress		
4	Classroom behavior	None	Completed	Some	Completed

For Goal #4 in the above example, the student did not achieve the first benchmark, completed the second, made some progress toward the third, but achieved the annual goal of less than 5 behaviors at the end of the year. The data that corresponds to goal #4 is as follows:

Benchmarks		<20	<15	<10	<5
4	Classroom behavior	None	Completed	Some	Completed
Performance PLP = 21		21	14	12	4

The progress report shown below illustrates a letter code format to indicate levels of performance. If desired, grades such as A,B,C, holistic percentages, or simple numerical equivalents could be used to indicate IEP progress.

Progress Report			
Student:			
Evaluation Codes: N = No progress S = Some Progress P = Progress G = Good Progress C = Completed			
Goal	STO	Description	Progress
1	1	Reading comprehension	N
1	2	"	C
1	3		S
1	4		
2	1	Study skills	G
2	2	"	S
2	3		
2	4		
3	1	Classroom behavior	N
3	2		P
3	3		C
3	4		
Parent comments: Please indicate any comments, questions or suggestions you might have concerning the above progress, and return to _____ or call _____ at _____			

If the final goal is completed during the course of the school year, the service provider or IEP team has several options. First, the goal and all preceding benchmarks could be labeled *Completed* and attention could be focused on other needs. Second, a new rating category such as *Maintenance* (or *Maintain*) could be used to show that the annual level of goal performance is being maintained. For example, if the goal is to reduce a behavior to 0 occurrences by the end of the year, and this is achieved in December, the various interventions could be maintained throughout the remainder of the year to ensure that the behavior has been eliminated. Third, an *Exceeded* (or *Exceed*) rating could be used to show that goal performance has been exceeded. If the goal is to learn 50 words by the end of the year and a child learns 100 by the end of September, performance above and beyond the goal could be developed to whatever level possible. By the end of the year, the child might learn 150 words, or 300, or 600 words. By keeping track of performance each reporting period, even though the goal has been achieved, the resulting data provide an excellent frame of reference for revising the goal for the following year. Finally, if a goal is clearly inappropriate, the IEP team can reconsider the task, difficulty level, short-term objectives or benchmarks, criteria, or a combination of these factors.

School report cards. A child with a disability is not restricted to an IEP report card. For academic areas in which the child is participating in the general curriculum, the child should also receive a regular school report card. The IEP Progress Report indicates progress for each measurable annual goal, short-term objectives or benchmarks; the school report card indicates performance in the regular curriculum. Reports to parents must be sent concerning progress toward goals during the year; a report card must also be given if the child is participating in the regular curriculum and the school sends report cards or computer-generated reports to children who are not disabled.

SUMMATIVE EVALUATION

Annual Review

The IEP team is required to review each child's IEP periodically, but not less than annually[21] to (1) determine whether annual goals are being achieved, (2) determine whether a reevaluation is necessary, (3) revise the IEP, and (4) address each child's anticipated needs.

Following the school year, a determination must be made whether the child is still a child with a disability under IDEA or whether the IEP must be revised. The IEP team must consider the need for IEP services and modifications, and each goal must be evaluated to determine whether the goal and/or the criteria for each goal should be maintained, modified, or eliminated. If an IEP is not revised, the validity of the IEP is certainly suspect. In almost all situations, an annual review that does not result in the revision of measurable annual goals or short-term objectives or benchmarks is insensitive to the individual learning needs of the child. If the goal has been achieved, the task, the difficulty level, or the content will need to be reevaluated and modified. If the benchmark is a score on a test of 50 for the current year, the benchmark for the following year might be reset to 75 or 80. Or, instead of changing the benchmark, the difficulty level might be increased.

Other situations might occur such as when benchmarks of 40, 60, and 80 percent are defined but actual measured performance results in scores of 43, 41, and 46 percent or very little progress. In this case, the content, the content difficulty, the method of instruction or a combination of these factors might be modified. Specially designed instruction is not simply repeating goals, and specially designed instruction is certainly not ignoring performance or the relation between performance, content and instructional methodology.

Overall IEP Program Review

The purpose of the IEP program review is to evaluate the overall progress toward achieving goals and objectives, and to evaluate the overall satisfaction with the IEP process. If one child made no progress toward all the objectives, there might be a very rational explanation for this occurrence. However, a careful examination by the IEP team would be required if all children made no progress. At the very least, the number of goals achieved, almost achieved, etc. must be evaluated on a programwide level. The below example shows the goal performance for five children. Each goal is evaluated using a four point scale: 0 (No Progress) to 4 (Completed). There are a total of 30 goals and the average rating is 3.26 (98/30). The percent of goal achievement is 81.5% (3.26/4(100). For the 30 ratings, the sum of these rating is 98, the overall summated mean is 30/98=3.26, and the overall summated percent is 3.26/4=81.5%.

Student				
A	B	C	D	E
4	0	3	2	4
4	3	3	4	3
4	4	4	3	4
	4	3	4	
	1	4	3	
		1	4	
		4	4	
		3	3	
		3	4	
		4		

As shown below, frequency table is useful for describing how goals are rated:

Category	Rating	f	f(Rating)
No Progress	0	1	0
Some Progress	1	2	2
Progress	2	1	2
Good Progress	3	10	30
Completed	4	16	64
Sums		30	98
Mean			3.26

The number of short-term objectives or benchmarks achieved is also useful when comparing goal performance to objective performance. A child might have completed 75 percent of the objectives but none of the goals, or 75 percent of the objectives and all of the goals. Comparing goals and short-term objectives achieved indicates whether the goals are too high in relation to the objectives, or whether the objectives provide a reasonable hierarchy for progressing toward goal achievement.

Summative Benchmarks

Scriven (1993) made an interesting observation that "formative evaluation is attractive, but summative evaluation is imperative" (p. 59). What is meant by this is that ongoing program evaluation is useful, but an overall summative evaluation is essential for making important program decisions that reflect changing and emerging program philosophy. For example, an annual review of a child's regular classroom participation might reveal that a level of 40 percent participation is very appropriate. However, an evaluation of all IEPs might show that the level of participation is 70 percent or 80 percent. This overall index does not signify that the level or participation for a particular child is either too low or too high, but rather this index can be used as a benchmark for developing strategies, programs and processes to increase the overall level of participation.

Each state that receives assistance under IDEA-1997 is required to provide data each year relating to disabilities, race, ethnicity, and services. For example, ethnicity is used to determine if there is a significant disproportion of children receiving services because of ethnicity.[22] These data should be reviewed to determine disproportionate patterns in providing IEP services that might be the result of factors other than meeting disability needs.

There are many additional indicators that can be used to evaluate the overall direction and quality of the IEP process. In the Twentieth Annual Report to Congress, one of the most important factors for predicting graduation rates was 4th grade reading proficiency (and the least important, interestingly enough, was current expenditure per pupil).[23] Although critical indicators will vary from state to state and from district to district, attempting to discern important predictor variables is, in itself, an important undertaking. When all is said and done, there is no single score or index that will indicate IEP process quality, but a consideration of many different factors will often provide insight into needed overall IEP modifications and revisions.

Although most indicators do not directly signify program quality, several come very close to achieving this goal. If the drop-out rate of students with disabilities is high, the IEP team might consider this factor when providing transition services to reduce the number of students with disabilities leaving school. Participation in state and districtwide assessment is an explicit goal of IDEA-1997 so that the number of students with disabilities who participate in these assessments, and their performance, provides critical program data.

There are many other indicators that can be used to evaluate the IEP process such as attendance, number of declassifications, number of complaints, mediations and hearings, regular classroom participation, state and districtwide test performance, IEP measurable annual goal performance, number of students receiving IEP and high school diplomas, and postschool employment. Above all, the IEP team must be aware that the development of the IEP has consequences in terms of what occurs during the year, annual performance, and certainly the long-term effects of IEPs (e.g., graduation from high school). All data cannot be evaluated, but the consequences of IEP development should be considered.

Evaluating IEP quality. The IEP team represents an invaluable source for evaluating the IEP process and the quality of the IEPs. Using a checklist as shown in Table XXV, each IEP member could evaluate the overall IEP process at the end of the year. By considering the quality of the different IEP components, IEP members will develop a better understanding of the components and the problems perceived by others. Individual IEP team members can evaluate IEPs to determine the overall quality of IEPs. For the following survey, the eight primary components of an IEP have been identified and each is rated on a scale from 0 (unacceptable) to 4 (acceptable). Instead of evaluating specific IEP elements (e.g., Present Levels of Educational Performance), each item could be in the form of a question or refer to more general IEP processes (e.g., Did all IEP team members participate? Are goals appropriate? Do services meet individual needs?).

Table XXV. General IEP Evaluation Rating Scale

General IEP Evaluation

Evaluate each IEP category:	Unacceptable				Acceptable
Present Levels of Educational Performance	0	1	2	3	4
Measurable Annual Goals and Short-term Objectives	0	1	2	3	4
Special Education and Related Services	0	1	2	3	4
Statement of Nonparticipation	0	1	2	3	4
State and District-wide Assessment Modifications	0	1	2	3	4
Date, Frequency, Location and Duration of Services	0	1	2	3	4
Measuring and Reporting Progress Toward Goals	0	1	2	3	4
Transition Services	0	1	2	3	4

The following rating scale (Table XXVI) is expanded version of the rating scale shown in Table XXV and includes specific IEP requirements (e.g., supplementary aids and services, the short-term objective data and criteria).

Table XXVI. Overall IEP Evaluation

Indicate your overall satisfaction with the IEP team's ability to address each of the following:

	Poor		Good		Excellent
1. General levels of educational performance	1	2	3	4	5
2. How the disability affects general curriculum involvement	1	2	3	4	5
3. How the disability affects nonacademic performance	1	2	3	4	5
4. Measurable annual goals	1	2	3	4	5
5. Measurable goals for each identified need	1	2	3	4	5
6. Measurable annual goals meet disability-related needs	1	2	3	4	5
7. Short-term objectives (STOs) or benchmarks	1	2	3	4	5
8. STOs or benchmarks as intermediate steps	1	2	3	4	5
9. Each STO or benchmark has a measure	1	2	3	4	5
10. Each STO has completion date and criterion	1	2	3	4	5
11. Special education services	1	2	3	4	5
12. Related services	1	2	3	4	5
13. Supplementary aids and services	1	2	3	4	5
14. Program modifications or supports	1	2	3	4	5
15. Regular curriculum involvement	1	2	3	4	5
16. Nonparticipation statement	1	2	3	4	5
17. Test accommodations	1	2	3	4	5
18. Alternate assessments (if necessary)	1	2	3	4	5
19. The beginning date of services	1	2	3	4	5
20. Location, duration, and frequency of services	1	2	3	4	5
21. How goal progress will be measured	1	2	3	4	5
22. How progress will be reported to parents	1	2	3	4	5
23. Age 14 school transition plan	1	2	3	4	5
24. Age 16 school-to-work transition plan	1	2	3	4	5
25. Transfer of rights statement (if appropriate)	1	2	3	4	5

Rather than using a rating scale, a simple short-question Yes/No survey can be used by the IEP team to evaluate IEPs:

1. Do the Present Levels of Educational Performance (PLEP) describe each area of need?   Yes   No

2. Does the PLEP show how the child's disability affects involvement and progress in the general curriculum or other appropriate activities?   Yes   No

3. Is there a measurable annual goal for each area of need?   Yes   No

4. Is each goal measurable?   Yes   No

5. Do the measurable annual goals meet needs that enable the child to be involved and progress in the general curriculum?   Yes   No

•

Overall, the exact format for evaluating IEPs is less important than actually implementing a process whereby IEPs are evaluated and deficiencies in the IEP process identified. When the intent is to honestly evaluate and revise IEPs, either a qualitative or a quantitative approach, an extensive survey, or simply a series of agreed upon questions will be more than adequate to implement a program directed toward meaningful and reflective IEP improvement.

NOTES

1 The Government Performance and Results Act of 1993, PL 103-62(2)(b)(3).
2 34 CFR 300.343(c)((1).
3 34 CFR 300.343(c).
4 20 USC 1414(d)(1)(A)(viii)(II))(bb).
5 34 CFR 300.343(c).
6 *Ibid.*
7 Hudson v. Rowley 458 U.S. 176 (1982).
8 34 CFR 300.343(b)(2).
9 34 CFR 300.345(a).
10 New York State, (1998). State Education Department, Office of Vocational and Educational Services for Individuals with Disabilities, Policy 97-09, Albany, N.Y.
11 Individual Education Program (IEP) Checklist 1981-82, Evaluating special education, Appendix A (1983). Skokie, Illinois School District (J. Joseph, Project Coordinator). ERIC #ED 227 176.
12 Nebraska Department of Education, Nebraska IEP Technical Assistance Guide, September, 1998, Lincoln, Nebraska.
13 Stevens, F., Lawrenz, F., and Sharp, L. *User-Friendly Handbook for Project Evaluation.* National Science Foundation, 1997.
14 Individual Education Program (IEP) Checklist 1981-82, Evaluating special education, Appendix A (1983). Skokie, Illinois School District (J. Joseph, Project Coordinator). ERIC #ED 227 176.
15 34 CFR 300.343(c).
16 These data can be used to compute a reliability coefficient (coefficient Alpha) as is demonstrated by the below BASIC program although this might be a situation where less rather than

more statistics are most beneficial.

```
10 REM COEFFICIENT ALPHA
20 CLS
30 DIM SX(20),SXS(50)
40 READ NRATERS, ITEMS
50 FOR J = 1 TO NRATERS: READ X$
60 FOR K = 1 TO ITEMS
70 X = VAL(MID$(X$,K,1))
80 SX(K) = SX(K) + X: XT = XT + X
90 SXS(K) = SXS(K) + X^2: NEXT K
100 T = T + XT: ST = ST + XT^2
110 XT = 0: NEXT J
120 MT = T / NRATERS: XT = ST / NRATERS - MT^2
130 FOR K = 1 TO NRATERS
140 SX(K) = SX(K) / NRATERS: SXS(K) = SXS(K) / NRATERS - SX(K)^2
150 SXS = SXS + SXS(K): NEXT K
160 CALPHA = ITEMS / (ITEMS-1) * ((XT - SXS) / XT)
170 PRINT "ALPHA = "INT(CALPHA*1000)/1000
180 END
190 DATA 6,5
200 DATA 54444
210 DATA 33333
220 DATA 54433
230 DATA 43342
240 DATA 33332
250 DATA 43343
```

17 34 CFR 300.534 Determination of eligibility.
18 Senate Report 105-17, p. 22.
19 *Ibid.*, p. 22.
20 34 CFR 300.347(a)(7)(ii)(B).
21 34 CFR 300.343(c).
22 20 USC 1400(c)(8)(B), (C), and (D).
23 Table IV-4 (p. IV-37).

REFERENCES

Bateman, B. D. *Writing Individualized Education Programs (IEPs) for Success.* Secondary Education and Beyond, Learning Disabilities Association, 1995. Retrieved September 22, 2000 from the World Wide Web: http://ldonline.org/ld_indepth/iep/success_ieps.html.

Barraga, N., and Erin, J. *Visual Handicaps and Learning.* Austin, Tex., Pro-Ed, 1992.

Brigance, A. H. *Brigance Diagnostic Assessment of Basic Skills - Spanish Edition.* North Billerica, Mass., Curriculum Associates, 1983.

British Columbia. *Special Education Services: A Manual of Policies, Procedures and Guidelines.* Victoria, B.C.: Author, 1996.

Burns, E. *The Development, Use and Abuse of Educational Tests.* Springfield, Thomas, 1979.

Burns, E. Linear regression and simplified reading expectancy formulas. *Reading Research Quarterly, 17,* 446–453, 1982.

Burns, E. *Test Accommodations for Students With Disabilities.* Springfield, Thomas, 1998.

Camp, R. C. *Benchmarking: The Search for Industry. Quality Performance Accreditation Manual.* Topeka, Kansas, Kansas State Department of Education, 1989.

Carr, E. G. Emerging themes in the functional analysis of problem behavior. *Journal of Applied Behavioral Analysis, 27,* 393–399, 1994.

Choate, J. S., Enright, B. E., Miller, L. J., Poteet, J. A. and Rakes, T. A. *Curriculum-based assessment and programming.* 3rd ed. Boston: Allyn and Bacon, 1995.

Connolly, A. *Keymath - Revised.* Circle Pines, Minn., American Guidance Service, 1988.

Council of Administrators of Special Education. *Student Access: A Resource Guide for Educators. Section 504 of the Rehabilitation Act of 1973.* Albuquerque, N.M., Author, 1992. (ERIC No. 349 769).

Cronbach, L. J. and Furby, L. How we should measure change—or should we? *Psychological Bulletin, 74,* 68-80.

Evaluating Special Education. Washington D.C., Department of Education, 1983. (ERIC #ED 227 176).

Dunn, L. M. Special education for the mildly retarded—Is much of it justifiable? *Exceptional Children, 35,* 5–22, 1968.

Dunn, L. M. and Dunn L. M. *Peabody Picture Vocabulary Test–Revised.* Circle Pines, Minn., American Guidance Service, 1981.

Foster-Johnson, L., and Dunlap, G. Using functional assessment to develop effective, individualized interventions for challenging behaviors. *Teaching Exceptional Children, 56,* 44–52, 1993.

Friend, M., and Bursuck, W. *Including Students With Special Needs: A Practical Guide for Classroom Teachers.* Boston, Allyn and Bacon, 1996.

Goldberg, S. S. *Special Education Law.* New York, Plenum, 1982.

Gottlieb, J., Alter, M., Gottlieb, B., and Wishner, J. Special education in urban America: It's not justifiable for many. *Journal of Special Education, 27,* 453–465, 1994.

Hammill, D, and Larsen, S. *Test of Written Language-2.* Austin, Tex., ProEd, 1988.

Hargrove, L., and Poteet, J. *Assessment in Special Education.* Englewood Cliffs, N.J., Prentice-Hall, 1984.

Haynes, S., and O'Brien, W. Functional analysis in behavior therapy. *Clinical Psychology Review, 10,* 649–668, 1990.

Hewett, F. M. *Education of Exceptional Learners.* 2nd ed. Boston: Allyn and Bacon, 1977.

Horn, A. The uneven distribution of the effects of special factors. *Southern California Education Monograph,* No. 12, 1941.

Individual Education Program (IEP) Checklist

1981-82, Evaluating special education, Appendix A. Skokie, Illinois School District (J. Joseph, Project Coordinator), 1983. (ERIC #ED 227 176).

Iowa Technical Assistance Guide for Learning Disability. Des Moines, Iowa Department of Education, Bureau of Special Education, 1997.

Iwata, B. A., Dorsey, M. F., Slifer, K. J., Bauman, K. E., Richman, G. S. Toward a functional analysis of self-injury. *Journal of Applied Behavioral Analysis, 27,* 197–209, 1994.

Kaufman, A. S. and Kaufman, N. L. *Kaufman Assessment Battery for Children.* Circle Pines, Minn., American Guidance Service, 1983.

Kerlinger, F. N. *Foundations of Behavioral Research* 2nd ed. New York, Holt, Rinehart and Winston, 1973.

Markwardt, F. C. *Peabody Individual Achievement Test–Revised.* Circle Pines, Minn., American Guidance Service, 1989.

Massachusetts Department of Education. *Question and Answer Guide on the New Special Education Individualized Educational Plan (IEP) and Related Chapter 766 Regulations.* Malden, Mass., Author, 1995.

McLaughlin, M, and Warren, S. *Individual Education Programs: Issues and Options for Change.* Alexandria, Va., National Association of State Educators of Special Education, 1995. (ERIC #ED 385 8).

McLoughlin, J. and Lewis, R. *Assessing special students.* 3rd ed. Columbus, Ohio: Merrill, 1990.

Mehrens, W. A. and Lehmann, I. J. *Measurement and Evaluation in Education and Psychology.* New York, Holt, Rinehart and Winston, 1973.

Meyen, E., and Skratic, T. *Special Education and Students Disability,* 4th ed. Denver, Love, 1995.

Miller, J., Tansy, M., and Hughes, T. Functional behavioral assessment: The link between problem behavior and effective intervention in schools. *Current Issues in Education, 1,* (1), 1998.

New York State Education Department. *Regulations of the Commissioner of Education,* Part 200, 200.4(a)(1)(vi), January, 1998a.

New York State Education Department. *Guidelines for Completing the Sample IEP,* 1998.

Phillips, S. Legal *Implications of High-Stakes Assessment: What States Should Know.* Oak

Brook, Il., North Central Regional Educational Laboratory, 1993.

Psychological Corporation. Stanford *Achievement Test.* 8th ed. San Antonio, Tex., Harcourt Brace Jovanovich, 1992a.

Psychological Corporation. *Wechsler Individual Achievement Test.* San Antonio, Tex., Harcourt-Brace Jovanovich, 1992b.

Pyecha, J. N., Cox, J. L., Conaway, L. E., Hocutt, A., Jaffe, J., Pelosi, J., and Wiegerink, R. *A National Survey of Individualized Education Programs (IEPs) for Handicapped Children. Volume I: Executive Summary. Final Report.* Durham, N.C., Research Triangle Institute, Durham, N.C., 1980. (ERIC #199 970).

Rothstein, L. F. *Special Education Law.* 2nd ed. New York, Longman, 1995.

Salvia, J., and Ysseldyke, J. E. *Assessment.* 6th ed. Boston, Houghton Mifflin, 1995.

Schipper, W., and Wilson, W. *Implementation of Individualized Education Programming: Some Observations and Recommendations.* Washington, D.C. National Association of State Directors of Special Education, 1978. (ERIC #ED 155 881).

Scriven, M. Hard-Won *Lessons in Program Evaluation.* San Francisco, Jossey-Bass, 1993.

Smith, S. Comparison of individualized education programs (IEPs) of students with behavioral disorders and learning disabilities. *Journal of Learning Disabilities, 24,* 85–100, 1990.

Smith, T., Polloway, E., Patton, J., and Dowdy, C. *Teaching Children with Special Needs in Inclusive Settings.* Boston, Allyn and Bacon, 1995.

Stevens, F., Lawrenz, F., and Sharp, L. *User Friendly Handbook for Project Evaluation.* National Science Foundation.

Texas Education Agency. *Frequently Asked Questions.* Austin, Author, 1997.

Tilly, W. D., Knoster, T. P., Kovaleski, J., Bambara, L., Dunlap, G., and Kincaid, D. *Functional Behavioral Assessment: Policy Development in Light of Emerging Research and Practice,* Created at the request of the National Association of State Directors of Special Education (NASDSE), Iowa Department of Education, Des Moines, Iowa, 1998.

Twentieth Report to Congress on the Implementation of the Individuals with Disabilities Education Act. Washington, D.C.,

U.S. Department of Education, 1998.

Wiles, J., and Bondi, J. *Curriculum Development: A Guide to Practice* 5th ed. Upper Saddle River, N.J, 1998.

Wilkinson, G. *The Wide Range Achievement Test-3.* Wilmington, Del., Jastak Associates, 1993.

Woodcock, R. *Woodcock Reading Mastery Tests–Revised.* Circle Pines, Minn., American Guidance Service, 1987.

Wright, P. D., and Wright, P. *Your Child's IEP: Practical and Legal Guidance for Parents.* The Special Ed Advocate, 2000. Retrieved September 22, 2000 from the World Wide Web: http://;www.wrightslaw.com/advoc/articles/iep_guidance.html and at http://www.ldonline.org/ld_indepth/iep/iep_guidance.html.

INDEX